Legal and Ethical Implications of Drone Warfare

Over the last decade, the U.S., U.K., Israel and other states have begun to use Unmanned Aerial Vehicles (UAVs) for military operations and for targeted killings in places like Pakistan, Yemen and Somalia. Worldwide, over 80 governments are developing their own drone programs, and even non-state actors such as the Islamic State have begun to experiment with drones. The speed of technological change and adaptation with drones is so rapid that it is outpacing the legal and ethical frameworks which govern the use of force. This volume brings together experts in law, ethics and political science to address how drone technology is slowly changing the rules and norms surrounding the use of force and enabling new, sometimes unprecedented, actions by states. It addresses some of the most crucial questions in the debate over drones today. Are drones a revolutionary form of technology that will transform warfare, or is their effect merely hype? Can drone use on the battlefield be made consistent with international law? How does drone technology begin to shift the norms governing the use of force? What new legal and ethical problems are presented by targeted killings outside of declared war zones? Should drones be considered a humane form of warfare? Finally, is it possible that drones could be a force for good in humanitarian disasters and peacekeeping missions in the near future?

This book was previously published as a special issue of *The International Journal of Human Rights*.

Michael J. Boyle is an Associate Professor of Political Science at La Salle University and a Senior Fellow at the Foreign Policy Research Institute in Philadelphia. He is the author of *Violence after War: Explaining Instability in Post-Conflict States* (2014).

Legal and Ethical Implications of Drone Warfare

Edited by
Michael J. Boyle

LONDON AND NEW YORK

First published 2017
by Routledge
2 Park Square, Milton Park, Abingdon, Oxon, OX14 4RN, UK

and by Routledge
711 Third Avenue, New York, NY 10017, USA

Routledge is an imprint of the Taylor & Francis Group, an informa business

© 2017 Taylor & Francis

All rights reserved. No part of this book may be reprinted or reproduced or utilised in any form or by any electronic, mechanical, or other means, now known or hereafter invented, including photocopying and recording, or in any information storage or retrieval system, without permission in writing from the publishers.

Trademark notice: Product or corporate names may be trademarks or registered trademarks, and are used only for identification and explanation without intent to infringe.

British Library Cataloguing in Publication Data
A catalogue record for this book is available from the British Library

ISBN 13: 978-1-138-20261-0

Typeset in Times New Roman
by RefineCatch Limited, Bungay, Suffolk

Publisher's Note
The publisher accepts responsibility for any inconsistencies that may have arisen during the conversion of this book from journal articles to book chapters, namely the possible inclusion of journal terminology.

Disclaimer
Every effort has been made to contact copyright holders for their permission to reprint material in this book. The publishers would be grateful to hear from any copyright holder who is not here acknowledged and will undertake to rectify any errors or omissions in future editions of this book.

Contents

Citation Information	vii
Notes on Contributors	ix

1. The legal and ethical implications of drone warfare   1
   Michael J. Boyle

2. Getting drones wrong   23
   Stephanie Carvin

3. A means-methods paradox and the legality of drone strikes in armed conflict   38
   Craig Martin

4. Clashing over drones: the legal and normative gap between the United States
   and the human rights community   72
   Daniel R. Brunstetter and Arturo Jimenez-Bacardi

5. Drones to protect   95
   David Whetham

6. Virtuous drones?   107
   Caroline Kennedy and James I. Rogers

Index   125

Citation Information

The chapters in this book were originally published in *The International Journal of Human Rights*, volume 19, issue 2 (February 2015). When citing this material, please use the original page numbering for each article, as follows:

Chapter 1
The legal and ethical implications of drone warfare
Michael J. Boyle
The International Journal of Human Rights, volume 19, issue 2 (February 2015), pp. 105–126

Chapter 2
Getting drones wrong
Stephanie Carvin
The International Journal of Human Rights, volume 19, issue 2 (February 2015), pp. 127–141

Chapter 3
A means-methods paradox and the legality of drone strikes in armed conflict
Craig Martin
The International Journal of Human Rights, volume 19, issue 2 (February 2015), pp. 142–175

Chapter 4
Clashing over drones: the legal and normative gap between the United States and the human rights community
Daniel R. Brunstetter and Arturo Jimenez-Bacardi
The International Journal of Human Rights, volume 19, issue 2 (February 2015), pp. 176–198

Chapter 5
Drones to protect
David Whetham
The International Journal of Human Rights, volume 19, issue 2 (February 2015), pp. 199–210

CITATION INFORMATION

Chapter 6
Virtuous drones?
Caroline Kennedy and James I. Rogers
The International Journal of Human Rights, volume 19, issue 2 (February 2015),
pp. 211–227

For any permission-related enquiries please visit:
http://www.tandfonline.com/page/help/permissions

Notes on Contributors

Michael J. Boyle is Associate Professor of Political Science at La Salle University and a Senior Fellow at the Foreign Policy Research Institute in Philadelphia, USA. He is the author of *Violence after War: Explaining Instability in Post-Conflict States* (2014).

Daniel R. Brunstetter is Associate Professor in the Department of Political Science at the University of California, Irvine, USA. His work on the ethics of drones has appeared in *Ethics & International Affairs, The Atlantic* and the *Journal of Military Ethics*. He has two upcoming volumes: *Just War Thinkers from Cicero to Today* (Routledge, 2017, co-edited with Cian O'Driscoll) and *The Ethics of War and Peace in an Era of Contested and Fragmented Sovereignty,* co-edited with Jean-Vincent Holeindre.

Stephanie Carvin is an Assistant Professor of International Relations at the Norman Paterson School of International Affairs. Her research interests are in the area of national security, foreign policy, critical infrastructure protection, international law, terrorism and technology. Stephanie holds a Masters and PhD from the London School of Economics and her most recent book is *Science, Law, Liberalism and the American Way of Warfare: The Quest for Humanity in Conflict* (Cambridge, 2015) co-authored with Michael J. Williams.

Arturo Jimenez-Bacardi is an Assistant Professor of International Relations in the History and Politics Department at the University of South Florida, St. Petersburg. His current book project, *Speaking Law to War: International Law, Legal Advisers, and Bureaucratic Contestation in U.S. Defense Policy* examines how the domestic institutionalization of international law into the U.S. national security system affected its use of torture during the Vietnam War and the War on Terrorism.

Caroline Kennedy is Professor of War Studies at the University of Hull, U.K.. She was previously Professor of War Studies at the University of Warwick. She has published extensively on the issue of contemporary security and especially on improvised explosive devices in contemporary wars as well as on Russia and the cold war. She has a First Class Honours Degree in History, an MscEcon in Strategic Studies and a D.Phil. in International Relations.

Craig Martin (B.A.(R.M.C.), J.D. (Univ. Toronto), LL.M. (Osaka Univ.), S.J.D. (Univ. Pennsylvania)), is a Professor of Law at Washburn University School of Law. He specializes in the use of force and the law of armed conflict in international law, and war powers in comparative constitutional law.

NOTES ON CONTRIBUTORS

James I. Rogers is Associate Lecturer in International Politics at the University of York. His work has appeared in the *International Journal of Human Rights, International Peacekeeping* and the *Guardian*. James' monograph, entitled *The Evolution of Precision Warfare*, is forthcoming in 2017.

David Whetham is Reader in Military Ethics in the Defence Studies Department of King's College London, based at the U.K.'s Joint Services Command and Staff College. He is the Director of the King's Centre for Military Ethics and has held Visiting Fellowships at the Stockdale Center for Ethical Leadership, Annapolis, the Centre for Defence Leadership and Ethics at the Australian Defence College in Canberra and at the University of Glasgow.

The legal and ethical implications of drone warfare

Michael J. Boyle

Department of Political Science, La Salle University, Philadelphia, PA, USA

This article examines whether American drone-based targeted killing program represents a fundamentally new challenge to the traditional legal and ethical standards of armed conflict. It argues that the novelty of drones flows less from the technology itself than from the Obama administration's articulation of a presumptive right of anticipatory self-defense, which allows it to strike anywhere in the world where al Qaeda and its allies are present. It highlights five new legal and ethical dimensions to the Obama administration's drones policy, all of which may lower the traditional barriers to the use of force if other actors begin to follow contemporary American practice.

In a speech at the National Defense University in May 2013, President Barack Obama described the US drone campaign in Pakistan, Yemen and elsewhere as part of 'a just war – a war waged proportionally, in last resort, and in self-defense'.[1] Emphasising the dilemmas associated with confronting the threat of modern terrorism, President Obama cast the American drones programme as a legally and morally superior alternative to using Special Forces or ground troops to capture or kill terrorist suspects in places where the United States (US) was not formally at war. This address, along with an earlier speech by Obama's chief counterterrorism advisor John Brennan in April 2012, showed the Obama administration on the defensive against a rising tide of criticism about the civilian casualties associated with American drone strikes.[2] In describing its response to what it called a new, de-territorialised form of armed conflict against terrorist groups, the Obama administration fell back upon long-established concepts of the law of armed conflict and just war theory to argue that its drone strike campaign was legally appropriate and ethically sound. Yet beyond the rhetoric, its actual position on drones has long been marked by ambiguities and internal contradictions. At some points, the administration has been insistent that it is fully complying with all applicable law, including the laws of war, in its drone strike policies.[3] At others, it has denied that some bodies of law – for example, international human rights law – should be applied to these conflicts.[4] At still others, it has implied that the law of armed conflict, and traditional notions of self-defence, need to be updated to reflect the realities of twenty-first century warfare.[5] Throughout its term in office, the Obama administration has tried to use the traditional legal and moral standards of armed conflict as a shield to protect itself from criticism, while simultaneously suggesting that the shield itself is fundamentally inadequate for the threats that the US and its allies face in the twenty-first century.

The fact that the Obama administration has continued to rely on the same legal and ethical frameworks used to restrain the behaviour of states during wars in the nineteenth and twentieth centuries to defend its drone campaign against a range of critics is not surprising.[6] These standards have proven invaluable in checking the cruelty and moral callousness of armies and government states for over a hundred years; indeed, they have proven resilient in light of the vast technological changes in warfare that have occurred since the first Geneva Convention in 1864. Although they do pose some new legal and ethical dilemmas, drones do not fundamentally undermine the applicability of traditional legal and ethical standards of armed conflict.[7] Drones are merely the latest iteration of a process of rapid technological change in warfare that has continued for much of the last one hundred years, and they are not the biggest technological change during this period. The challenges posed by drones are not larger than those posed by nuclear weapons or other twentieth-century innovations such as inter-continental ballistic missile systems (ICBM). As Stephanie Carvin argues in her contribution here, there is no reason to assume that the legal and ethical problems posed by drones are wholly unprecedented or unique to this form of technology.[8] Some of the literature on drones makes this mistake by assuming that the new aspects of drone technology mean that unprecedented legal and ethical questions are now being raised. In fact, the opposite is true. Even more than nuclear weapons and or ICBMs, drones can be discussed within the traditional legal and ethical frameworks governing armed conflict because they are so analogous to conventional or manned aircraft. For many of the relevant ethical questions, such as how many were killed and why, drone strikes can be measured in a straightforward way against bombing done by conventional manned aircraft. In most respects, there is not much of a difference between a bomb dropped by a piloted aircraft and one dropped by a drone provided that both are done by declared combatants in a recognised armed conflict.[9]

Further, some of the charges that are levelled against drones on the basis of the technology itself – for example, that drones automate killing, or that they produce a moral distance between the operator and the target that facilitates gratuitous killing – are either overstated or unproven. For example, while it is true that fully autonomous weapons would produce a new set of legal and ethical challenges for warfare, this is not the situation that prevails today.[10] In all major or well-established drones programmes, the technology remains under the firm control of an individual from the military or intelligence services of an established government.[11] No modern drones programme is fully automated, and in all cases it remains the decision of a single individual – often located in a military chain of command – to strike a target and be held accountable for the consequences. The allegation that there is a 'Playstation mentality' to targeted killings by drones remains to be proven.[12] There is some evidence that the moral distance between the drone operator and target desensitises the operator from the act of killing and may make targeted killings easier.[13] Some drone operators' use of derogatory terms for their targets – 'bug splats' and 'squirters' – points to this dynamic at play.[14] But equally there is evidence that drone operators feel a surprising degree of intimacy with their targets because they monitor them for such long periods of time. Drone operators report relatively high rates of post-traumatic stress disorder (PTSD) in part because they are so acquainted with their target.[15] Further, many of these charges of moral distance are not, strictly speaking, new as they were levelled against automated weapons systems such as cruise missiles and nuclear weapons during the Cold War. The possibility of an individual callously ending a life by pressing a button is as real with cruise missiles as it is with a drone, and even more real with the prospect of a nuclear strike.[16] None of these forms of lethal violence preserve the direct confrontation between perpetrator and target that characterises most depictions of honour in warfare, yet all have been a reality of modern warfare for over half a century.[17]

Still, there may be something new about drone warfare that requires rethinking some of the rules of armed conflict in the twentieth century. While the technology itself may not present wholly new moral and legal dilemmas, it may exaggerate some of them and accelerate other trends – towards speed, precision, and targeting those who blur the distinction between combatants and civilians – present in other forms of armed conflict. If so, while it is certainly not necessary to rewrite the rulebook on armed conflict, it may be necessary to adapt it in ways that reflect the reality of the legal and ethical dilemmas that drones pose, either due to the technology itself or the way that the technology is used. This is the challenge that has yet to be fully met despite a decade of drone-based targeted killing. Although the Obama administration has implied that the rules of armed conflict need to change to meet the new threat of terrorism, and has stated on multiple occasions that the domestic legal authority for drone strikes (the Authorization to Use Military Force, passed in 2001) needs to be revised, it has shied away from explicitly stating what is new about the drone technology and why it requires changes in the rules of war for the twenty-first century. It has left this debate open for scholars and outside experts to identify what is new about drones and to spell out the legal and ethical implications of this technology.

The articles in this special edition identify and analyse the new legal and ethical implications of drones and illustrate how they relate to the existing legal and ethical frameworks that govern armed conflict. This introduction and the article by Stephanie Carvin wrestle with the key conceptual question about what is new with drones: the technology, or the policies surrounding the use of them? The second set of articles, by Craig Martin and by Daniel Brunstetter and Arturo Jimenez Bacardi explain why the legal and ethical debate over drone-based targeted killing remain so contested after nearly a decade of operation. The third set of articles, by David Whetham and by Caroline Kennedy and James Rodgers, look at some of the legal and ethical issues surrounding the next generation uses of drones for humanitarian relief and United Nations (UN) peacekeeping. Taken together, these articles show how American policies surrounding drone usage have themselves produced the dilemmas that the Obama administration now confronts while charting a way in which drone usage might be reconciled with the traditional legal and ethical frameworks in international politics.

This introductory article will address the central conceptual question about what is new with drone warfare, with a focus more on the new dimensions of the policy of targeted killing than the technology itself. Echoing some of Craig Martin's arguments here, it argues that the Obama administration is correct that drones have begun to challenge some of the assumptions that underlie the traditional legal and ethical frameworks for the use of force, but that it is American policy, rather than the technology itself, which is producing this challenge. The US drone-based targeted killing programme has five different characteristics which produce new challenges to the traditional interpretations of the legal and ethical standards for armed conflict. They are: (1) the *legal authority* for drone strikes under both domestic and international law; (2) the *nature of the targets* that the US engages with drone strikes – specifically non-state actors operating outside recognised conflict zones, including those with an indirect link to the original combatants; (3) the *regular deployment* of drones for near-perpetual surveillance and targeted killing, as opposed to periodic or time-limited kinetic action; (4) the *institutional framework* governing drone strikes, which can give rise to transparency and accountability problems; and (5) the *precedent* set by lowering the bar against assassinations and by allowing a state a presumptive right to violate the sovereignty of another state on the basis of a generally articulated threat. Each of these issues flow more from the American use of drones – and the precedent of presumptive self-defence that it sets – than from the technology itself.

Legal authority

The Obama administration has deployed a number of different arguments to provide a legal foundation for its drone programme under domestic and international law. The primary claim of legal authority is based on the Authorization to Use Military Force (AUMF), passed on 14 September 2001. The Congress provided this authorisation following the 9/11 attacks to permit the president to 'to use all necessary and appropriate force against those nations, organizations, or persons he determines planned, authorized, committed, or aided the terrorist attacks that occurred on September 11, 2001, or harbored such organizations or persons, in order to prevent any future acts of international terrorism against the United States by such nations, organizations or persons'.[18] The Bush administration interpreted the AUMF broadly as a legal rationale for worldwide operations against terrorist operatives. It also unsuccessfully cited it as legal authority for employing military tribunals at Guantanamo Bay in *Hamdi* v. *Rumsfeld*.[19]

The position of the Obama administration on the AUMF has been marked by ambivalence. Like his predecessor, President Obama has interpreted the AUMF broadly to allow for maximum discretion in pursuing terrorists abroad, including through the use of drone strikes. Even more than the Bush administration's interpretation of the AUMF, the Obama administration's interpretation has allowed for the US to pursue 'associates' of al-Qaeda wherever they are located, even if that is far from the original theater of war in Afghanistan. The Obama administration has recently extended this argument to suggest that it may pursue successor groups to al-Qaeda on the basis of the AUMF even if they did not exist at the point of the 11 September attacks. For example, under pressure from Congress, the Obama administration argued that it had the right to target the al-Nusra front, an al-Qaeda linked insurgent group located in Syria but operating only since 2012, on the basis of the 2001 AUMF.[20] Similarly, the Obama administration used the AUMF as the legal basis for aiding the Libyan rebels in the overthrow of Muammar Gaddafi and for engaging in air strikes against the Islamic State of Iraq and Syria (ISIS).[21] Both of these objectives are not directly related to al-Qaeda or to the 11 September attacks, yet drone strikes for these purposes have been conducted on the basis of the 2001 AUMF.

The Obama administration has regularly cited the AUMF as the basis for expanding the use of drone strikes in Pakistan, Yemen, Somalia and elsewhere, and argued that its authority has no specified temporal or geographic limit. The Obama administration has defended these strikes as legitimate attacks against al-Qaeda or the Taliban, declared enemies of the US, who as a transnational enemy must be attacked even outside the original theatre of war. In a March 2012 speech at Northwestern Law School, Attorney General Eric Holder remarked that:

> Indeed, neither Congress nor our federal courts has limited the geographic scope of our ability to use force to the current conflict in Afghanistan. We are at war with a stateless enemy, prone to shifting operations from country to country. Over the last three years alone, al Qaeda and its associates have directed several attacks – fortunately, unsuccessful – against us from countries other than Afghanistan. Our government has both a responsibility and a right to protect this nation and its people from such threats.[22]

Similarly, John Brennan has argued that 'there is nothing in the AUMF that restricts the use of military force against al-Qaida to Afghanistan'.[23] This interpretation of the AUMF has come under criticism for effectively providing a greenlight for US action anywhere in the world until some unspecified point in the future when al-Qaeda and its co-belligerents are defeated.[24]

The administration has further implied that it has a series of additional criteria that determine whether a drone strike should take place against a prospective target outside a declared combat zone, such as Afghanistan. Former Legal Advisor for the State Department, Harold Hongju Koh, has said that the US drone policy takes into account specific conditions of that case, including 'those related to the imminence of the threat to the sovereignty of the states involved, and the willingness and ability of those states to suppress the threat that the target poses'.[25] The measurements for each of these criteria – in other words, how the US government assesses whether a government is willing and able to respond to a terrorist threat – have never been released. Similar additional criteria also apply when determining if a drone strike may be used against an American citizen. According to an internal document with the legal justification for killing Anwar al-Awlaki, an American citizen, the US considers itself 'in a non-international armed conflict against al-Qaida and its associated forces', and believes that the determination of whether a proposed strike would require 'consideration of the particular facts and circumstances of each case' rather than a prior determination of the geographic scope of the AUMF.[26] For strikes against both foreign and American citizens, the criteria used to decide when a state is not willing or able to address the terrorist threat on their territory have never been made public. This information would be particularly important in cases like Pakistan, where it remains unclear which of the operative criteria – lack of ability or political will – is the deciding factor in enabling US drone strikes.

There are three major concerns with the interpretation of the AUMF adopted by the Obama administration. First, the lack of a temporal scope for the AUMF, and the fact that its termination is premised on the defeat of al-Qaeda, raises the question of whether any future American administration will ever be constrained from launching drone strikes against al-Qaeda or its associated forces. At this point, the AUMF has operated as an effective green light for worldwide terrorist operations for over 13 years. There is no sign that this war, or the AUMF's applicability, will end soon. In 2013, Michael Sheehan, the assistant secretary of defense for special operations, suggested that the defeat of al-Qaeda could take 'at least 10 to 20 years'.[27] Similarly, former Defense Secretary Leon Panetta has predicted that the US faces a '30 year war', with a campaign extending to Libya, Somalia, Yemen and other locations.[28] Despite a thoughtful effort by former counsel for the DoD Jeh C. Johnson to wrestle with the question of what defeating al-Qaeda would look like, the Obama administration has never articulated what strategic defeat of al-Qaeda and its forces would look like, or what will happen to American counterterrorism operations when that point is reached.[29] In other words, no one knows what the defeat of al-Qaeda would look like or what happens to American counterterrorism policy the day after. There is some evidence that the US would be reluctant to give up the broad remit of authority provided by the AUMF no matter what happens to al-Qaeda. Even when Panetta announced in 2011 that al-Qaeda was on the verge of strategic defeat, the Obama administration never relented on its use of the AUMF as the legal basis for drone strikes, and in fact increased the tempo of these strikes.[30]

Second, the lack of geographic limits to the administration's interpretation is a broad remit for military action, including full-scale combat operations and preventive attacks, in any country where al-Qaeda may be present and planning an attack. Given that al-Qaeda and its affiliates are officially in as many as 30 or more countries, the US has effectively pre-authorised itself for drone strikes in any place it sees a growing threat and little evidence of a local government with the ability to deal with it.[31] The administration has already shown that it will extend drone strikes to countries where there were no plotters of the 11 September attack and no evidence of prior knowledge of that attack, such as Somalia. While the US is less likely to use drones against terrorist targets in Europe, it has used drones across the Middle East (for example, in Iraq and Libya) for reasons unrelated, or only indirectly related, to the 11 September attacks. It remains unclear whether drone strikes in regions far outside South Asia, such as Indonesia and the Philippines, could be conducted on the basis of the legal authority of the AUMF, but the Obama administration's argument implies that it would be permitted to do so if the target was linked in some way to al-Qaeda or the Taliban.

Third, the administration's implication that it has private criteria for determining both the ability and willingness of a government to deal with terrorist threats on its own soil is troubling. On one level, its arguments echo the principal argument of the Responsibility to Protect (R2P) doctrine, which suggests that external states can decide when a sovereign state forfeits its right to non-interference on its territory. For many humanitarian activists, a state's systemic abuse of the human rights of its population can give rise to a duty to intervene for well-intentioned states to rescue a victimised group of civilians. For many R2P advocates, if a government cannot or will not protect its citizens, other actors are entitled to step in and do so as long as the UN or another legitimate body approves. In an ironic twist, the Obama administration has retrofitted this argument – designed to instill fear in dictators and enable states to intervene for legitimate humanitarian purposes – into a rationale for the American drone programme in ungoverned spaces around the world. According to what is known about the Obama administration's criteria, the forfeiture of the sovereign right of non-interference is based on a state's inability, or unwillingness, to address a growing terrorist threat within its borders. The right to make this determination is accorded solely to the US government without any explicit standards or outside authority to adjudicate the decision to violate another state's sovereignty. This raises the prospect that this decision to violate the sovereignty of another state will be used in an inconsistent or capricious manner, with deleterious consequences for the sovereign right of non-interference in the international system.

The Obama administration's ambivalence on the AUMF has also been reflected by different statements from key administration officials on whether a new, revised AUMF is desirable or necessary. In his May 2013 speech, President Obama said:

> The AUMF is now nearly 12 years old. The Afghan war is coming to an end. Core al Qaeda is a shell of its former self. Groups like AQAP must be dealt with, but in the years to come, not every collection of thugs that labels themselves al Qaeda will pose a credible threat to the United States. Unless we discipline our thinking, our definitions, our actions, we may be drawn into more wars we don't need to fight, or continue to grant Presidents unbound powers more suited for traditional armed conflicts between nation states. So I look forward to engaging Congress and the American people in efforts to refine, and ultimately repeal, the AUMF's mandate. And I will not sign laws designed to expand this mandate further. Our systematic effort to dismantle terrorist organizations must continue. But this war, like all wars, must end. That's what history advises. That's what our democracy demands.[32]

Yet the administration has done nothing to revise or amend the AUMF; moreover, it has since invoked the AUMF to justify military operations in Iraq and Syria against ISIS, a group that did not exist in 2001 and that is not formally allied with al-Qaeda. As Jack Goldsmith has argued, 'if this remarkably loose affiliation with al Qaeda brings a terrorist organization under the 2001 law, then Congress has authorized the President to use force endlessly against practically any ambitious jihadist terrorist group that fights against the United States. The President's gambit is, at bottom, presidential unilateralism masquerading as implausible statutory interpretation.'[33] Other Obama administration officials have expressed scepticism about the need for a new AUMF, noting that even a new legal authorisation for drones under a new AUMF would be neither necessary nor wise.[34] Despite growing pressure from some of his Democratic allies in Congress, the president has made no moves towards repealing or revising the AUMF, thus allowing this framework to stand as the predominant legal authority for drone strikes.[35]

The Obama administration has also invoked international law to provide an additional legal foundation for its drone strike programme, arguing that it has the right to strike at al-Qaeda under the inherent right for self-defence provided by the UN Charter.[36] The interpretation of self-defence offered by the administration argues that individuals who are part of a group like al-Qaeda and the Taliban can be considered belligerents, and become targetable, even if they are not located in the country where the original self-defence justification was invoked. By this logic, an al-Qaeda member in Yemen could be killed by a US drone strike authorised in part on a claim of self-defence for an attack prepared and organised from Afghanistan. In the administration's view, this strike would not qualify as an assassination because, in the words of Koh, 'under domestic law, the use of lawful weapons systems – consistent with the applicable laws of war – for precision targeting of specific high-level belligerent leaders when acting in self-defense or during an armed conflict is not unlawful, and hence does not constitute "assassination"'.[37] This argument has been backed by some scholars who argue that when a country is facing a potential attack, a self-defence rationale may be invoked for drone strikes against transnational actors, no matter where they are located.[38]

This assertion of a right of anticipatory self-defence – which allows for an unrestricted geographic scope of military action, even in the absence of evidence of an immediate threat – has not been widely accepted by the international community. Even if one concedes that states are entitled to self-defence against non-state actors not controlled by another state – and the International Court of Justice has suggested that they are not – this argument has at least two major limitations.[39] First, as Philip Alston has pointed out, the self-defence argument implies higher standards for necessity and proportionality than the US government typically applies with its drones programme.[40] Specifically it would require that the government would only use force for defensive objectives, and for that it would only do so once other non-lethal options had been exhausted. There is no evidence in many drone strikes that the US is using them defensively or that they have exhausted other options before electing to strike. In many cases the Obama administration's arguments have emphasised preventive, rather than defensive, actions in that drone strikes are authorised before an attack can be launched or even fully planned. Moreover, the Department of Justice (DoJ) White Paper on drone strikes showed how the Obama administration adopted tendentious readings of 'imminence' and 'necessity' to superficially meet these requirements. According to this memorandum, 'the condition than an operational leader presents an "imminent" threat of violent attack against the United States does not require the United States to have clear evidence of a specific attack in the future'.[41] Similarly, the definition of necessity, according to the Obama administration's interpretation in the DoJ White Paper, requires only that it make the determination that a capture mission or some other non-lethal option be considered infeasible or too risky.[42] The evidentiary standard for a capture operation to be deemed infeasible has never been publicly released.

Second, the case most often cited as providing precedent for using drone strikes for anticipatory self-defence – the *Caroline* case, from 1837 – requires that a state must show that there was an 'instant, overwhelming, and leaving no choice of means, and no moment for deliberation' situation before invoking a right of preventive self-defence.[43] This depiction is at odds with the narrative depiction of the Obama administration's drones programme, which shows a deliberate, non-hurried process to identify potential targets with the president's direct input before the drone strike occurs.[44] Although this explanation is an additional one to the AUMF, the anticipatory self-defence rationale adopted by the Obama administration leaves the US as an outlier in the international system, according for itself a right of anticipatory self-defence that it opposes for other states, with some exceptions.[45] Senior administration officials have recognised this fact. Former CIA Director Michael Hayden remarked in 2012 that 'right now, there isn't a government on the planet that agrees with our legal rationale for these operations, except for Afghanistan and maybe Israel'.[46] The Obama administration is not an outlier due to its possession of drones and use of them for targeted killing, but rather due to its legal interpretation that enables it to continually strike against targets only indirectly related to the original combatants on the grounds of self-defence.

Nature of targets

The approach that the Obama administration has taken to identify the targets of drone strikes is also new and stands in stark contrast with the American approach during previous armed conflicts. According to the law of armed conflict, the identification of a target in an armed conflict involves a positive determination of their conflict status – i.e., whether that individual serves as a direct combatant, such as a soldier, in a recognised armed conflict. This determination, supported by both state practice and customary international law, involves designating as a combatant all those involved in combatant armies, even those not directly fighting, with the exception of religious and medical personnel.[47] In classical interstate wars, this is a relatively straightforward determination as the combatant is typically clothed as a soldier, carries some clear national identification, and is participating in conflict in a direct way. In these cases, states are not generally required to pinpoint the precise identity of an individual before targeting them, but they are required to determine if their actions are materially related to the armed conflict before attacking. They are also not required to provide combatants with access to legal process if they are in *hors d'combat*, but they must treat them as a privileged combatant and accord them prisoner of war status if captured.

For irregular wars, the designation of combatant status has always been more complex. The chief problem with these conflicts is that insurgents and other irregular fighters have often not been clothed or self-identified as combatants. For many insurgent groups, blurring their combatant status by hiding amidst the civilian population has allowed them to fight a stronger power and exploit the fact that governments are obliged to use force with the principle of distinction, avoiding civilian casualties if at all possible. Nevertheless, Article 4 of the Third Geneva Convention requires governments to accord to these irregular fighters prisoner of war status if they fulfil the following conditions: (1) that of being commanded by a person responsible for his subordinates; (2) that of having a fixed distinctive sign recognisable at a distance; (3) that of carrying arms openly; (4) that of conducting their operations in accordance with the laws and customs of war.[48] During the Vietnam War, the US generally applied the Geneva Conventions to the Viet Cong forces and accorded captured insurgents humane treatment, though not always full prisoner of war status. During the Bush administration, the US adopted a different approach and unsuccessfully advanced the argument that al-Qaeda and Taliban members were unlawful combatants because they failed to fulfil these conditions and should not enjoy trial by jury in civilian courts. Their argument – that unlawful combatants should be tried by military tribunals at Guantanamo Bay and elsewhere – was ultimately rejected by the Supreme Court.[49]

The Obama administration has confronted similar problems with its drones programme. Many of the targets of drones do not wear uniforms and are part-time combatants, fighting at one moment but engaging in peaceful civilian activities at the next. The fact that many insurgent and terrorist groups do not have a clear command structure or distinction between political and military leaders produces a series of important moral dilemmas.[50] Many facilities and vehicles used by insurgents are dual use: they are used for military activity at one moment, and for combat at another. Even more so than guerrillas during the Cold War, today's insurgents are embedded in the civilian population, intermixing with them in ways that make analytically separating combatants and civilians difficult, if not impossible, in some cases.[51] How governments can justly and carefully fight non-state actors, while maintaining the principle of distinction and not slipping into the barbarism that its abandonment would imply, is a key question that any government facing insurgent warfare in the twenty-first century must answer.

The Obama administration has acknowledged these problems but has maintained that the difficulties associated with identifying combatants in today's messy intra-state wars should not be an insurmountable barrier against using drones for targeted killings. It insists that the monitoring technology associated with its drones allows operators to abide by the principle of distinction and carefully distinguish between combatants and civilians.[52] Koh has argued that the American drone strike programme easily meets the international humanitarian law requirements of necessity, distinction and proportionality. On the question of necessity, the US has consistently argued that it is legally permitted to attack members of al-Qaeda and the Taliban as irregular combatants because they are engaged in a protracted armed conflict with the US. For distinction and proportionality, the Obama administration has insisted that it has carefully avoided civilian casualties and abided by the principle of proportionality in its drone strikes, killing relatively few civilians compared to other available military means.[53] President Obama has admitted that some civilian casualties are inevitable with drone strikes, but has insisted that reports of high levels of civilian casualties are overstated. From an ethical vantage point, the Obama administration argues that the drones programme is humane in that it kills relatively few civilians, all of whom would be covered under the principle of double effect given the military necessity of the strikes.

Yet the Obama administration's arguments both presume, and are dependent upon, a novel definition of the nature of the enemy not widely accepted by the international community. Recognising the problems associated with the Bush approach, the Obama administration has expanded the definition of the target in a way which avoids the difficulties associated with using the terms illegal or enemy combatants. In 2009, the Attorney General announced the Obama administration was abandoning the term 'enemy combatant' while reaffirming its broad powers to fight and detain terrorist suspects.[54] This allowed the Obama administration to avoid many of the legal headaches that the Bush administration experienced with that definition, although in practice it meant little for those held as prisoners in Guantanamo Bay. At the same time, the Obama administration advanced, without fanfare, a more expansive definition of the potential targets of American military action

LEGAL AND ETHICAL IMPLICATIONS OF DRONE WARFARE

than President Bush articulated. First, the Obama administration rejected the notion that it was limited to striking only al-Qaeda and the Taliban and insisted that it could also target 'associated forces'. Although the AUMF language requires some connection be drawn to the 11 September attacks or that the enemy be at the least a co-belligerent of al-Qaeda and the Taliban, the Obama administration has in practice attacked groups linked to al-Qaeda or the Taliban in a variety of indirect, often immaterial, ways.[55] These 'associated forces' are not precisely defined by the US government and in practice have ranged from Pakistani Taliban to even Somali militants. All are now considered co-belligerents of al-Qaeda under the Obama approach. In effect, it has drawn a functional equivalence between 'associated forces' and 'co-belligerents', thus providing legal cover to strike a growing array of targets. It has used this expansive definition of the enemy to target the Islamic State in Iraq and Syria (ISIS), which was expelled from al-Qaeda in February 2014 and had no contemporary organisational link to it.[56] In fact, its authorisation for the Iraq operation declared that ISIS was a successor to al-Qaeda, and thus it can be considered a co-belligerent, a determination now also supported by the UN.[57] Its expansive interpretation of 'associated forces' or 'co-belligerents' is also not public, as the US refuses to make the list of what it considers an associated force of al-Qaeda or the Taliban public.[58] While the Pentagon maintains that a target must be defined as a co-belligerent of al-Qaeda or the Taliban, it does not specify how an actor operating far outside a recognised theater of conflict (Afghanistan) can be considered a co-belligerent of an actor in that conflict. While there is a plausible case that transnational terrorist groups could be considered co-belligerents even if they are not physically co-located with a combatant, the legal standard for making that determination remains a mystery. By equating the term 'associated force' with 'co-belligerent', the Obama administration has enabled itself to attack any group operating in the same radical Islamist milieu as al-Qaeda by deeming it an 'associated force'.

Second, the Obama administration has adopted vague language about a group being 'linked' to a recognised combatant group without explaining exactly what that link is.[59] If the linkage was material support, that connection could be considered relatively obvious as a group supplying weapons or key equipment to a fighting group could be considered a combatant under the normal interpretation of the laws of war. Equally, groups that are fighting alongside an original combatant – for example, the Haqqani network and the Islamic Movement of Uzbekistan (IMU) in Afghanistan – could plausibly be considered a combatant, and hence a target, under international law. Yet the administration has acted in ways that suggest that the linkage could consist of purely ideological or political support for al-Qaeda or the Taliban, rather than direct material support. For example, the Obama administration has reportedly used drone strikes to target elements of al-Shabaab in Somalia without specifying how it is materially linked to the original combatants in Afghanistan and Pakistan. Similarly, some Pakistani Islamist groups have been targeted on the basis of a tangential connection to al-Qaeda or the Taliban. This administration's expansive definition of linkage allows for many possible connections, even political or ideological links, to be sufficient to make a group 'linked' to al-Qaeda and hence targetable.

Third, the Obama administration has adopted a policy of engaging in periodic signature strikes, directing drone strikes against training camps and compounds which were suspected of harbouring militants.[60] These strikes are premised on the basis that the patterns of behaviour of the potential target are sufficient to indicate that they intended to engage in combat against American or local allied forces. Critics have argued that signature strikes carry with them a greater risk of civilian casualties than so-called personality strikes, as the risk of false positives – that is, a mistaken identification of a target – is

LEGAL AND ETHICAL IMPLICATIONS OF DRONE WARFARE

greater in these cases.[61] This approach may also fall below the standard for distinction that is required under international law, as it is generally accepted that the person launching the strikes must be certain, within reason, that the activity witnessed is materially aiding the enemy's military effort. Conducted at a substantial remove from the actual target, signature drone strikes do not always achieve that standard and can fall afoul of the principle of proportionality, depending on the nature of the target and what they appear to be doing. For example, striking people simply because they were moving towards a conflict zone, or stopping at a rest area known to be used by al-Qaeda, is insufficient as grounds for a signature strike.[62] Although he did not mention signature strikes by name, President Obama promised to employ a higher standard for drone strikes, which would eliminate many of these strikes, after his May 2013 speech. It remains unclear whether this has taken place, although drone strikes in Pakistan and Yemen declined sharply after that speech.

Drone usage

A third new aspect to the American policy on drones has to do with the way in they are used for monitoring, and striking, populations in foreign countries. Since 2009, the US has used drones as a regular form of surveillance in places such as Pakistan, Afghanistan and Yemen. This usage takes advantage of one of the significant technological features of drones: that they can loiter for significant periods of time over territories and provide detailed readouts on the movements of people and equipment. This means that unlike manned surveillance flights – where the time in the air is limited by human endurance and difficulties loitering – drones are able to remain over a territory for a long time. For example, the Predator B drone (otherwise known as the Reaper) can stay airborne for up to 14 hours while fully loaded with cargo.[63] Others have an even greater endurance capacity. The RQ-1A Predator drone can remain airborne for up to 40 hours and cover a large area at a distance of 400 miles from its operating base.[64]

The US has taken advantage of the endurance capacity of these drones to extend the length of its surveillance in ungoverned spaces, such as Pakistan and Yemen, and in Afghanistan and Iraq. It has also deployed some of its more capable lethal drones, such as Predators and Reapers, as a semi-regular presence in these territories as the drones scan for known targets. Unlike surveillance flights during the Cold War, surveillance drones can loiter over a territory and provide a constant feed of data on what is occurring below. In this respect, they operate more like hyper-capable, low-altitude modern satellites than the manned overflights that occurred over major nuclear and defence installations during the Cold War. The regular deployment of drones for target killings is crucially different than the use of cruise missiles or other temporary, time-limited kinetic (or lethal) options. A cruise missile attack, like the US launched against alleged al-Qaeda sites in Sudan and Afghanistan in 1998, is by definition a limited event, where the destruction is over in a matter of moments. Even systematic bombing campaigns, like the Rolling Thunder campaign in the Vietnam War, occurred over a period of hours but then ceased on a daily basis as the manned aircraft returned to bases for refueling and rest. In these cases, it was certainly the case that bombers were seen over the territory on a semi-regular basis, but the duration of the operations, and the attendant risks to civilians, were relatively short-lived.

By contrast, the deployment of drones over ungoverned spaces in places like Pakistan and Yemen has become a regular event, where a foreign population is routinely monitored, and sometimes killed, by the US on an ongoing basis. The effect of the near-constant presence of drones on the wider population has been noted by a number of critics. The journalist

David Rohde, for example, has described the effect of hearing drones whirring above him for hours on end and called them a 'potent, unnerving symbol of unchecked American power'.[65] Similarly, the Stanford/NYU report, *Living under Drones*, has described the waves of fear that individuals feel from drones hovering overhead and the extent to which their presence has begun to interrupt normal political, economic and social life in these countries.[66] Others have reported from Yemen that drones fuel a pervasive sense of helplessness for those under their flight paths.[67] This sense of fear is clearly not universal; some critics have found evidence that drones are not as disruptive or hated as these accounts imply, for many educated, urban-dwelling Pakistanis and Yemeni see drones as preferable to the greater evils confronting them from local militants and their own government.[68] The actual psychological effect of drones may vary by social class and location, with rural dwellers in the ungoverned spaces where drones operate feeling their effects most directly.[69] But even given this fact, it is hard to dispute that for those living under the flight paths drones have become a constant, enduring reminder that they are being watched, and may be killed, by a foreign government. According to Human Rights Watch, some Yemenis have even concluded that they fear the US as much as they fear al-Qaeda in the Arabian Peninsula.[70]

The key question that arises from this particular use of drones is whether the American routine deployment of drones over ungoverned spaces – and the psychological effect that this deployment has on the subject populations – has produced novel ethical and legal problems. If drones have the effect of terrorising parts of the rural population in the areas where militants are active, there may be a prima facie case that drone deployments are violating the fundamental criterion of proportionality, even if many of the strikes do not. The administration has employed a narrow calculation of proportionality, focusing exclusively on the body count associated with the drones. The US has insisted that drones are not violating the principle of proportionality because the tallies of civilian deaths have been low and that the ratio of civilians killed per combatant is favourable.[71] The Obama administration's method of calculating civilian casualties has run into a wide array of critics, but even many of its critics implicitly accept that body counts should determine whether drones are more proportionate than other weapons of war.

Yet there are three reasons why a narrow calculation of proportionality – which focuses exclusively on measuring body counts, both of 'bad guys' and civilians – provides a misleading account of the real effects of drones. First, as John Kaag and Sarah Kreps argue, the typical calculation of proportionality is sometimes skewed as the goals associated with drone strikes – for example, ending 'evil' and preventing catastrophic terrorist attacks – are inflated, thus making civilian casualties and other psychological costs associated with the strikes more palatable.[72] Seen from this vantage point, the psychological costs associated with drones would be considered more acceptable if they were in the service of countering a greater 'evil'. Second, as Daniel Brunstetter and Arturo Jimenez Bacardi point out in their article in this volume, the principle of proportionality is difficult to measure when the psychological consequences of drones are added into the equation.[73] Much of the debate is conducted with a narrow calculation of proportionality, which measures only civilian deaths against the military gains associated with a strike, and engages in a form of 'proportionality relativism' that uses impertinent comparisons to claim that drones are proportionate.[74] Such calculations tend to downplay many of the psychological effects of drones and the longer-term consequences on America's global image, treating them as 'off the books' costs when measuring the casualties associated with each strike. Third, the degree of fear inflicted on the wider population from drone strikes may be disproportionate to the military advantages accruing from the drone strike itself. According to Geneva Conventions, if the

LEGAL AND ETHICAL IMPLICATIONS OF DRONE WARFARE

incidental harm to the civilian population exceeds the advantages of removing an operational leader from the battlefield, a military operation may be deemed disproportionate
even if its intention was not to terrorise the civilian population.[75] The Obama administration's decision to keep drones as a near-constant presence in areas in Pakistan and
Yemen could constitute a violation of proportionality if the generalised fear in the population were seen as producing real costs, exceeding the advantages of removing some terrorist operatives from the battlefield.

If the psychological effects of drones are real and widespread, the regular deployment of
drones by the US may also constitute a violation of the principle of distinction, which
requires governments to shield non-combatants from the direct effects of conflict as
much as they can. By using drones as near-constant force over these ungoverned territories,
as opposed to an occasional presence, the US may be subjecting the civilian population to
an environment of constant fear and uncertainty that is at variance with the normal interpretation of non-combatant immunity. While this action would not nearly be as egregious a
legal and ethical violation of the principle of distinction as the actual bombing of civilian
targets, it would still stand in contrast to a traditional interpretation of non-combatant immunity which requires those using violence to direct their attacks only at open participants in
the conflict. By making the American deployment of drones a regular, nearly constant
feature of life in these countries, and by allowing the psychological consequences of that
decision to impact upon the local population outside the circumstances of a supreme
emergency, the US may be violating the spirit of the principle of distinction even if it is
not violating the letter of it.[76]

Transparency and accountability

A further element of novelty in the Obama administration's drones policy has to do with its
relatively weak mechanisms for transparency and accountability. As described by the
Geneva Convention, the use of military force should be conducted by recognised armies
who have clear chains of command and standards for releasing information about their
operations. These government-led military forces are considered 'lawful combatants' and
they have clear rights and responsibilities on the battlefield. Information on battlefield
activities should flow up the chain of command and should be released, albeit selectively,
to the wider public. No government has ever been perfectly transparent about its use of military force or willing to show ugliness of war to its population; in wartime, censorship and
the manipulation of information for propaganda purposes has always been a serious
problem. Yet on balance democracies have gone further than other states towards providing
clear mechanisms of transparency and accountability to ensure that their use of force is governed by applicable legal and ethical principles. Throughout the twentieth century advanced
democracies in Europe and North America created sophisticated mechanisms of transparency and accountability to ensure that progress of a military campaign was regularly
assessed through legislative scrutiny and through the investigation of an active media.
For most of the Cold War, the US government conducted armed conflict under the watchful
eye of Congress and of the media, which demanded a regular release of information on their
activities. These mechanisms of transparency and accountability were flawed and often met
with government-led evasions and outright lies, as most famously happened with the
Pentagon Papers during the Vietnam War. But even the Nixon administration conceded
the basic principle that American military activity should be subject to harsh scrutiny
from external forces, including academia and non-profit organisations, as well as Congress
and the courts. Recognising that the domestic need for transparency was crucial, the US

government built its own set of public relations bureaucracies to relay information about its military campaigns and hopefully keep the balance of public opinion on its side.

With the targeted killing programme, the Obama administration has reversed much of this trend and kept most of its activities out of the gaze of Congress, the courts and the independent media. Former White House spokesperson Robert Gibbs has admitted that he was told to not even admit the existence of a drones programme.[77] Even after President Obama admitted in a town hall meeting that there was a drones programme in 2012, White House spokesperson Jay Carney rebuffed questions about its existence.[78] By May 2012, the Obama administration began to open up the drones programme and to engage in a selective public relations campaign to release some information about it. It emphasised that the administration had a careful, deliberative process for selecting targets, but shied away from laying out the details of that process in the public domain.[79] By May 2013, President Obama promised to be more forthcoming with details about the drones programme, yet concrete action on revealing details of it have been very limited. Although the government has released some information on personality strikes, and on strikes against US citizens, it has failed to acknowledge publicly that it even engages in signature strikes, despite how often that allegation is made.[80] Moreover, it has released few details on key issues surrounding the targeted killings of non-Americans, despite the fact this group constitutes the vast majority of those targeted by drone strikes. The administration has not even confirmed the number of countries where drones are present or where al-Qaeda or 'associated forces' have been attacked.

The Obama administration has not been much more forthcoming with Congress or the courts. The administration has regularly argued that Congress is fully briefed about the fundamental elements of the drones programme, but in practice only select members of Congress on the Intelligence Committees are briefed on the fundamentals of the drone operations. Relatively few Congressional briefings have been held on the mechanics or effects of the drones programme, although sparely attended hearings on the drones programme began to increase as the administration contended with a wave of public criticism.[81] These hearings have largely been directed to the administration's assertion that it is entitled to target American citizens with drone strikes, despite the fact that strikes against American citizens are far less common than strikes against foreign citizens. With respect to the rest of the programme, Congress has 'essentially abdicated oversight responsibility' for much of the drones programme.[82] There has never been a single vote for or against the drones programme, as most of it has been conducted with tacit Congressional approval.[83] Until 2013, American courts regularly refused to hear drone cases and met administration opposition that they lacked jurisdiction over the matter. The Obama administration has only recently allowed the courts to weigh in on drone strikes, though they have signalled some willingness to consider a drones court to weigh up the justness of a proposed strike.

The administration also has uneven mechanisms for Congressional accountability in the event of a mistake or careless use of a drone strike. The US drones programme is divided into two parallel programmes, one under the control of the Joint Special Operations Command (JSOC) and another under the control of the Central Intelligence Agency (CIA). The JSOC programme is governed by the military's rules and standards for targeting individuals and goes through a rigorous process of target selection and review. In other words, the JSOC programme has a chain of command that allows for proper accountability.[84] There is some evidence that this pays off in more careful discrimination about civilian casualties.[85] The CIA programme, on the other hand, is entirely classified, with almost no data in the public domain about its activities. It remains unclear who is involved in the process of selecting targets and how the chain of command for the CIA drone programme is designed.[86] The absence of clear accountability for the CIA's portion of the drones programme is important because it raises key questions about whether the CIA will be as careful and discriminating as JSOC. It also raises some key questions about the legal accountability of the CIA officials involved in the programme. As Mary Ellen O'Connell points out, the CIA would not be considered a lawful combatant according to the law of armed conflict and may not be as well trained or mindful of the requirements of distinction, necessity and proportionality as military officers.[87] This means that unlike soldiers they may be later held criminally accountable in foreign courts for their involvement in the drones programme. The Obama administration is attempting to prevent this by denying the existence of the programme, by refusing to reveal the mechanics of its targeting decisions, and by trying to limit the applicability of international human rights law in countries where drones are used frequently.

The result of the Obama administration's approach is that the drones programme has become an anomaly: an unaccountable and non-transparent form of democratic warfare. The administration has argued that the programme is accountable, but it has emphasised that the accountability for it should be relegated to the executive branch and select Intelligence Committees, as opposed to Congress, the courts or the general public. In this respect, it is treating the drones programme as analogous to spying, which receives scant Congressional and judicial oversight and remains a preserve of the Executive Branch. Yet it is hard to argue that the drones programme – which has killed as many as 4000 people, according to a leaked government estimate – is closer to spying than it is to armed conflict.[88] Moreover, this effort by the Obama administration to keep drones in the shadows stands in opposition to many of the global trends towards greater accountability seen with warfare around the globe, as other democratic governments are increasingly holding the agents of violence, including soldiers, criminally responsible for war crimes and other acts that violate the laws of war. Whether a democracy can engage in this kind of sustained violence in the absence of mechanisms for transparency and accountability, and remain democratic, is an open question. But there is a serious possibility that the drones programme will become corrosive of the democratic character of the US government as long as these two conditions remain unfulfilled.

Precedent

The final new dimension of the Obama administration's use of drones concerns the precedent that it sets for the use of assassination and targeted killings abroad. In general, the use of assassinations is not widely accepted by states, as relatively few governments – notably Israel – have argued publicly that they should be permitted outside of armed conflict. This is not to say that assassinations are rare; governments and intelligence agencies conduct assassinations from time to time, and in rare cases, such as Israel, make a policy of it.[89] Yet most governments are loathe to articulate publicly that this should be permissible by others for two reasons. First, it is widely accepted that assassinations and targeted killings are legally prohibited. Under international law, assassinations are forbidden outside the context of armed conflict because they violate international human rights law, as well as an array of domestic laws.[90] Assassinations are generally considered a violation of customary international law and of a state's obligation to protect the right to life. They are permitted only during the context of armed conflict and under exceptional circumstances, where overwhelming necessity to prevent further loss of life dictates that they should be conducted.[91] The US government is officially barred from conducting assassinations by both domestic law (for example, the 1976 executive order signed by President Gerald Ford) and by international law. Although the CIA has committed extrajudicial killings, it operates under a legal authority (Title 50 of the United States code) that requires it be consistent with the US constitution and all other applicable laws.[92] Second, there is a strong norm against assassinations that is widely respected by states, if only for reasons that they fear others will engage in assassinations against their officials.[93] This norm has proven to be durable despite the growth of informal violence in the system, as even states that conduct assassinations are reluctant to concede that this should become a generalisable right. Even during wartime, when some assassinations would arguably be permitted, states have been reluctant to kill wartime leaders, in part because it would deprive them of someone who could negotiate an end to the war.

The use of drones for targeted killings challenges this legal and normative prohibition on assassinations and targeted killings outside of armed conflict. The Obama administration has maintained that its drone programme does not constitute a form of assassination, and therefore it is not in violation of legal and ethical prohibitions on that act.[94] By declaring that it is in a geographically unrestricted state of armed conflict against al-Qaeda, the US has argued that its drone strikes should be considered as part of wartime conduct, rather than an assassination conducted in peacetime. This interpretation enables the US to strike at the leaders and operatives of non-state actors around the world under the broad rubric of armed conflict, while avoiding the legal restrictions on assassinations. The problem with this argument is that the US is not at war with the governments in the territories in which it is conducting targeted killings; its interpretation is essentially that it can be at war with non-state actors in foreign countries and strike them without being in a state of war against the government which is legally sovereign in the territory where the non-state actor is present. By this logic, a state at war with an ideological or nationalist terrorist group could kill their operatives on the territory of another state, without declaring war on that government or admitting that it is a form of assassination. In other words, the US policy creates a gray area between war and assassination that enables a variety of different forms of informal violence, especially government on non-state actor targeted killing.

From a legal and ethical vantage point, this articulation of a space for killing between war and peace poses a number of challenges. The Obama administration's position is not consistent with international law which requires states to either declare war on a government or leave it to that government's responsibility to deal with armed threats emanating from its borders. To articulate a generalised right to strike within another state's territory, without first declaring war on that state, could be interpreted as an act of aggression unless the state granted consent to do so. Even if they did, some have argued that states cannot grant other governments the right to strike on their territory in this way outside an official armed conflict.[95] Arguably, the US may be articulating a new form of state practice, as recognised by a number of legal scholars, which permits assassinations or targeted killings to regularly occur in the gray area between armed conflict and peacetime.[96] One danger of this approach is that recurring state practice may itself begin to produce followers and generate new norms of customary international law that undermines the strict prohibition on assassinations and enables a new range of prospective targets for targeted killings. In other words, the US may be gradually normalising the practice of extrajudicial murder by states, particularly if other states do not accept that the right of anticipatory self-defence belongs to the US alone.

There is already some evidence that this loosening of the barriers against assassinations or targeted killings is now in play. The US has already begun to expand its range of targets beyond traditional insurgents by drawing up a 'hit list' of Afghan drug lords.[97] Other states have begun to follow suit and adapt extrajudicial killings to their own purposes. For example, Israel has begun to use drones to strike at militants in the Sinai and in the Palestinian territories.[98] According to a *New York Times* report, China seriously considered using a drone strike to kill a notorious drug lord in Myanmar.[99] At present, the chief reason that more states have not joined the practice of using drones to target their enemies is that their technology has lagged behind industry leaders such as the US and Israel. But as more states catch up, the prospect of an increasing number of states engaging in targeted killings against their domestic enemies becomes a real one. A high-level panel at the Stimson Center recently sketched out a number of scenarios where drones could be used by others for targeted killings, such as Russia using drones to kill its enemies in Ukraine without admitting its legal reasoning for doing so. The danger of the American practice of drones is that it has produced a new pattern of state behaviour that may lead more states to join the assassination game. The Stimson Center report asks: 'is the United States inadvertently handing abusive foreign regimes a playbook for murdering those it considers politically inconvenient under the guise of combating terrorism?'[100]

A growing number of ethics scholars have also begun to recognise that this gray area between war and peace may be necessary, but should not be seen as a free-for-all zone where any form of violence is permitted. In the areas which Michael Walzer calls the 'in between zones', where terrorists are operating in ungoverned or less governed spaces, drone strikes must still be assessed on the basis of *jus en bello* standards or, as Braun and Brunstetter argue, a modified form of *jus en bello* with even stricter standards of proportionality and discrimination.[101] In this realm, increasingly called *jus ad vim*, Braun and Brunstetter argue that the resort to force in these ethical gray zones should not be permissible on the basis of a generally articulated threat, as is often the case with the US targeted killings programme. In these areas, harm to civilians must be measured in a way that stretches beyond body counts and incorporates a wider notion of harm, including psychological harm. Even if one concedes that the US may be right that there is a space short of war where some form of force should be permitted, it does not follow that the standards currently applied by the CIA's drone programme, which presume a broadly articulated threat and a narrowly articulated standard of proportionality, must be accepted.

In this context, the technology of drones becomes relevant once more and interacts with American policy in dangerous ways. One of the chief ethical dangers arising from drones is moral hazard, where the fact that drone technology is low-cost and increasingly accessible to a number of states means that targeted killings becomes easier and therefore more frequent. As Kaag and Kreps argue, the expediency of drone-based targeted killing can be confused with the moral justification for it; just because something can be done quickly and with a modicum of personal risk does not mean that it is justified.[102] Drone technology is seductive because it can create the illusion of riskless war and lead more states into taking risks to kill more enemies with drone strikes in other lands. Here the US policy on targeted killing is perilous if it creates a precedent and leads other states to follow suit with their own drones-based targeted killing programmes. The spread of drone technology and the American precedent could combine to create a world in which more and more states engage in targeted killings because they are easy and because so many of their rivals do it. Such a world would be closer to the rule of the jungle than to the rule-based international order that the US sought to create and sustain over the last 50 years.

Conclusion

One of the unfortunate consequences of the rise of drone-based targeted killings is that much of the debate over the technology and its uses focuses exclusively on that function and its legal and moral consequences. It is important to remember that targeted killings are not the only function of drones; they can be put to a wide range of other, often beneficial purposes. For example, as David Whetham points out in his contribution here, drones could play an important role in complex humanitarian emergencies as they can conduct surveillance in regions (like the Syrian civil war today) where outside monitors find it too difficult to operate.[103] Similarly, Caroline Kennedy and James Rodgers argue that drones can provide a solution for the UN in peacekeeping operations, both by reducing the risks that peacekeepers face and by monitoring the compliance of signatories to peace agreements.[104] Kennedy and Rodgers go even further by suggesting that armed drones might be able to play a useful role in peace enforcement. Both of these uses of drones have legal and ethical questions; there are important issues surrounding the legal authority for their use, the control of the drones, the legal accountability for their use, and the moral hazard that flows from their employment by the UN or other actors. But they point to an important fact: a world of drones is not inevitably one in which targeted killings are their only, or even primary, function.

Whether this world ever emerges has to do largely with what the US – as a leader in the research and development of drones and as the world's largest and most innovative user of drones – does next. In other words, the legal and ethical implications of drones are not set in stone but are in fact being created and reinforced by discrete American policies. At present, the use of drones by the Obama administration has been directed towards establishing a right of anticipatory self-defence, enabled and accelerated by drone technology, which is accorded exclusively to the US government. Such an articulation of the purpose of drones is dangerous because it may begin to crowd out other, more beneficial, uses of drones, and to produce a set of precedents that may be exploited by other states. The policies employed by the Obama administration for drone-based targeted killings have begun to slowly erode some of the traditional legal and ethical restraints on the use of force, creating a growing gap between current American practice and how armed force should be used according to the law of armed conflict. Such an approach is short-sighted for it surrenders the opportunity for the US to take the lead in articulating precisely what the legal and ethical implications of drones are and how the rules on the use of force must be adapted to accommodate and control them. By developing a targeted killing programme as an exceptional, US-only proposition, and by keeping that programme in the shadows, the Obama administration may be hastening a day in which others use drones in ways hostile to both American interests and to a just international order.

Acknowledgements

The author is grateful to Emma Leonard Boyle for feedback on this piece and wishes to thank all of the authors and reviewers who made this special edition possible.

Disclosure statement

No potential conflict of interest was reported by the author.

Notes

1. President Barack Obama, 'Remarks by the President at the National Defense University', The White House, 23 May 2013. http://www.whitehouse.gov/the-press-office/2013/05/23/remarks-president-national-defense-university (accessed 28 September 2014).
2. John Brennan, 'The Ethics and Efficacy of US Counterterrorism Strategy', Address at the Woodrow Wilson Center, Washington DC, 30 April 2012. http://www.wilsoncenter.org/event/the-efficacy-and-ethics-us-counterterrorism-strategy (accessed 28 September 2014).
3. See, for example, Harold Hongju Koh, 'The Obama Administration and International Law', 25 March 2010. http://www.state.gov/s/l/releases/remarks/139119.htm (accessed 28 September 2014).
4. See Daniel R. Brunstetter and Arturo Jimenez Bacardi, 'Drones and Human Rights: A Clash of Discourses', in this volume.
5. Barack Obama, 'Nobel Lecture', 10 December 2009. http://www.nobelprize.org/nobel_prizes/peace/laureates/2009/obama-lecture_en.html (accessed 3 November 2014).
6. For example, former General Counsel of the Department of Defense, Jeh Charles Johnson, remarked that 'this is a new kind of war. It is an unconventional war against an unconventional enemy. And, given its unconventional nature, President Obama – himself a lawyer and a good one – has insisted that our efforts in pursuit of this enemy stay firmly rooted in conventional legal principles.' See Jeh Charles Johnson, 'The Conflict Against Al Qaeda and Its Affiliates: How Will It End', Speech to the Oxford Union, 30 November 2012.
7. This article refers to these standards in general terms, but they are comprised of the Geneva Conventions and the *jus ad bellum* and *jus in bello* requirements.
8. Stephanie Carvin, 'Getting Drones Wrong', in this volume.
9. This point is made well by Bradley Jay Strawser, 'Moral Predators: The Duty to Employ Uninhabited Aerial Vehicles', *Journal of Military Ethics* 9, no. 4 (2010): 352–68. See also Strawser's debate with Asa Kasher in 'Distinguishing Drones: An Exchange', in *Killing by Remote Control: The Ethics of an Unmanned Military*, ed. Bradley Jay Strawser (Oxford: Oxford University Press, 2013), 47–65.
10. For good discussions of some of the philosophical and ethical questions arising if fully autonomous drones emerge, see Peter Finn, 'A Future for Drones: Automated Killing', *The Washington Post*, 19 September 2011; Patrick Lin, 'Drone-Ethics Briefing: What a Leading Robot Expert Told the CIA', *The Atlantic*, 15 December 2011.
11. For Robert Sparrow, this fact means that drones are permissible, but fully autonomous drones would not be due to a lack of clear human accountability. See Robert Sparrow, 'Killer Robots', *Journal of Applied Philosophy* 24, no. 1 (2007): 62–77.
12. Human Rights Council, 'Report of the Special Rapporteur on Extrajudicial, Summary or Arbitrary Executions, Philip Alston', Fourteenth Session, 28 May 2010, para. 84.
13. Mary Ellen O'Connell, 'Unlawful Killing with Combat Drones: A Case Study of Pakistan 2004–2009', Notre Dame Law School, Legal Studies Research Paper No. 09-43, July 2010, 8–10.
14. Glenn Greenwald, 'Bravery and Drone Pilots', *Salon*, 10 July 2012.
15. See Matthew Power, 'Confessions of a Drone Warrior', *GQ Magazine*, 22 October 2013; Mark Bowden, 'The Killing Machines', *The Atlantic*, 14 August 2013.
16. David Whetham, 'Killer Drones', *RUSI Journal* 158, no. 3 (2013): 22–33.
17. This fact has led a number of scholars to argue that we are now living in a world of post-heroic warfare. See particularly Edward Luttwak, 'Towards Post-Heroic Warfare', *Foreign Affairs* (May/June 1995); and for an application to drones see Christian Enemark, *Armed Drones and the Ethics of War: Military Virtue in a Post-Heroic Age* (London: Routledge, 2013); and Robert Sparrow, 'War Without Virtue', in *Killing by Remote Control: The Ethics of an Unmanned Military*, ed. Bradley Jay Strawser (Oxford: Oxford University Press, 2013), 84–105.
18. Authorization to Use Military Force, Pub L. 107-40, 115 Stat. 224, 14 September 2001.
19. For an effective summary, see *Hamdi* v. *Rumsfeld* (2004), 542 U.S. (507), Lawfare, 12 November 2012. http://www.lawfareblog.com/wiki/the-lawfare-wiki-document-library/post-911-era-materials/post-911-era-materials-court-cases/hamdi-v-rumsfeld-542-u-s-507-2004/ (accessed 21 October 2014).
20. Jack Goldsmith, 'Congress Must Figure Out What Our Government is Doing in the Name of the AUMF', *Lawfare*, 17 May 2013. http://www.lawfareblog.com/2013/05/congress-must-figure-out-what-our-government-is-doing-in-the-name-of-the-aumf/ (accessed 8 October 2014).

LEGAL AND ETHICAL IMPLICATIONS OF DRONE WARFARE

21. Charlie Savage, 'White House Invites Congress to Approve ISIS Strikes, but Says It's Not Necessary', *The New York Times*, 10 September 2014.
22. Remarks by Attorney General Eric Holder, Northwestern Law School, 5 March 2012.
23. Brennan, 'The Ethics and Efficacy of US Counterterrorism Strategy'.
24. Jennifer Daskal and Stephen I. Vladeck, 'After the AUMF', *Harvard National Security Journal* 5 (2014): 115–46.
25. Hongju Koh, 'The Obama Administration and International Law'.
26. Department of Justice White Paper, 'Lawfulness of a Lethal Operation Against a U.S. Citizen Who is A Senior Operational Leader of al Qai'da or an Associated Force', obtained by NBC News, quotes at pp. 3, 4.
27. Quoted in Andrew Rosenthal, 'The Forever War', *The New York Times*, 17 May 2013.
28. Susan Page, 'Panetta: "30 Year War" And a Leadership Test for Obama', *USA Today*, 6 October 2014.
29. Jeh Charles Johnson, 'The Conflict Against Al Qaeda and Its Affiliates: How Will It End', Speech to the Oxford Union, 30 November 2012.
30. Craig Whitlock, 'Panetta: U.S. "Within Reach" of Defeating al Qaeda', *The Washington Post*, 9 July 2011.
31. The number of 30 countries where al-Qaeda operates comes from *The New York Times*, 'Map of Countries Where al Qaeda and Its Affiliates Operate', 12 May 2011.
32. Obama, 'Remarks by the President at the National Defense University'.
33. Jack Goldsmith, 'Obama's Breathtaking Expansion of a President's Power to Make War', *Time Magazine*, 11 September 2014.
34. Harold Hongju Koh, 'How to End the Forever War', Speech at the Oxford Union, 7 May 2013. DoD backs up, see Goldsmith.
35. Ed O'Keefe, 'Kaine: If Congress Doesn't Authorize Military Action, "We Will Have Created a Horrible Precedent"', *The Washington Post*, 23 September 2014.
36. Hongju Koh, 'The Obama Administration and International Law'.
37. Ibid.
38. For a good statement of this view, see Jordan J. Paust, 'Self Defense Targetings of Non-State Actors and the Permissibility of US Use of Drones in Pakistan', *Journal of Transnational Law and Policy* 19, no. 2 (2009): 237–80.
39. United Nations General Assembly, Human Rights Council, 'Report of the Special Rapporteur on Extrajudicial, Summary or Arbitrary Executions, Philip Alston', 14.
40. Ibid.
41. Department of Justice White Paper, 'Lawfulness of a Lethal Operation Against a U.S. Citizen Who is A Senior Operational Leader of al Qai'da or an Associated Force', quote at p. 7.
42. Ibid., 8–9.
43. Thomas M. McDonnell, 'Sow What You Reap? Using Predator or Reaper Drones To Carry Out Assassinations or Targeted Killings of Suspected Islamic Terrorists', *George Washington International Law Review* 44 (2012): 243. http://digitalcommons.pace.edu/cgi/viewcontent.cgi?article=1857&context=lawfaculty, 289.
44. Jo Becker and Scott Shane, 'Secret "Kill List" Proves a Test of Obama's Principles and Will', *The New York Times*, 29 May 2012.
45. The US is generally supportive of Israel's right to preventive self-defence to strike terrorist operatives in the West Bank and Gaza, as well as in Lebanon, Syria and elsewhere.
46. Quoted in John Mearsheimer, 'America Unhinged', *The National Interest* (January/February 2014): 29.
47. International Committee of the Red Cross, 'Combatant Status'. https://www.icrc.org/customary-ihl/eng/docs/v1_rul_rule3 (accessed 11 October 2014).
48. Convention (III) Relative to the Treatment of Prisoners of War. Adopted on 12 August 1949 by the Diplomatic Conference for the Establishment of International Conventions for the Protection of Victims of War, held in Geneva from 21 April to 12 August 1949. Entered into force 21 October 1950.
49. Charles Lane, 'High Court Rejects Detainee Tribunals', *The Washington Post*, 30 June 2006.
50. Michael Walzer, 'Targeted Killing and Drone Warfare', *Dissent Magazine*, 11 January 2013. http://www.dissentmagazine.org/online_articles/targeted-killing-and-drone-warfare (accessed 7 November 2014).

51. General Sir Rupert Smith calls this 'war among the people'. See his *The Utility of Force* (London: Allan Lane, 2005).
52. Hongju Koh, 'The Obama Administration and International Law'.
53. See Koh for the administration's defence. Ibid.
54. Del Quintan Wilber and Peter Finn, 'US Retires "Enemy Combatant", Keeps Broad Right to Detain', *The Washington Post*, 14 March 2009.
55. Daskal and Vladeck, 'After the AUMF', 115–46.
56. Liz Sly, 'Al Qaeda Disavows Any Ties with Radical Islamist ISIS Group in Iraq, Syria', *The Washington Post*, 3 February 2014.
57. Marty Lederman, 'The Legal Theory Behind the President's New Initiative Against ISIL', *Just Security*, 10 September 2014.
58. Cora Currier, 'Who Are We At War With? That's Classified', *Pro Publica*, 26 July 2013.
59. Michael J. Boyle, 'Is the US Drone War Effective?', *Current History* 113, no. 762 (2014).
60. Becker and Shane, 'Secret "Kill List" Proves a Test of Obama's Principles and Will'.
61. Danya Greenfield, 'The Case Against Drone Strikes on People Who Only "Act" Like Terrorists', *The Atlantic*, 19 August 2013.
62. Kevin Heller, 'One Hell of a Killing Machine: Signature Strikes and International Law', Melbourne Legal Studies Research Paper 634, 2012.
63. MQ-9 Reaper Hunter/Killer UAV. http://www.defense-update.com/products/p/predatorB.htm (accessed 13 October 2014).
64. RQ-1A/MQ1 Predator UAV. http://defense-update.com/products/p/predator.htm (accessed 13 October 2014).
65. David Rohde, 'The Obama Doctrine: How the President's Secret War is Backfiring', *Foreign Policy* 192 (March/April 2012): 66.
66. Stanford Law School and NYU School of Law, *Living Under Drones* (2013): 73–99.
67. Adam Baron, 'In Yemen, Drones Ill Effects Linger Long After Dust Settles', *Christian Science Monitor*, 17 July 2013.
68. C. Christine Fair, Karl Kaltenhalter, and William J. Miller, 'Pakistani Opposition to American Drone Strikes', *Political Science Quarterly* 129, no. 1 (2014): 1–33; Christopher Swift, 'The Blowback Fallacy', *Foreign Affairs*, 1 July 2012.
69. C. Christine Fair, Karl Kaltenhalter, and William J. Miller, 'You Say Pakistanis All Hate the Drone War? Prove It', *The Atlantic*, 23 January 2013.
70. *The Telegraph*, 'Yemen Drone Strikes Cause Civilians to "Fear the U.S. As Much As al Qaeda"', 22 October 2013.
71. Becker and Shane, 'Secret "Kill List" Proves a Test of Obama's Principles and Will'; Michael J. Boyle, 'The Costs and Consequences of Drone Warfare', *International Affairs* 89, no. 1 (2013): 1–29.
72. John Kaag and Sarah Kreps, *Drone Warfare* (Cambridge: Polity Press, 2014), 97.
73. See Daniel R. Brunstetter and Arturo Jimenez Bacardi, 'Drones and Human Rights', article in this volume.
74. See Megan Braun and Daniel R. Brunstetter, 'Rethinking the Criterion for Assessing CIA-Targeted Killings: Drones, Proportionality and Jus ad Vim', *Journal of Military Ethics* 12, no. 4 (2013): 304–24.
75. Dieter Fleck, *The Handbook of International Humanitarian Law*, 3rd edition (Oxford: Oxford University Press, 2013), Section 509.
76. On supreme emergency, see Michael Walzer, *Just and Unjust Wars: A Moral Argument with Historical Illustrations*, 2nd edition (New York: Basic Books, 1992).
77. Michael Calderone, 'Robert Gibbs Told Not to Acknowledge Drone Program Exists As White House Press Secretary', *The Huffington Post*, 24 February 2013. http://www.huffingtonpost.com/2013/02/24/robert-gibbs-drones-white-house_n_2753183.html (accessed 20 October 2014).
78. Karen DeYoung, 'After Obama's Remarks on Drones, White House Rebuffs Security Questions', *The Washington Post*, 31 January 2012.
79. Becker and Shane, 'Secret "Kill List" Proves a Test of Obama's Principles and Will'.
80. Kaag and Kreps, *Drone Warfare*, 40.
81. Micah Zenko, *Reforming U.S. Drone Strike Policies, New York: Council on Foreign Relations*, Report No. 65, January 2013. See also Tim Starks, 'Unmanned Oversight', *The New Republic*, 7 February 2013.

82. Kaag and Kreps, *Drone Warfare*, 67.
83. Peter W. Singer, 'Do Drones Undermine Democracy?', *The New York Times*, 21 January 2012.
84. See the discussion in the Stimson Center, *The Task Force on Drone Policy* (Washington, DC: June 2014), 33.
85. Braun and Brunstetter, 'Rethinking the Criterion for Assessing CIA-Targeted Killings', 310–11.
86. Stimson Center, *The Task Force on Drone Policy*, 33.
87. O'Connell, 'Unlawful Killing with Combat Zones', 7.
88. Senator Lindsay Graham has estimated that drones have killed 4700 people. Spencer Ackerman, 'Senator Lists the Death Toll from Drones at 4,700 People', *Wired*, 21 February 2013.
89. See the discussion in Gabriella Blum and Philip B. Heymann, 'Law and Policy of Targeted Killings', *Harvard National Security Journal* 145 (2010): 145–70.
90. UN Special Rapporteur on Extrajudicial Assassinations, *Handbook* (Center for Human Rights and Global Justice, New York University), 'Chapter Two: Use of Force by Law Enforcement Officials'. http://www.extrajudicialexecutions.org/application/media/Handbook%20Chapter% 202%20use%20of%20force%20in%20LE.pdf (accessed 21 October 2014).
91. Philip Alston, 'The CIA and Targeted Killings Beyond Borders', *Harvard National Security Journal* 2 (2011): 283–446. See also Blum and Heymann 'Law and Policy of Targeted Killings'.
92. Stanford Law School and NYU School of Law, *Living under Drones*, 121.
93. Ward Thomas, 'Norms and Security: The Case of International Assassination', *International Security* 25, no. 1 (2000): 105–33.
94. Hongju Koh, 'The Obama Administration and International Law'.
95. O'Connell, 'Unlawful Killing with Combat Zones', 16.
96. See David Kretzmer, 'Targeted Killings of Suspected Terrorists: Extra-Judicial Executions or Legitimate Means of Self-Defence?', *The European Journal of International Law* 16, no. 2 (2005): 171–212.
97. Blum and Heymann, 'Law and Policy of Targeted Killings', 148.
98. Associated Press, 'Israeli Drone Kills Suspected Islamic Militants in Egypt', 9 August 2013.
99. Jane Perlez, 'Chinese Plan to Kill Drug Lord with Drone Highlights Military Advances', *The New York Times*, 20 February 2013.
100. Stimson Center, *The Recommendations and Report of the Task Force on Drone Policy* (Washington, DC: 2014), 37.
101. Michael Walzer, 'On Fighting Terrorism Justly', *International Relations* 21 (2007): 480–4; Braun and Brunstetter, 'Rethinking the Criterion for Assessing CIA-Targeted Killings', 306.
102. Kaag and Kreps, *Drone Warfare*, 112.
103. David Whetham, 'Drones to Protect', in this volume.
104. Caroline Kennedy and James Rodgers, 'Virtuous Drones', in this volume.

Getting drones wrong

Stephanie Carvin

Centre for International Policy Studies, University of Ottawa, Canada

Over the last several years there has been an explosion of scholarly interest in drones, their impact on armed conflict, and the ethics of using such unmanned weaponry. While this attention and inquiry is to be welcomed, an examination of this scholarship reveals that much of it frequently gets drones wrong – focusing too much on the questionable 'newness' of the technology, misunderstanding or misapplying the legal principles which govern such conventional weaponry (especially proportionality) and searching for definitive answers from problematic data. This article highlights the trouble with the contemporary debate over drones and sets out a research agenda in a world of murky campaigns and imperfect information.

Men could not make up their minds whether means of destruction were to be deemed unlawful because of their newness, or their unfairness, or their secrecy, or their cruelty, and they generally solved the difficulty by objecting to what they disliked, and regarding as unobjectionable what suited their tastes or work to their advantage (T.J. Lawrence, *Principles of International Law*, 1895).[1]

Introduction

'In most "drone" conferences, there comes an awkward moment when a panelist realizes that the category "drone" has very little to do with the question that they're asking.'[2] This observation, though somewhat glib, essentially summarises that which is key to the debate over drones: the weapon itself is seldom the true issue at hand. While the technology associated with drones is impressive and in many ways awe inspiring, the novelty of the technology overshadows the fact that international society has faced similar questions and dilemmas posed by technology before. The challenges posed by the rapid change in weapons technology in the mid-to-late nineteenth and early twentieth centuries, and the parallel efforts of humanitarians to tame such developments through law speaks to many of the debates and arguments put forward about drones today. In particular, the advent of long-range artillery and the possibility of remote killing posed new ethical challenges for armies that could now strike at 'invisible' targets over the horizon line.

This article looks at the lessons of weapons past and drone present in order to discuss the implication for both drone and weapons future. Essentially, it argues that the current debate gets drones wrong: first, that much of what is new is actually old and that there are lessons which we can apply to today's ongoing discussions. Second, the debate misunderstands or misconstrues some of the key principles regarding weapons regulation, especially that of proportionality. Finally, academic approaches to studying drones have generally applied methods that are inappropriate or problematic.

But to point out that we have 'been there, done that' before, or that research into drone warfare suffers from certain flaws is not to simply dismiss the conversation surrounding ethical, legal and moral concerns. Rather, it is to suggest that those interested in issues surrounding drones, their use and regulation, should take and apply the lessons of prior debates and apply them to today's discussions. Additionally, it suggests we need to question a disproportionate focus on drones, a weapon that constitutes a relatively small percentage of the current United States (US) arsenal and is responsible for an equally small percentage of casualties. Instead, the focus should be about the use of drones and similar weapons as a tactic – and to what extent they have evolved into a strategy, and meaningful measures of success that are context-specific, but highlight the areas from which we should draw lessons.

But first, there are some arguments which should be dismissed from the outset. Importantly, the idea that drones may be some kind of slippery slope to Terminator-style autonomous 'killer robots' is, at this point in time at least, pure speculation – more science fiction than science.[3] While there has been a certain amount of attention devoted to this issue by organisations such as the international 'Campaign to Stop Killer Robots',[4] as David Blair argues, 'using these fictions to reason about actual remote aircraft is much like using the Easter Bunny to think about the role of rabbits in ecosystem'.[5]

Remote killing: been there, done that, 1850–1918

Historical precedence for drones may be found in the modern period beginning in the mid-nineteenth century. Between 1750 and 1850 the development of weapon technology had been relatively stagnant. However, by the 1860s, sustained scientific and technological progress became the norm as new inventions, materials and techniques lead the way to a series of rapid developments in weapons technology. For example, the invention and perfecting of the metal-hulled warship, the machine gun and the national railway, which greatly enhanced the speed at which states could mobilise and deploy national armies, all had an effect on military matters of the period.[6] As van Creveld notes, this era marks a transition from an age where inventions were for the most part not only exceptional but accidental and unexpected, to one in which technological change – and the anticipation of technological change – became ordinary rather than extraordinary. As a result, states that wanted to stay secure had to constantly keep up with the latest developments in these areas. 'Applied to the military sphere, this means that war itself became an exercise in managing the future, and the most successful commanders were not those most experienced in the ways of the past but, on the contrary, those who realized that the past would not be repeated.'[7]

Of course the impact of these changes was bloody. Technology had facilitated an extraordinary increase in the size and scale of destruction and killing, as seen in the American Civil War where mass mobilisation and new inventions resulted in the deaths of hundreds of thousands of soldiers and civilians. Indeed, the dawn of modern warfare, with its mass, national armies, and mobilised citizens, placed considerable pressure on the norms that governed war in the West and began a process of breaking down a (theoretical) normative distinction between soldier and civilians and certain norms of what constituted a legitimate military target during the eighteenth century, or what Best refers to as the 'latter Enlightenment Consensus'.[8]

This is, in many ways, ironic, as was the motivation behind the creation of some of the technologies that eventually would make war so deadly. Consider for instance this excerpt from a letter that Richard Jordan Gatling, one of the early machine gun pioneers, wrote on developing the first machine gun during the US Civil War:

> It may be interesting to you to know how I came to invent the gun that bears my name … In 1861, during the opening events of the war … I witnessed almost daily the departure of troops to the front and the return of the wounded, sick and dead. The most of the latter's lost their lives, not in battle, but by sickness and sickness incident to the service. It occurred to me that if I could invent a machine – a gun – that would by its rapidity of fire enable one man to do as much battle duty as a hundred, that it would to a great extent, supersede the necessity of large armies, and consequently exposure to battle and disease would be greatly diminished.[9]

Gatling's belief that his invention would make war more humane rather than more inhumane was typical of the society in which he lived. 'Technical utopianism' was increasingly evident within American culture, as Howard Segal noted, 'a growing number, even majority, or Americans were … coming to take for granted: the belief in the inevitability of progress and in progress precisely as technological progress'.[10]

Obviously, Gatling's (professed) vision did not materialise. Although, increasingly, there were weapons to do work on the battlefield, this did not result in a decrease in the number of men who were required to fight battles for their country. There are no better examples of this than the First and Second World Wars where mass conscription and casualties became a central element of the conflict.[11]

The advent of long-range artillery and the emergence of remote killing around this time are key historical developments to consider. Brodie and Brodie note, 'The science of interior ballistics, which uses a combination of chemistry, mathematics and physics to study the various strains and reactions within the gun itself when fired, led to remarkable improvements in artillery.' For example, in 1850, the first rifle cannons could shoot within a 9500-yard range. However, by the First World War, the 420 mm 16.5 inch Howitzer, popularly known as 'Big Bertha' was successful at destroying Belgian forts up to nearly eight miles away. The 'Paris Gun' used by the Germans near the end of the war, was able to hurl a 250 pound shell 75 miles directly into the city of Paris.[12]

This period marked the first time that armies could target objects that were out of the line of sight from the position of attacking. While this development had important implications for both the tactics and battle strategy, there was (as noted above) a considerable impact on the laws and norms governing warfare. In brief, the capacity and impact of the guns raised new questions and ethical issues in a dramatic way. As Best argues:

> The laws of war had historically been developed on the assumption that the man trying to injure or kill an enemy could see what he was doing. Nor was this an unreasonable assumption. Until about the dawn of the twentieth century it was generally true in respect of all major weapons, except long-range artillery, and … it was precisely on the occasions when artillery was used in sieges against invisible targets that basic law-of-war principles were most likely to be thought at risk.[13]

There were at least three important questions/issues that arose from these developments. First, as Best notes, this period marks the first time in history where soldiers did not witness the immediate consequences of their actions. As such, concern was growing that soldiers might not realise the effects of what they were doing. This gave rise to the question whether technology that allows for remote killing lowers perceptions of responsibility? Not for the last time there was concern that it may be difficult for soldiers to experience feelings of common humanity with people 15 miles beyond or, with the advent of the airplane and the first aerial bombardments, five miles beneath.[14]

Second, although the technology allowed for distance, it did not yet allow for a great deal of accuracy. Armies that aimed their munitions at military targets frequently hit civilian objects instead. Under such circumstances how was it to be determined whether 'accidents' were deliberate or not, and whether any apology offered was truly genuine?[15] And even where it was established that civilian objects were accidently damaged as a part of a remote attack on a legitimate military target, how was fault and responsibility to be portioned out? The individuals who put the civilian object near a military one (or vice versa) or the armed forces that did the targeting? Or both?

Third, even if some of the impetus for the technology was humane, ideas and norms about what constituted a legitimate target came under pressure. As such, questions over what weapons were permitted on the battlefield and what could be done with them became of immediate importance not just to armies but also non-combatants who were now more likely to experience the consequences of armed conflict. It is therefore neither surprising nor entirely coincidental that the first humanitarian organisations, the International Committee of the Red Cross (ICRC) and the British and American Sanitary Commissions were all products of this period. And, of course, it is during this period that the first codified international treaties on the laws of war, including weaponry, emerge.

Responding to these issues, then – as now – would prove to be slow when it came to weapons, and any regulations tended to be generated for practical rather than humane reasons. The first codified weapons treaty, the 1868 St Petersburg Declaration aimed at banning the use of certain exploding bullets, was called for by the Russian Tsar on humanitarian grounds. Yet, it is also likely that the Tsar was also concerned over the impact of such bullets on his large, but technologically unsophisticated, manpower-driven forces. Clearly for Russia these bullets represented a real military disadvantage. Nevertheless, and important when considering the regulation of weapons, the declaration was able to establish principles in its preamble that have guided weapons law ever since:

> Considering that the Progress of civilization should have the effect of alleviating as much as possible the calamities of war;
> That the only legitimate object which States should endeavor to accomplish during war is to weaken the military forces of the enemy;
> That for this purpose it is sufficient to disable to greatest possible number of men;
> That this object would be exceeded by the employment of arms which useless aggravate the sufferings of disabled men, or render their death inevitable;
> That the employment of such arms would, therefore, be in contrary to the laws of humanity; …

Spelled out, these principles are *military necessity* and *humanity*. Military necessity is the principle which acknowledges the necessity of those measures which are indispensable for securing the ends of the war, and which are lawful according to the modern law and usages of war. In other words the laws of war recognise that states have to actually wage war in an effective manner so as to be able to achieve their aims.[16] Humanity, however, places limits on the means that states may use. Specifically, as a principle, it dictates that the employment of any kind or degree of force not required for the purpose of the partial or complete submission of the enemy with minimum expenditure of time, life and physical resources is prohibited.[17]

While these two principles might seem to be at cross-purposes, they work surprisingly well with one another. As Michael N. Schmitt notes, rather than permitting wanton death and destruction, military necessity exists in equipoise with the principle of humanity – proscribing any activity that is not strictly required to achieve a military end.[18]

Additionally, the idea of *unnecessary suffering/superfluous injury* as a governing principle emerged at this time. Translated from the original French '*maux superflus*', this principle recognises that weapons which uselessly aggravate suffering are prohibited. Typically, this is said to include exploding bullets and poisoned weapons.

Later, following the Second World War and the wars of decolonisation/national-self liberation, these three principles were joined by two more – *distinction* and *proportionality.* Distinction is the notion that a weapon should, as a matter of law, be capable of adequate control both as to the place of its impact and the nature and extent of its effects. It balances humanitarian concern for civilians and civilian objects and military interest in directing their destructive effects as accurately and reliably as possible.[19]

Proportionality is something of a trickier concept – not helped by the fact that it may refer to two separate ideas: (i) the proportionality of a military action in response to a grievance and (ii) proportionality in the conduct of hostilities. The former usage belongs in the realm of the law that governs the rights of states to wage war – the *jus ad bellum.* The latter relates to the *jus in bello* – manifesting itself in three ways: the proportionality of a military's response to an adversary's military actions, the proportionality of a military action in relation to the anticipated military advantage to be gained and proportionality in reprisals.[20]

As noted above, these principles acknowledge that militaries have a job to do and must be allowed to accomplish their goals within the boundaries of the law. They also clearly acknowledge and presuppose that some suffering is inevitable in warfare and a normal consequence of the use of weapons. At the same time, they also embrace a notion of humanity that reminds us that (in the words later codified in Article 22 of the 1907 Hague Convention) 'The right of belligerents to adopt means of injuring the enemy is not unlimited.' A state which engages in armed conflict is required to balance these principles when it chooses the instruments that it unleashes when it engages its enemies.

However, despite the codification and development of these principles, it cannot be denied that the response of the international community to the ever-growing and increasingly powerful arsenals of major states was lethargic. Where conventional weapons were banned, they were typically outdated and had fallen out of use in most modern militaries.[21] And while there were bans in place on certain exploding bullets and poisoned weapons on the grounds that they caused unnecessary suffering, other weapons that were subject to international regulation were hardly the ones which were responsible for most of the killing in modern warfare. As Christopher Greenwood notes, 'a 1973 survey of the law on weaponry by the United Nations Secretariat cited bayonets or lances with barbs, irregular shaped bullets, and projectiles filled with glass as examples of weapons considered to be outlawed by the unnecessary suffering principle'.[22]

This slow pace of progress is understandable, if not exactly satisfactory: having invested large amounts of money in developing powerful weapons that were deemed to provide a military advantage, states were not inclined to ban such technology. Yet, there are other less obvious reasons for the sluggish pace of legal regulation. For instance, although it is the case that humanitarian groups emerged during this period and contributed to a nascent humanitarian dialogue, their efforts were largely concentrated on elements of law that focused on the protection of victims rather than governing weapons. In other words, there was more emphasis on protecting prisoners of war rather than regulating artillery.[23] Instead, the perception existed that regulating weapons was the sole business of states. Even for most of the twentieth century, states were left to monitor themselves; assessments of the legal validity of a weapon have therefore been left to governments as their prerogative, a view that is actually reaffirmed in international law. And few states were inclined to make the regulation of weapons a foreign policy priority.

So, what can we learn from this brief history? First, despite the span of a century and a half, many of the legal, normative and ethical issues that come out of the modern drone debate are ones that have come before. The technology may be very different, but questions arising from distance, regulation and accountability challenged those debating the 1899 Hague Conventions as much as those seeking to establish the rules applicable to drone warfare. Technological innovation will inevitably raise challenging questions in many human endeavours, including armed conflict.

Second, given weapons that appear to provide a military advantage, states are unlikely to push for regulation and resist efforts at banning them. Yet, this does not mean that the activities these weapons are used for are without any form of legal parameters. As noted above, in the midst of the changes being brought about by the Industrial Revolution, principles emerged that have subsequently been codified into international treaties and applied to armed conflict. These same principles apply today, whether the weapon is a machine gun, daisy cutter or a drone. Drones have not produced some kind of 'Wild West' of unregulated warfare – there are rules that apply to how they are used, whether they are run by the Central Intelligence Agency (CIA), US Department of Defense (DoD), or another country entirely.[24]

Something shiny! Identifying the drone distraction

At the outset of this article it was argued that the current discussion about drones is lacking historical context, neglecting the fact that many, if not most of these conversations have come before. An additional problem is that the disproportionate attention paid to the weapon is on one small aspect of the US arsenal and political and military policy generally.

For example, of the large reports written about drone warfare by journalist or international organisations, the focus typically centres on questions related to proportionality and the effect on civilians who live in areas where there have been drone strikes. The work of the Bureau of Investigative Journalists has focused on documenting strikes, counting casualties, estimating civilian casualties and covering legislation/attempts at regulation.[25] Similarly, the United Nations (UN) has issued a number of reports focusing on similar issues, largely with a view to assessing the promotion and protection of human rights in the war against terrorism. At the time of writing, the most recent of these was a report that:

> examines the use of remotely piloted aircraft, or drones, in extraterritorial lethal counter-terrorism operations, including in the context of asymmetrical armed conflict, and allegations that the increasing use of remotely piloted aircraft, or drones, has caused disproportionate civilian casualties, and makes recommendations to States.[26]

Other human rights organisations such as Human Rights Watch (HRW) and Amnesty International have produced reports which investigate specific instances of alleged civilian casualties[27] as well as general advocacy against the use of drones in the war on terror.[28]

It is important to acknowledge that this work is valuable research and plays an important part in the debate about the use of drones in the war on terror or in armed conflict generally. Such studies help to put forward the points of view of those living in areas affected by drone strikes, and to raise questions about what constitutes proportionality. Further, it is fundamentally required in order to understand how drones will fit in with the principles of the laws of war.

Yet, in several ways, these reports stand out as an example of some of the more problematic elements of the debate over drones. One of these issues is the discussions of issues related to 'proportionality'. What actually constitutes disproportionality when it comes to drone strikes? Boothby notes that it is important to be careful when applying the question of 'proportionality' to weapons:

> This proportionality rule has, however, no direct applicability to the legitimacy of a weapon. It is not a criterion against which the legitimacy of a weapon can sensibly be considered, because what is proportionate can only meaningfully be determined in relation to an attack on a particular occasion, perhaps at a specific time, using particular weapons and specified attack profiles ... The case-specific nature of these factors means that the proportionality rule is not something of direct relevance to weapons law.[29]

In other words, proportionality depends on the attack – the *way* drones are being used, *not* the weapon itself. Any argument that drones are inherently disproportionate or indiscriminate weapons is mistaken. What then is an indiscriminate attack? Additional Protocol I to the 1949 Geneva Conventions states that an indiscriminate attack is 'an attack which may be expected to cause incidental loss of civilian life, injury to civilians, damage to civilian objects or a combination thereof, which would be excessive in relation to the concrete and direct military advantage anticipated'.[30] This leaves us with the dilemma as to what constitutes 'excessive'? There is no clear, general answer to this question. Yet, some peculiar answers have been offered in recent years. For example, the International Criminal Tribunal Yugoslavia (ICTY) ruled in 2011 that a 4% error rate in targeting in a complex military operation was tantamount to a war crime,[31] a finding that seems out of kilter with any understanding of the history of modern conflict.[32] (This decision was later overturned on appeal in 2012.[33])

Letta Taylor, a researcher with HRW, notes that there have been over 400 drone strikes since 2009. However, HRW bases its claims that drone strikes are causing major violations of international humanitarian law (IHL) on an examination of seven of the alleged 400 drone strikes in which two of the seven were found to have breached IHL. While the two attacks she describes are grim, she uses this survey of two out of 400 strikes to support a call for an investigation into every drone strike that may have caused a human rights violation.[34]

In fairness, most international organisations are sophisticated enough to realise that such a calculation of proportionality is too simplistic. However, it is clear that in some cases that *any* civilian deaths automatically raise accusations of wrongdoing. As Emmerson's UN report demands:

> Having regard to the duty of States to protect civilians in armed conflict, the Special Rapporteur considers that, *in any case in which civilians have been, or appear to have been, killed*, the State responsible is under an obligation to conduct a prompt, independent and impartial fact-finding inquiry and to provide a detailed public explanation. This obligation is triggered whenever there is a plausible indication from any source that civilian casualties may have been sustained, including where the facts are unclear or the information is partial or circumstantial.

The obligation arises whether the attack was initiated by remotely piloted aircraft or other means, and whether it occurred within or outside an area of active hostilities.[35]

The issue as to when there is an obligation to have an inquiry when civilians may have been killed in armed conflict is a complex one and outside the scope of this article.[36] Yet, despite a demand for an investigation into *any* circumstances where civilians are killed, there is no discussion of proportionality in the UN reports on these issues, other than that the law of proportionality is a principle that must be taken into consideration. The Interim Report offers a brief mention of the fact that the Israelis use proportionality to justify civilian casualties, but this is countered with a United Kingdom claim that any strike that could kill civilians will automatically be ruled out. What constitutes proportionality – a fundamental and constant principle of the laws of war – and whether any incidental death is permissible is an issue that the UN Special Rapporteur does not engage with.[37]

Instead, what seems to be the most egregious case of disproportionality is the large amount of attention given to death from one weapon and considerably less to others. The groups which are issuing these reports may reply that they are looking at a broader context, not specifically at the weapon itself. Yet, the sheer number of reports on drones, as opposed to other aspects of killing, seem to be the product of the fascination of the technology, rather than the difficulties of civilian casualties. For example, a recent UN report on civilian casualties in Afghanistan suggests that the vast majority were caused by 'anti-government elements' (such as the Taliban and militants sponsored by the Haqqani Network). Further, of these civilian casualties, the majority were killed by roadside bombs and other improvised explosive devices.[38] Regarding deaths attributable to the International Stabilization Afghanistan Forces (ISAF), of the 182 civilians allegedly killed in aerial operations (2% of the casualties overall) 32% were by drone strikes. The rest were by rotary wing or fixed wing aircraft or the aerial method was undetermined.

However, this focus on numbers – particularly surrounding strikes and casualties – has produced two further myopias: there is considerably less focus on the way drones are actually being used as a strategy by states and the way this technology has been integrated into the armed forces of states. While this may seem a side issue – less important than the death of children at a wedding – the way technology has been integrated is fundamental to appreciating, understanding and assessing their use. As Antoine Bousquet notes, the successful use of virtually all technological innovations normally has less to do with the quality and quantity of the device than 'with its integration within a new organizational and tactical scheme that could take advantage of it'.[39]

As such, while drone technology may provide new opportunities, it is ultimately its integration into the armed forces of states and resultant tactics and strategies that emerge that actually change warfare. As van Creveld notes:

> It was not the technical sophistication of the Swiss pike that defeated the Burgundian knights, but rather the way it meshed with the weapons used by the knights at Laupen, Sempach and Granson. It was not the intrinsic superiority of the longbow that won the battle of Crécy, but rather the way in which it interacted with the equipment employed by the French on that day and at that place. Using technology to acquire greater range, greater firepower, greater mobility, greater protection, greater whatever is very important and may be critical. Ultimately, however, it is less critical and less important than achieving a close 'fit' between one's own technology and that which is fielded by the enemy.[40]

Finding the right 'fit' is key, as is demonstrated by the last 100 years of warfare. As noted above, large artillery guns provided the German army with the capacity to hit cities from

LEGAL AND ETHICAL IMPLICATIONS OF DRONE WARFARE

great, unprecedented distances – well beyond the line of sight of those firing the weapon. Yet, there is a general agreement that these weapons were largely ineffective in the German war effort, amounting to little more than an over-priced terror weapon that solved nothing.[41] Adolf Hitler, allegedly impressed with the might and potential of the V2 rocket, focusing the efforts of the German war machine at a crucial time from the cheaper and arguably more efficient V1 rocket, in order to produce a weapon that would help him win the war. However, the V2 rocket, though an impressive invention, was unstable and of limited use. While it may have caused chaos in southern England by the end of the Second World War, the unpredictability of the V2 and the considerable resources it required ultimately did little for, and arguably great harm to, the German war effort.[42]

Research challenges

The above discussion dances around what should be the main focus of the debate: are drones being used effectively and can we offer any evidence regarding the consequences of their use – ethical and otherwise?

The positive news is that we can ground research into these questions in the work that has been done on assassination and the research on 'targeted killing' (the planned direct killing of an individual because of their perceived membership – and often perceived leadership – of a terrorist movement[43]), which has continued apace over the last decade. Obviously, though this bears repeating, not all incidents of targeted killing are carried out with drones. Night raids by armed forces (such as the one that killed Osama bin Laden in 2011) or missile strikes by planes are similar and frequent forms of this activity. However, much of the recent attention on targeted killing has come from the US drone programme in Yemen, Afghanistan and East Africa. And, for the reasons discussed above, it is important to contextualise the drone debate into larger questions of counter-terrorism strategy.

For example, one useful line of questioning of this debate has been whether or not targeted killing/drones are as effective as their proponents claim. A number of scholars argue that targeted killing/drone campaigns are able to eliminate terrorists with highly valuable skills that are not easily replaced, disrupt terrorist organisations – throwing them into chaos and preventing them from planning future attacks – and provide an option for states rather than sending troops into harm's away and when it is not possible to bring the leaders of terrorist groups to trial.[44]

On the other hand, opponents argue that targeted killing/drones cause more problems than they solve and undermine the stability of communities where the strikes take place.[45] For example, Michael L. Gross argues that such operations are guided by intelligence that disrupts societies and generates mistrust within.[46] Exum et al. argue that the campaign 'has created a siege mentality among the Pashtun population of northwest Pakistan'.[47] Additionally, opponents raise concerns about the unpredictability of targeted killing/drone strikes. Although terrorist leaders may be taken out by such operations, there is no way of knowing what the 'blow-back' may be. Enraged terrorist groups may seek to strike back against the West and affected societies may become more difficult to work with on other crucial counter-terrorism initiatives. Further, contrary to the point that drone strikes eliminate skilled terrorists that are hard to replace, they raise the possibility that any replacements may in fact be worse or more capable.[48]

Finally, as Audrey Kurth Cronin notes, 'dead men tell no tales'. When the purpose of counter-terrorism is to gather further intelligence on other activities, a live terrorist is far more useful than a dead one. Arrested terrorists may be interrogated for information on future plots and, as Kaplan et al. argue, the discovery of links to more nodes in terrorist networks.[49]

So, given these arguments, are drones effective? The less positive news is that determining an answer has proved to be extremely challenging. Certainly there have been a series of quantitative studies in an attempt to answer this question of effectiveness, whether for or against drones/targeted killing.[50] However, these and many of the qualitative/normative arguments about effectiveness struggle with three issues which prevent us from drawing definitive or even preliminary answers to the question of effectiveness.

First, there is a dearth of data available to the public. As most countries do not provide information on their drone programmes, most studies rely on news reports – raising doubts over the accuracy of the studies. As Peter Bergen and Katherine Tiedemann note, one of the main challenges in producing an accurate count of fatalities from the strikes is that different sides in the drone debate have different motives for presenting evidence. While the US claims that almost all of those killed are militants, others (including the Pakistani government and the militants themselves) claim the victims are always civilians. Given the difficulty of obtaining accurate information in the remote, mountainous regions of Pakistan, 'determining who is a militant and who is a civilian is often impossible'.[51]

Yet, even if scholars and advocates were provided with solid numbers, a second major problem is that definitions as to what constitutes 'success' in a targeted killing/drone campaign varies widely.[52] Further, these definitions are often tweaked so as to produce a level of quasi-scientific certainty or gamed to suit the argument being made. In these circumstances the bar for what constitutes success is set unrealistically high.[53] For example, in Jordan's study, the threshold for success is 'where an organization was inactive for two years following the incident of decapitation'.[54] Considering the scope and size of modern terrorist networks, this is a fairly difficult standard to achieve.

But more importantly, success is unavoidably subjective. For some, merely degrading the capabilities of a terrorist organisation, making it more difficult for them to conduct operations against the West, would be sufficient. Others may claim only drone strikes that eliminate a terrorist group entirely should be considered successful. And there are other questions in terms of scope. For example, should researchers be looking at the impact of individual drone strikes or entire campaigns? And how wide should our view of success be? How should we weigh the perceived success of a drone campaign with potential second- or third-level consequences such as difficult bi-lateral relations, upset populations, etc.?

Finally, there is a tendency to generalise the use of drones across different campaigns, by different states. Yes, the US may be using drones in Afghanistan/Pakistan and Yemen all as a part of a 'War on Terror', and Israel has used them against Palestinian targets. Yet, these are different campaigns against different kinds of targets in different areas. Making sweeping generalisations about the effectiveness of drones based on one campaign is problematic. Trying to assess if drones will work in a campaign against a target in Country A cannot entirely rest upon what has previously happened in Country B and whether the effectiveness of 'smart bombs' against Serbia will work against Iraq.

Conclusion: a normative drone research agenda

Bearing these challenges in mind, how should we think about developing a drone research agenda? First, researchers are going to have to deal with the fact that they are not likely to obtain perfect information on drones anytime soon. The US government will probably not release details or statistics on its drone programmes in the near future – if ever. Further, information on casualties, particularly in remote areas of South Asia, will likely be flawed, problematic and politicised for at least the medium term. However, this does not mean that analysis of such programmes is impossible – rather, that the focus will have to be on the strategic rather than the tactical level. This means scholars could and should be focusing on the second- and third-order effects of drone/targeted killing campaigns, rather than getting caught up in the nitty-gritty details. Such research would have to be long-term in scope, but would be more successful in providing a bigger-picture analysis that is less focused on the immediacy of the moment.

Second, as a part of a bigger-picture approach, scholars should consider questions such as when is it appropriate to apply the lessons learned from one drone/targeted killing campaign to another? Can scholars identify any underlying circumstances or factors that would make comparison less superficial and more systematic/comprehensive? While circumstances may necessitate the need to compare apples and oranges, we should avoid comparing apples to toasters – and scholars will be instrumental in developing methodologies to avoid doing so.

Third, even if scholars do not wish to contextualise their research historically, they should at least be aware of the lessons of previous innovations in weaponry outlined above: technological change in warfare and weaponry will, and always will, exert pressure on norms related to restraints on the waging of force. However, if history is any guide, this technological change will not break these norms and conventions. Instead, in order to deal with these pressures, states may engage in actual, formal legal change by adopting new laws or adapting old ones or, alternatively, they may adapt a previous understanding of a particular law and principle in order to apply it to the new technological challenge. Following, discussing and debating how this occurs is and will continue to be an important normative issue for researchers and scholars.

Fourth, scholars researching drones should question research that is overly focused on the weapon itself rather than the effects that it causes. As noted above, drones constitute a small part of the US arsenal and are not even likely responsible for most of the targeted killing that has taken place in the last decade. By avoiding a magpie-like distraction from the 'shiny object' that in the drone, scholars can focus on the larger issues at stake, such as proportionality (broadly speaking) and necessity.

Finally, good questions and useful inquiry about drones will focus on overall strategy. Are drones being used as a tactic in an overall counter-terrorism campaign? Or are they becoming a strategy in and of themselves? If it is the latter, what are the consequences of this? How do drones impact on gathering intelligence? Or the core functions of intelligence agencies? In finding diplomatic/political solutions? Or the stabilisation of territories? Contextualising the drone debate and refocusing research on larger strategic questions does not guarantee that social science will get drones right, but it will likely lead to a more informed discussion, better suited to addressing human rights concerns and issues that have and will inevitably arise.

Disclosure statement

No potential conflict of interest was reported by the author.

Notes

1. Cited in Geoffrey Best, *Humanity in Warfare: The Modern History of the International Law of Armed Conflicts* (London: Methuen, 1983), 160.
2. Dave Blair, 'Remote Aviation Technology – What Are We Actually Talking About?', Centre for International Maritime Security Blog. http://cimsec.org/remote-aviation-technology-actually-talking/
3. Of course this would not be the first time that there have been efforts to ban weapons which do not yet exist. Protocol I of the 1980 Convention on Certain Conventional Weapons (CCW) prohibits 'weapons the primary effect of which is to injure by fragments which in the human body escape detection by X-rays'. Such weapons did not exist at the time that the CCW was drafted, were not under development and do not exist today.
4. See the Campaign to Stop Killer Robots: http://www.stopkillerrobots.org/
5. Blair, 'Remote Aviation Technology'.
6. Best, *Humanity in Warfare*, 159. See also Martin van Creveld, *Technology and War: From 2000 BC to the Present* (London: The Free Press, 1989), 217.
7. van Creveld, *Technology and War*, 218.
8. It may, of course, be argued that such a distinction had historically been honoured more in the breach than in reality. After all, neither medieval nor Napoleonic warfare has been noted for its humanity. However, the idea that non-combatants should be protected in war had gained traction during the Enlightenment period and was arguably an important norm by which international society could and often did judge the conduct of armies. See Best, *Humanity in Warfare*, especially Chapter I: 'The Later Enlightenment Consensus'.
9. P. Whal and D.R. Toppel, *The Gatling Gun* (London: Herbert Jenkins, 1966), 18. See also, C.J. Chivers, *The Gun* (New York: Simon & Schuster, 2010), especially Chapter 1.
10. Howard P. Segal, *Technological Utopianism in American Culture* (Chicago: University of Chicago Press, 1985), 1.
11. It is worth noting that the creators of the First World War's gas weapons seem to have applied similar logic as Gatling to their inventions. The German chemist, Fritz Haber argued that gas weapons were humane alternatives to the other technologies that had been deployed on the battlefield. W. Lee Lewis, the inventor of Lewisite (a systematic poison that can kill by being deposited on a person's skin or exposure in a concentration of only 50 parts per million) argued that the gas was 'the most efficient, most economical, and most humane single weapon known to military service'. See P.D. Smith, *Doomsday Men: The Real Dr Strangelove and the Dream of the Superweapon* (London: Allen Lane, 2007), especially Chapter 5. Smith cites W. Lee Lewis, 'Is Prohibition of Gas Warfare Feasible?', *Atlantic Monthly* 129 (June 1922): 834, in Gilbert F. Whittemore, Jr, 'World War I, Poison Gas Research, and the Ideals of American Chemists', *Social Studies of Science*, no. 5 (May 1975): 135–63, 158.
12. Bernard Brodie and Fawn M. Brodie, *From Crossbow to H-Bomb: The Evolution of the Weapons and Tactics of Warfare* (Bloomington and Indianapolis: Indiana University Press, 1973), 139–40, and 191.
13. Geoffrey Best, *Law and War Since 1945* (Oxford: Oxford University Press, 1994), 53.
14. There is an interesting question that may be raised here regarding whether or not this period was really the first occasion where soldiers did not witness the immediate consequences of their actions. For example, it could be argued that this has been a feature of certain weapons (i.e. cross-bow) and tactics (i.e. siege warfare) for centuries. However, I think it may be argued that the difference in the physical distances experienced for the first time in the late nineteenth century – from yards to many miles away – created a situation that was unique for armed forces on the ground. Sieges were difficult and time-consuming (not to mention expensive and frequently ineffective). Armies besieging a castle would have had to be within line of sight to employ any siege weapons they were using – something that made their task very difficult from the well-defended fortresses of the medieval period. Additionally, a besieging army would likely have to have been in relatively close range, surrounding their target fortress to ensure it was completely isolated (another difficult feat to accomplish effectively). In this sense, while medieval soldiers may not have experienced the absolute immediate effects of their actions, by the late nineteenth century soldiers might not have seen their target at all. I do, however, concede that this is a relative point, open for debate. Thanks to Michael Boyle for raising this point. On siege warfare see C.W.C. Oman, *The Art of War in the Middle Ages*, ed. John H. Beeler (Ithaca, NY: Cornell University Press, 1953), especially Chapter

LEGAL AND ETHICAL IMPLICATIONS OF DRONE WARFARE

IV; John Keegan, *A History of Warfare* (London: Pimlico, 1993), 150–2; and Konstantin Nossov, *Ancient and Medieval Siege Weapons: A Fully Illustrated Guide to Siege Weapons and Tactics* (Guilford: The Lyons Press, 2005), especially Chapter 10.

15. Best, *Law and War Since 1945*, 53.
16. It is worth noting that this is true regardless of what those aims might be. The laws that govern when a state is permitted to engage in armed conflict, the *jus ad bellum*, is separate and distinct from the law which governs the means states use to achieve their goals, the *jus in bello*.
17. The definitions here are based on those found in Adam Roberts and Richard Guelff, *Documents on the Laws of War*, 3rd edition (Oxford: Oxford University Press, 2005), 10.
18. Michael N. Schmitt, 'Military Necessity and Humanity in International Humanitarian Law: Preserving the Delicate Balance', *Virginia Journal of International Law* 50, no. 4 (2010), 796–837, 796.
19. William H. Boothby, *Weapons and the Law of Armed Conflict* (Oxford: Oxford University Press, 2009), 69.
20. Roberts and Guelff, *Documents on the Laws of War*, 9–10.
21. It is important to note that the idea that states only ban weapons that they tend not to use or that are out of date tends to apply better to conventional weapons rather than weapons of mass destruction. There have been several international treaties which govern the use of biological, chemical and nuclear weapons – weapons still clearly in the arsenal of many states. Thanks to Michael J. Boyle for raising this point.
22. Christopher Greenwood, 'The Law of Weaponry at the Start of the New Millennium', in *The Law of Armed Conflict: Into the New Millennium*, ed. Michael N. Schmitt and Leslie C. Green, International Law Studies, Vol. 71 (Newport: Naval War College, 1998), 185–232.
23. And of course most modern states felt that they had a strategic interest in protecting their captured soldiers.
24. There is an important debate as to whether the CIA's drone programme is legitimate as it is unclear as to whether their operators have any training in the laws of war or follow a responsible chain of command as required by the 1949 Geneva Conventions. This would have implications on the legal protections afforded CIA operators in the drone programme. As of 2013, the Obama administration reportedly began to transfer responsibility for this programme over to the DoD, although at time of writing it is not clear to the extent this has occurred. However, the point here is that regardless of who is operating the drones, the principles governing their use remain the same. Though it was unlikely the CIA programme was conducted without extensive legal guidance, the question of accountability/responsibility is important. It would be addressed by the transfer of responsibility to DoD.
25. See the series of stories and reports by the Bureau of Investigative Journalism, http://www.thebureauinvestigates.com/category/projects/drones/. There is, of course, a considerable normative component to the work of the bureau, with considerable attention devoted to speaking with victims and anti-drone activists.
26. At the time of writing, the most recent of these was 'Report of the Special Rapporteur on the Promotion and Protection of Human Rights and Fundamental Freedoms While Countering Terrorism', 28 February 2014, A/HRC/25/59. http://www.ohchr.org/EN/HRBodies/HRC/RegularSessions/Session25/Documents/A-HRC-25-59.doc
27. Human Rights Watch, 'A Wedding That Became a Funeral: US Drone Attack on Marriage Procession in Yemen', 20 February 2014. http://www.hrw.org/node/123245
28. Amnesty International, '"Will I be Next?" US Drone Strikes in Pakistan', 22 October 2013. http://www.amnestyusa.org/research/reports/will-i-be-next-us-drone-strikes-in-pakistan
29. Boothby, *Weapons and the Law of Armed Conflict*, 79.
30. Additional Protocol I 51(5) b.
31. Gotovina et al. (2011). A summary of the original ruling can be found at the ICTY website: http://www.icty.org/x/cases/gotovina/tjug/en/110415_summary.pdf
32. This argument was raised by a series of former military lawyers from several countries in an Amicus Brief to the Appeals Chamber in January 2012. Available online at: http://icr.icty.org/LegalRef/CMSDocStore/Public/English/Application/NotIndexable/IT-06-90-A/MSC7958R0000353013.pdf
33. *Prosecutor* v. *Ante Gotovina, Mladen Markač*, November 2012. http://www.icty.org/x/cases/gotovina/acjug/en/121116_judgement.pdf
34. Letta Taylor, 'The Truth about the United States Drone Programme', *Policy Review*, March 2014. http://www.policyreview.eu/the-truth-about-the-us-drone-programme/. Taylor refers to

LEGAL AND ETHICAL IMPLICATIONS OF DRONE WARFARE

a HRW report she researched and authored, 'Between a Drone and Al Qaeda: The Civilian Cost of US Targeted Killings in Yemen', 22 October 2013. The report notes that there may have been violations in the other incidents but they cannot draw a definitive conclusion. Available online at: http://www.hrw.org/reports/2013/10/22/between-drone-and-al-qaeda-0

35. 'Report of the Special Rapporteur on the Promotion and Protection of Human Rights and Fundamental Freedoms While Countering Terrorism'. Emphasis added.

36. For example, there is no such legal obligation in the laws of war but there is in human rights law under the guarantee of 'right to life'. Whether such an investigation would be possible in the tribal areas of Afghanistan/Pakistan and Yemen is, likewise, another issue entirely.

37. See the 'Interim Report of the Special Rapporteur on the Promotion and Protection of Human Rights and Fundamental Freedoms While Countering Terrorism', 25 October 2013. http://www.lawfareblog.com/wp-content/uploads/2013/10/Emmerson-Report.pdf

38. Of the remaining 26%, 11% were by 'pro-government' forces, of which 8% were the Afghan national forces and 3% international forces. A further 10% seem to have been caught in the cross-fire between anti- and pro-government forces and the remaining 5% the result of unknown causes, but mostly explosive remnants of war. United Nations, 'Afghanistan Annual Report 2013: Protection of Civilians in Armed Conflict', February 2014. http://unama.unmissions.org/Portals/UNAMA/human%20rights/Feb_8_2014_PoC-report_2013-Full-report-ENG.pdf; see also, Tim Craig, 'Civilian Casualties Are Up in Afghanistan, a New U.N. Report Says', *Washington Post*, 8 February 2012. http://www.washingtonpost.com/world/asia_pacific/civilian-casualties-are-up-in-afghanistan-a-new-un-report-says/2014/02/08/de7389f0-90e5-11e3-878e-d76656564a01_story.html

39. Antoine Bousquet, *The Scientific Way of Warfare: Order and Chaos on the Battlefields of Modernity* (London: Hurst, 2009), 96.

40. van Creveld, *Technology and War*, 319–20.

41. Brodie and Brodie, *From Crossbow to H-Bomb*, 192.

42. van Creveld, *Technology and War*, 76 and 221–2.

43. The author has written about the effectiveness of targeted killing in greater detail in Stephanie Carvin, "The Trouble with Targeted Killing", *Security Studies* 21, no. 3 (2012): 529–55. This section draws on some of the research and conclusions reached in that article.

44. See Kenneth Anderson, 'Predators over Pakistan', *The Weekly Standard*, 8 March 2010, 26–34; Daniel Byman, 'Do Targeted Killings Work?', *Foreign Affairs* 85, no. 2 (2006): 95–111; Steven R. David, 'Fatal Choices: Israel's Policy of Targeted Killing', *Mideast Security and Policy Studies* 51 (2002); and Steven R. David, 'Israeli's Policy of Targeted Killing', *Ethics and International Affairs* 17, no. 1 (2003), 111–26; Amitai Etzioni, 'Unmanned Aircraft Systems: The Moral and Legal Case', *Joint Force Quarterly* 57, no. 2 (2010): 66–71.

45. Philip Alston, 'The CIA and Targeted Killings Beyond Borders' (New York University School of Law: Public Law & Legal Theory Research Paper Series Working Paper No. 11-64). http://papers.ssrn.com/sol3/papers.cfm?abstract_id=1928963; Michael L. Gross, 'Fighting by Other Means in the Mideast: a Critical Analysis of Israel's Assassination Policy', *Political Studies* 51 (2003): 350–68; and Michael L. Gross, 'Assassination and Targeted Killing: Law Enforcement, Execution or Self-Defence?', *Journal of Applied Philosophy* 23, no. 3 (2006): 323–35; Mary Ellen O'Connell, 'Unlawful Killing with Combat Drones: A Case Study of Pakistan, 2004–2009' (Notre Dame Legal Studies Paper No. 09-43, 2010). http://papers.ssrn.com/sol3/papers.cfm?abstract_id=1501144; Yael, Stein, 'By Any Name Illegal and Immoral', *Ethics and International Affairs* 17, no. 1 (2003): 127–37.

46. Gross, 'Fighting by Other Means in the Mideast'.

47. Andrew M. Exum, Nathaniel C. Fick, Ahmed A. Humayun, and David Kilcullen, *Triage: The Next Twelve Months in Afghanistan and Pakistan* (Washington, DC: Center for a New American Security, 2009). http://www.cnas.org/files/documents/publications/ExumFickHumayun_TriageAfPak_June09.pdf, 18.

48. Brian Michael Jenkins, 'Should Our Arsenal Against Terrorism Include Assassination?' (RAND Paper P-7303, January 1987). http://www.rand.org/pubs/papers/P7303.html, 8.

49. Audrey Kurth Cronin, *How Terrorism Ends: Understanding the Decline and Demise of Terrorist Campaigns* (Princeton, NJ: Princeton University Press, 2009), 232.

50. See Cronin, *How Terrorism Ends*; Mohammed M. Hafez and Joseph M. Hattfield, 'Do Targeted Assassinations Work? A Multivariate Analysis of Israeli Counter-Terrorism Effectiveness during Al-Aqsa Uprising', *Studies in Conflict & Terrorism* 29, no. 4 (2006): 359–82; Jenna

Jordan, 'When Heads Roll: Assessing the Effectiveness of Leadership Decapitation', *Security Studies* 18, no. 4 (2009): 719–55; Edward H. Kaplan, Alex Mintz, Shaul Mishal, and Claudio Samban, 'What Happened to Suicide Bombings in Israel? Insights from a Terror Stock Model', *Studies in Conflict & Terrorism* 28, no. 3 (2005): 225–35; and Aaron Mannes, 'Testing the Snake Head Strategy: Does Killing or Capturing its Leaders Reduce a Terrorist Group's Activity?', *Journal of International Policy Solutions* 9 (2008) 40–9.

51. Peter Bergen and Katherine Tiedemann, 'Washington's Phantom War: The Effects of the U.S. Drone Program in Pakistan', *Foreign Affairs* 90, no. 4 (2011).

52. The same point from a more critical perspective can be found in Michael J. Boyle, 'Is the US Drone War Effective?', *Current History* 113, no. 762 (2014): 137.

53. This is a point also made by Patrick B. Johnston, 'Does Decapitation Work: Assessing the Effectiveness of Leadership Targeting in Counterinsurgency Campaigns', *International Security* 36, no. 4 (2012): 47–79.

54. Jordan, 'When Heads Roll', 731–2.

A means-methods paradox and the legality of drone strikes in armed conflict

Craig Martin

Washburn University School of Law, Topeka, USA

This article examines the legality of drone strikes. It limits the analysis to conduct within a traditionally defined armed conflict, in order to focus more clearly on the question of whether features inherent to the drone as a weapons system might make it conducive to violations of international law. The article reviews the applicable legal principles from international humanitarian law and international human rights law, and examines the record of civilian deaths caused by drone strikes in Afghanistan. While transparency and accountability are a problem, the study suggests that the drone strike operations may be characterised by more direct systemic violations of international law. In examining such potential violations the article considers the features inherent to the drone as a 'means' of warfare, and the features of the policy and practices that underlie the 'methods' of warfare related to drone strikes, with the aim of determining which is more responsible for any violations. The features of the armed drone as a weapons systems appear to make it more conducive to compliance with international humanitarian law than competing aerial weapons systems. Conversely, aspects of the policy governing drone operations, such as the criteria used for 'signature strikes', are more likely to contribute to violations of international law. However, examining the issue from the perspective of a particular strike, and viewed through the lens of cognitive consistency theory on misperception, the article suggests that the picture may be more complex. Paradoxically, the very features that are most likely to make the drone compliant with international humanitarian law – its ability to linger undetected for protracted periods over potential targets, feeding intelligence back to an operations team that can make targeting decisions in a relatively stress-free environment – may facilitate targeting errors caused by misperception and misinterpretation of the target data. In short, both the 'means' and 'methods' of drone strikes may combine to facilitate violations of international humanitarian law.

I. Introduction

The legality of targeted killing with armed unmanned aerial vehicles (UAVs – commonly referred to as drones) is a hotly debated issue.[1] It is also a fiendishly complex one. The debate is particularly complicated because it tends to encompass operations of varying kinds conducted by different actors in a range of very different circumstances.[2] The US drone-based targeted killing programme stretches from operations conducted by the military in openly acknowledged non-international armed conflict in Afghanistan, to CIA operations in the tribal areas of Pakistan, in Yemen, and in Somalia, none of which constitutes an armed conflict as traditionally defined, or in which the US is a belligerent.[3] A number of different legal regimes are thus implicated, and the extent to which each one is operating and whether or how they may interact is both complicated and the subject of dispute.[4]

Nonetheless, one of the questions that arises in the broader debate is whether there is anything inherently unlawful about drones themselves. This special volume of the journal sets out to explore this question by restricting the focus of analysis to the use of drones in traditionally defined armed conflicts. It asks whether the use of drones for the conduct of lethal strikes in a traditionally defined armed conflict is giving rise to systemic violations of international law; and if so, is there something inherent in the nature of the weapons system itself that is causing or contributing to such unlawful conduct? This focus on the legality of drone strikes exclusively in a traditionally defined armed conflict is relatively rare. But this narrow focus helps to better isolate, for purposes of analysis, the issue of whether any unlawfulness under international humanitarian law (IHL, also commonly referred to as the law of armed conflict, and the laws of war), may be related to the nature of the weapon system itself.

The use of armed drones to kill suspected terrorists and members of organised armed groups taking part in an acknowledged non-international armed conflict such as Afghanistan, may implicate less complicated legal issues than such conduct in Yemen and Somalia. Nonetheless, it may still give rise to violations of IHL, international human rights law (IHRL), and even domestic criminal and constitutional law. Indeed, there is sufficient evidence of civilian killings in drone strikes in Afghanistan to raise significant questions in this regard. By exploring some of this evidence and examining the potential causes of what may constitute systemic violations of law in these operations, it may be possible to identify the extent to which such violations are attributable to something inherent in the nature of the weapons systems, or rather the extent to which it is more attributable to the manner in which the drone strikes are being conducted.

This question implicates two different specialised areas of law within the laws of war. IHL places limits on the 'means of warfare', by which is meant the weapons used to engage in armed conflict, through a body of law commonly referred to as weapons law.[5] Certain types of weapon are considered to be inherently unlawful, while others may be deemed unlawful in particular circumstances. Other weapons are not inherently unlawful in any way, but may of course be used in an unlawful manner. IHL also limits the 'methods of warfare', which refers in part to how weapons are used. The body of law that governs the methods of warfare relevant to our study here is the law of targeting.[6] In considering the legality of drone strikes in armed conflict, we must assess both the nature of the weapon and the manner of its use. We must analyse the extent to which possible unlawfulness in drone strikes arises principally from the means of warfare, that is from something inherent in the nature of the weapon itself, and to what extent it is more attributable to the methods of warfare employed in the conduct of drone strikes. The answer to these questions could help provide some insight into how the incidence of such violations of law might be reduced.

The analysis below will suggest that while any illegality would appear at first glance to be primarily a consequence of how the drone is employed, upon deeper reflection the issue may be more complicated, and there may indeed be something of a paradox. It may be that some of the features of the armed drone that are most likely to make it compliant with IHL may, counter-intuitively, facilitate violations of international law. For it is indeed the case that many of the features of the current drone weapons system, as an air-to-ground anti-personnel weapon, would seem to make it more compliant with the relevant IHL principles than most other competing aerial weapons systems, such as manned fixed-wing aircraft or cruise missiles. The drone is highly precise and surgical in the actual delivery of missiles to the target. But more importantly, it has an enormous advantage in its ability to linger undetected for protracted periods of observation over a potential target, feeding detailed visual and other sensory intelligence back to an operations team that is able to engage in a targeting decision-making process under little stress, at a relatively leisurely pace, and with zero risk. This should militate in favour of better decision-making and fewer targeting errors.

To the extent that there are systemic violations of IHL or IHRL in the implementation of drone strikes in Afghanistan, these would seem to be more likely attributable to the policies and practices governing how the weapon system is being used. This begins with the lack of transparency and accountability in the programme, which may constitute an independent violation of law, and is compounded by the involvement of the CIA and Joint Special Operations Command (JSOC) in the process.[7] But more relevant to the possible specific violations flowing from targeting errors, are the concerns over intelligence failures and the possible employment of improper targeting criteria for so-called signature strikes. Even more intriguing is the possibility that drone crews are making targeting errors due to systemic misperception and misinterpretation of the target behaviour and pattern of life information received from the drone. This issue is explored through an examination of one of the few strikes about which a detailed account is publicly available, and through the lens of psychological theory relating to misperception and confirmation bias. And herein lies the paradox – for it may be that it is precisely the features of the armed drone that are most likely to make it highly compliant with IHL, that facilitate or make more likely the kind of systemic misperception and misinterpretation that is leading to targeting errors resulting in violations of international law. At this stage this proposition is an untested suggestion that certainly requires further empirical and theoretical work to confirm, but it raises a question that surely deserves further inquiry.

The article begins, in Part II, by providing a brief account of certain well-known drone strikes and reviewing the broader data available on the killing of civilians in drone strikes in Afghanistan. Part III engages in a review of the legal regimes that apply to drone strikes within an armed conflict. In Part IV the article turns to explore the extent to which the drone strike operations in Afghanistan comply with these legal regimes, and the extent to which there is evidence of possible systematic violations of international law. It is as part of this assessment that the article examines the features of the armed drone as a weapons system, to evaluate its inherent legality, followed by an analysis of the features of the policy and methods by which the drone systems are used, focusing on the nature of the targeting criteria used in strikes, and the status and nature of the operators. In Part V the article introduces the ideas underlying cognitive consistency theory and attribution theory as explanations for misperception and confirmation bias, and explores the extent to which targeting errors in drone strikes may be explained, in part, as being caused by such misperception. It is here that the arguments about the means-method paradox discussed above are developed and advanced.

II.   Drone strikes and civilian casualties in Afghanistan

The US drone-based targeted killing programme is commonly regarded as having commenced in November 2002, when a CIA operated Predator drone was used to target and kill the suspected al-Qaida leader Ali Qaed Senyan al-Harithi, along with five other men, in Yemen.[8] This may have been the first acknowledged strike resulting in the successful killing of an identified target, but it was not the first lethal drone strike.

Illustrative drone strikes

The first lethal drone strike was likely in Afghanistan, in February 2002, when a Predator drone was used by the CIA in a Hellfire missile strike targeting a tall man and two other men who were acting deferential towards him – leading the operators to believe it might be Osama Bin Laden – at an old Mujahedeen base called Zhawar Kili.[9] The target was not Osama Bin Laden of course, but the three men were killed in the strike. Speaking for the Pentagon, Rear Admiral John D. Stufflebeem later acknowledged that the target had not been Bin Laden after all, but suggested that the targets were 'not innocent', and that 'initial indications afterward would seem to say that these [were] not peasant people up there farming'.[10] Another spokesperson later added that the Pentagon was 'convinced that it was an appropriate target' but that 'we do not know yet exactly who it was'.[11] There was no indication of the basis for such conviction, or indeed what criteria had been used for determining that the three men were legitimate targets. The *New York Times* later identified the three men, and determined that they had been civilians from nearby villages scavenging for scrap metal.[12]

This strike illustrates a number of features common to other drone strikes that have been documented over time in Afghanistan, and which raise significant questions about compliance with IHL and IHRL. To take a couple more examples, in September 2013 a drone strike in Watapur district, Kunar province, targeted a vehicle thought to be carrying insurgents. It was later determined that there were indeed six insurgents in the vehicle, but also eleven civilians, including four women and four children. Along with the six insurgents, ten of the civilians were killed, leaving a young girl seriously injured. The NATO-led International Security Assistance Force (ISAF) media liaison initially denied the presence of civilians, and would not disclose what pre-engagement measures were taken to verify the identity or status of the targets, or whether the insurgents targeted were of strategic value, saying only that one of the insurgents had 'most likely' been 'high level'.[13]

Another strike, which became famous because it was one of the few strikes to be made subject to a publicly disclosed investigation, which resulted in administrative action, occurred in Uruzgan province in February 2010. The missiles were actually fired from a helicopter, but a Predator drone and its crew played an integral part in the operation and the drone crew was determined to have been responsible for serious targeting errors that resulted in the strike. The targets were a group of over 20 people who gathered in the pre-dawn hours and set out in a convoy of vehicles across the province. They were later determined to have been civilians, among whom were women and children, who were travelling together for security in order to traverse a dangerous region. The Predator drone observed them as they set out, and shadowed them for more than three hours, providing data on the group to an American ground commander who was leading a unit that was moving to engage a Taliban force in the area. We will return to this incident in the discussion below, but in short the drone crew misinterpreted the data being received from the drone, leading to the conclusion that the group comprised targetable insurgent men. The entire group comprised civilians, including several women and children, and 23 of them were killed in the strike. The military conducted a rare publicly disclosed investigation, and several senior officers, along with the Predator crew operating out of an Air Force base in Nevada, received administrative sanctions.[14]

The data on drone strikes and civilian casualties

There are several other known incidents that involve the killing of civilians, which reflect and share to varying degrees a number of features that will be explored here, and indeed features that are common to drone strikes reported from Pakistan and Yemen. Yet, having said that, there is surprisingly little data on the drone strikes in Afghanistan. Much of the focus of research and analysis of the drone-based targeted killing programme has been on operations in countries other than Afghanistan. Yet, the use of drone strikes in both 'personality strikes' and 'signature strikes' has been robust in Afghanistan as well. Unfortunately, it is difficult to precisely account for the number of drone strikes, the number of casualties resulting, or the number of civilian casualties among those totals, in Afghanistan. The US government does not report such data,[15] notwithstanding that its operations there, unlike the covert operations in Pakistan and Yemen, are in an open armed conflict in which the US is an acknowledged belligerent.

There are more detailed ongoing studies of drone strikes in Pakistan and Yemen, and while they are not consistent with one another regarding the numbers and rate of civilian casualties, most report significantly higher numbers of civilian casualties, and higher rates of civilian deaths per insurgent killed, than the US government reports.[16] It has been argued that the upshot of these studies is that we really do not know how many people have been killed, or how many of those killed are civilian, which raises serious problems of transparency and accountability. These patterns of government under-reporting and insufficient disclosure hold true for operations in Afghanistan.

There are far fewer independent reports providing drone strike data for Afghanistan. The United Nations Assistance Mission in Afghanistan (UNAMA) reports annually on the numbers of civilian casualties in Afghanistan, along with details of how they died and at whose hands. But the UNAMA reports did not separate casualties caused by drone strikes from other aerial attack numbers until 2012.[17] Nonetheless, it has reported that there was a steady rise in the numbers of weapons fired by drones from 2009 through 2013.[18] UNAMA reported that in 2012 there were 506 drone strikes in Afghanistan, which resulted in only five incidents of civilian casualties, involving 16 deaths and three injured, which included the killing of four children through an apparent targeting error.[19] It reported that in 2013 there were 261 civilian casualties (147 deaths, 114 injured), attributable to the international forces, of which, as far as could be determined, 59 casualties (45 deaths, 14 injured) were the result of 19 separate aerial operations conducted by drones – which constitutes a fairly significant increase in both the number of drone strikes causing civilian casualties, and the total numbers of such casualties.[20]

The Bureau of Investigative Journalism, well-known for its work in Pakistan, has only very recently turned its attention to Afghanistan, obtaining access to some of the US Central Command (CENTCOM) drone-related data.[21] It reported in July 2014 that there have been over 1,000 drone strikes in Afghanistan since 2008,[22] but noted that there is no public record of these strikes or their effects.[23] Moreover, it reported that ISAF data on the number of civilian casualties caused by drone strikes suffer from systemic underreporting.[24] Perhaps the most astonishing report published recently, and most significant for our purposes, was a classified report compiled by the Joint and Coalition Operational Analysis (JCOA), a component of the US Joint Forces Command. It similarly found that (according to the unclassified executive summary), coalition forces suffered from 'inaccurate assessments of civilian harm'.[25] What is more, and of particular importance for our analysis, the JCOA report concluded that:

Drone strikes in Afghanistan were seen to have close to the same number of civilian casualties per incident as manned aircraft, and were an order of magnitude more likely to result in civilian casualties per engagement.[26]

This finding by the US military, that drone strikes are much more likely to cause civilian casualties per engagement than manned airstrikes, both raises serious questions about compliance with IHL and would seem counterintuitive given the features of the armed drone, issues that we will return to below.

III. The applicable law

Questions regarding what legal regimes apply and how precisely they may govern the conduct of drone strikes in a traditionally defined armed conflict, even a non-international armed conflict such as Afghanistan, are much less complex and less disputed than similar questions regarding strikes in countries such as Yemen and Pakistan. Having said that, there remain some disputes over which legal regimes apply to drone strikes in a traditionally defined and acknowledged non-international armed conflict, and over the nature of the relationship among such regimes. In order to properly assess the issue of legality it is necessary that we briefly review the substance and operation of the legal principles that may apply to the drone strikes in Afghanistan.

International humanitarian law

It is undisputed that the primary legal regime governing drone strikes in a traditionally defined armed conflict is IHL. It is worth recalling, at the outset, that IHL is animated by two fundamental but somewhat conflicting rationales and purposes. One of these is to require armed forces to engage in hostilities in accordance with specific limits and constraints, in order to reduce human suffering, and in particular to minimise harm to civilians and civilian objects. The second is to provide legal authority for the conduct of such hostilities, and to thereby immunise the lawful combatants from prosecution or other action under different legal regimes, and to immunise the states on whose part they fight, for conduct that is undertaken in accordance with the principles and rules of IHL.[27] IHL thus both limits and legitimises the conduct of hostilities in armed conflict.

The bulk of the IHL regime applies primarily to international armed conflict – that is conflict between or among sovereign states. This body of IHL comprises a host of treaties, the most important of which are the Hague Conventions of 1899 and 1907,[28] the four Geneva Conventions of 1949,[29] and Additional Protocol I of 1977,[30] together with an extensive body of customary international law principles.[31] Only a subset of these rules and principles applies to conduct in a non-international armed conflict, by which is meant hostilities of a sufficiently intense nature between the armed forces of the state and well-organised armed groups (or hostilities among such groups), within some geographically limited theatre of conflict (the exact parameters of which are the subject of some debate).[32] Nonetheless, the customary international law principles relating to the law of targeting, and to weapons law, which in turn reflect the core principles of IHL, apply in both international and non-international armed conflict. In particular, the principles of necessity, distinction, humanity, discrimination, proportionality, and precautions in attack, all apply to drone strikes whether in non-international or international armed conflict.[33]

Means and methods of warfare

It will be helpful to briefly review the substance of these principles, and to also identify more specifically how they relate to both the law of targeting and to weapons law, which as mentioned earlier are two separate aspects of IHL. They find their origins in one of the earliest treaty provisions that explicitly articulated constraints on the conduct of war, which stipulated that neither the *means* nor the *methods* of warfare are unlimited.[34] The term 'means of warfare' here is understood to refer to weapons, and is the subject of weapons law,[35] while 'methods of warfare' relates to how weapons are used, which includes targeting decisions and is governed in part by the law of targeting.[36] This of course maps onto our inquiry into whether there is something inherent in the weapon system that contributes to illegality, or whether any such illegality can be explained by how it is being used. Virtually any weapon can be used in a manner that violates IHL, but relatively few are inherently unlawful.[37] Where a weapon is deemed to be inherently unlawful, the reason typically flows from a determination that any use of the weapon would by definition result in a *per se* violation of one of the core principles. Thus, chemical weapons and biological weapons are prohibited as being inherently unlawful because they are so indiscriminate that it is virtually impossible for them to be used in a manner compliant with the principle of distinction (to be discussed next). Other weapons, such as the use of white phosphorous on personnel, or exploding bullets more generally, are prohibited because they violate the principle of humanity, in that they cause unnecessary suffering.[38]

Principles of necessity and distinction

The principle of military necessity reflects the duality of IHL's rationales, both authorising belligerents to use the requisite force to achieve any military advantage that will advance the cause of winning the conflict, while inherently limiting the use of force to lawful means, and to the extent that such force is actually necessary to achieve a specific military objective.[39]

More specifically central to targeting issues, at least for the purposes of our analysis, is the principle of distinction, which is also one of the core principles of IHL. Codified in both Additional Protocols, it provides that armed forces must distinguish between combatants and civilians, and between military objectives and civilian objects.[40] In particular, the principle of distinction requires that armed forces refrain from making civilians or civilian objects the direct object of targeting or attack. This does not mean that the killing of civilians in a strike in and of itself violates the principle of distinction. This is so even when it was known at the time of the targeting decision that the killing of civilians would be a likely or even a sure consequence of the strike. So long as the killing is incidental to a strike in which the primary target is a legitimate military objective, it does not violate the principle of distinction. Such killing would be 'collateral damage', which is the focus of the principle of proportionality, to which we will turn presently.

Individual status in armed conflict

Before examining proportionality, it is necessary to pause and consider the question of who is actually targetable as a 'combatant', and who is protected as a 'civilian', as part of the principle of distinction. This is an issue over which there continues to be considerable dispute in the context of non-international armed conflict. However, it is well-accepted that the concept of 'combatant' as a legal status is unique to international armed conflict. The Geneva Conventions also provide, and it is generally accepted, that in both international and non-international armed conflict civilians may be targeted for such time as they take direct part in hostilities.[41] The dispute arises over precisely how insurgents, militants, terrorists and the like should be classified in a non-international armed conflict (which would, of course, include Afghanistan today). There is no question that they are targetable for such time as they are taking direct part in hostilities, though even then there remains debate over the precise parameters of this concept. The International Committee for the Red Cross (ICRC) has published guidelines that attempt to crystallise the elements required of the acts taken by the individual to qualify as taking direct part in hostilities (which include a certain level of harm, direct causation between the act and such harm, and a belligerent nexus), as well as to clarify the scope of the temporal component (which is limited to the duration of each act but also includes preparation for those acts), in order for the individual's conduct to be considered as taking direct part in hostilities.[42]

There are arguments, however, which have been recently supported by the ICRC, that members of organised armed groups party to a non-international armed conflict may fulfil a 'continuous combat function', making such individuals analogous to 'combatants' in an international armed conflict, and thus targetable based on their status as members of the organised armed group rather than their acts at any given moment.[43] Some apply the term 'fighters' to group members fulfilling this continuous combat function, as distinguished from but analogous to 'combatants'.[44]

Principle of discrimination

Related to the principle of distinction, but considered by some to be a distinct principle, is the principle of discrimination. Armed forces may not engage in indiscriminate attacks, by which is meant the conduct of strikes that are not directed at any specific military objective, or which employ a means of warfare that cannot be so directed, or the effects of which cannot be limited to the military objective.[45] This is reflected more specifically in weapons law in the prohibition on weapons that are indiscriminate, such as chemical weapons, and in targeting law by prohibiting the indiscriminate methods of using otherwise legitimate weapons, such as carpet bombing civilian populations. In addition to the principle of distinction, another overarching principle of IHL that provides part of the foundation for this prohibition against indiscriminate attacks is the principle of humanity, also sometimes called the principle of unnecessary suffering. The corollary to the principle of necessity, the principle of humanity prohibits the infliction of suffering, injury, or destruction that is not necessary for the achievement of legitimate military objectives or purposes.[46]

Principle of proportionality

We can now return to the principle of proportionality, mentioned above and closely related to both necessity and distinction. This principle provides that armed forces are prohibited from launching attacks that would be expected to cause incidental death or injury to civilians, or damage to civilian objects, which would be *excessive* in relation to the concrete and direct military advantage anticipated.[47] Implicit in this, as discussed earlier, is the idea that incidental death, injury, and damage are permissible so long as civilians and civilian objects were not the object of the attack (which would of course be contrary to the principle of distinction). It is only necessary to ensure that such harm is not excessive in relation to the advantage to be gained by attacking the military objective (which itself must be necessary, pursuant to the principle of necessity). There continues to be some debate over the scope and precise definition of 'military advantage', and even leaving that aside, the calculation of how much civilian life is to be considered excessive in relation to the rather incommensurate notion of military advantage is a difficult business. It should also be noted that any ex post assessment of compliance with the principle of proportionality focuses on what was known and anticipated at the time the decision was made.[48]

Principle of precautions in attack

The final principle directly relevant to our analysis of drone strikes is that of precautions in attack. This builds on the rationale underlying the principles of distinction, discrimination, and proportionality, creating a positive obligation to take care to spare the civilian population, civilians, and civil objects from harm. It provides that 'all feasible precautions' must be taken to avoid or to minimise incidental harm to civilians and civilian objects.[49] There are more specific related obligations, which include: a duty to take all feasible measures to ensure that targets are military objectives; to ensure that the means and methods of attack are selected with a view to minimising incidental harm to civilians; to do everything feasible to assess whether the attack may be expected to cause excessive harm to civilians in violation of the principle of proportionality; and finally, the obligation to do everything feasible to cancel any attack if it becomes apparent that the target is not a military objective, or that the attack will cause excessive loss of life or injury to civilians, or damage to civilian objects.[50]

As we turn our attention to the use and effects of armed drones, their attributes as a weapons system, and some aspects of the policy that governs the manner in which they have been employed, we will consider how these principles apply to the conduct of drone strikes. But it is worth observing here that the principles and rules apply to drones in exactly the same way that they apply to any other weapon or method of attack.[51]

International human rights law and domestic law

In the context of an ongoing armed conflict, IHL is the *lex specialis* that governs the conduct of armed forces operating in the hostilities. Nonetheless, more general legal regimes continue to operate alongside IHL, and they may apply to some conduct within the conflict notwithstanding the operation of IHL. The most relevant of these legal regimes, for our purposes here, is IHRL (international human rights law). The extent to which and precisely how IHRL may operate alongside IHL in the theatre of armed conflict is, however, the subject of some dispute. On the one hand, there are those who argue that IHRL will operate to govern conduct in situations where IHL does not provide a specific rule, or when the rule is unclear or ambiguous in the particular circumstances.[52] On the other hand, there are those who lean much further in the direction of holding that the *lex specialis* of IHL largely displaces and prevails over all more general legal regimes, such that IHRL has little if any application in an armed conflict, regardless of whether IHL is silent in a particular situation.[53] What is more, there is sometimes confusion, even on the part of institutions and international organisations operating within these legal regimes, in employing distinct concepts and principles that are unique to each of IHL and IHRL – such as applying the concept of 'combatant' from IHL in a human rights analysis.[54]

Nonetheless, there is a growing acceptance that IHRL operates at least to some extent alongside IHL in the theatre of armed conflict. This position has been confirmed by the International Court of Justice (ICJ) in its advisory opinions in the *Legality of Nuclear Weapons* case, and the *Legal Consequences of the Construction of a Wall in the Occupied*

Palestinian Territory case.[55] Moreover, it has been argued that the relationship between the two is more involved and complicated in the context of a non-international armed conflict, in part because the members of armed groups against which the state is fighting will often be nationals or residents of that state. As such these individuals will come squarely within the state's jurisdiction for purposes of triggering IHRL rights and obligations. As will be returned to below, the due process obligations imposed by IHRL may potentially influence the application of IHL principles, and vice versa. Thus, IHL principles may, for instance, inform the analysis of what constitutes an arbitrary denial of the right to life under IHRL, where the right is implicated in the context of an armed conflict.[56]

Extraterritorial operation of IHRL and the right to life

Even apart from this more general conceptual debate over the extent to which IHRL operates in an armed conflict, there is the more specific dispute over the extent to which IHRL has extraterritorial effect, so as to create binding obligations on a state in its relations with non-nationals when operating in the territory of another state. For instance, does the US have IHRL obligations in relation to non-Americans in the conduct of its operations in the non-international armed conflict in Afghanistan? The central right at issue, of course, is the right to life, which is enshrined as a matter of treaty law in Article 6 of the International Covenant of Civil and Political Rights (ICCPR).[57] The corollary obligation created by this right is a prohibition against the arbitrary killing of any person by the state. But the ICCPR imposes obligations on states to respect and ensure the rights enshrined in the treaty 'to all individuals in its territory and subject to its jurisdiction',[58] which the US has interpreted to mean that the US only has obligations in relation to persons who are both subject to US jurisdiction and who are within the territory of the US.[59]

This interpretation has been rejected by the UN Human Rights Committee,[60] as well as the ICJ,[61] and it is not shared by many other countries. Indeed, it has been controversial within US government.[62] But quite aside from the specific language of the ICCPR, the right to life exists as a principle of customary international law, and there are strong arguments that the armed forces of one state that are operating in a separate state would at a minimum have obligations to respect the customary international law right to life of persons within that state, if not an obligation to ensure the protection and enforcement of the right.[63] In the *Armed Activities on the Territory of the Congo* case the ICJ suggested that, under both treaty law and customary international law, not only will IHL and IHRL have to be taken into consideration in some contexts in an armed conflict, but that IHRL may also have extra-territorial application.[64] This was followed by the European Court of Human Rights in *Al-Skeini and Others* v. *The United Kingdom*, in finding that the European Convention on Human Rights applied to the actions of the British forces in relation to Iraqi nationals during the conflict there after the 2003 invasion.[65]

The UN Special Rapporteur on the Protection of Human Rights and Fundamental Freedoms while Countering Terrorism likely captured the current state of the law accurately when he recently wrote that '[i]t is now reasonably well settled that, in a situation of armed conflict (whether of an international or non-international character), the international human rights law prohibition on arbitrary killing continues to apply, but the test of whether a deprivation of life is arbitrary must be determined by the applicable targeting rules of international humanitarian law'.[66] This may seem to suggest that in an armed conflict the default standards for assessing compliance with respect for the right to life are provided by IHL principles. It should be noted, however, when the killing is conducted by civilian agencies such as the CIA, as we will discuss below, then IHL principles will not necessarily provide such standards for what is arbitrary. Moreover, the consequences and remedies under state responsibility for the resulting violations of IHRL may differ. Thus, in short, the operation of IHRL separate and apart from IHL is not insignificant, and is relevant to drone strikes in Afghanistan.

Domestic law

In addition to IHRL the domestic criminal and constitutional law of the state in which the armed conflict is taking place will continue to operate, and in some circumstances may apply to conduct undertaken in relation to the armed conflict. Moreover, the criminal and constitutional law of the state operating abroad in a non-international armed conflict will also be operating in the background – meaning that, of course, US criminal and constitutional law may apply to some conduct undertaken in the theatre of war in Afghanistan. In what circumstances could the domestic criminal or constitutional law, or for that matter IHRL, apply? It was mentioned above that (according to the predominant view) the *lex generalis* could apply when the rule from the *lex specialis* of IHL is ambiguous or non-existent. In other words, these other legal regimes would potentially apply when the conduct undertaken is clearly not authorised or governed by IHL, such that the immunities and privileges that IHL confers on combatants would not operate to protect the actor from the application of other legal regimes. This may be due, for instance, to the nature of the act, or the status of the actor – issues we will return to shortly in examining the role of the CIA in drone strikes.

Transparency and accountability

Transparency and accountability has become a significant legal issue in relation to drone strikes. The drone-based targeted killing programme conducted in countries such as Yemen and Pakistan continues to be classified, with the US government refusing to formally acknowledge its existence in court filings, even as government representatives, including President Obama himself, nonetheless make reference to it.[67] While the military's drone operations in Afghanistan are not formally classified there is insufficient transparency and accountability in relation to drone strikes in Afghanistan as well, as will be discussed in more detail below. The argument is being increasingly made that IHL and IHRL impose distinct obligations regarding transparency and accountability. Special rapporteurs reporting to the UN General Assembly, the UN Human Rights Council, and the European Parliament, have all argued that both IHL and IHRL obligations require states to provide some degree of transparency, and to develop formal mechanisms of accountability, in the conduct of lethal drone strikes – and that the failure to do so constitutes a separate violation of international law.[68]

The starting point for such arguments is that transparency and accountability are integral to the very essence of the rule of law. Accessibility and intelligibility of the law, as well as assurance that the law is enforced equally throughout the system, are central ideas to all conceptions of the rule of law.[69] But there are more specific obligations relating to accountability in both IHL and IHRL. The UN Secretary General's expert panel on Sri Lanka asserted in its 2011 report that accountability for serious violations of both IHL and IHRL is a duty under both domestic and international law.[70] With respect to IHL, Philp Alston has argued that the obligations of accountability arise directly from the undertakings of state parties in Common Article 1 of the 1949 Geneva Conventions to 'respect and *ensure respect*' for the Geneva Conventions, which requires states to implement the obligations in internal law, and to develop mechanisms to enforce compliance.[71] Moreover, in the context of targeted killing, the Geneva Conventions and customary international law require states to implement specific procedural safeguards in order to comply with the principles of distinction, proportionality, and precautions in attacks, as reviewed above. In order to comply with those obligations states must have in place specific mechanisms for implementation, assessment, and enforcement, all of which are aspects of accountability, and these in turn require a minimum level of transparency.[72]

Special Rapporteur Ben Emmerson reached similar conclusions in his report to the UN General Assembly, arguing that transparency and accountability require fact-finding inquiries in the aftermath of all incidents that appear to have caused unanticipated civilian casualties; and that where any such assessment reveals the possibility of violations, a full investigation is required, adhering to transparency principles of promptness, effectiveness, independence, and impartiality.[73] All of these obligations relating to accountability necessarily require states to demonstrate, to both domestic audiences and the international community, that they are in compliance with legal obligations and that they have mechanisms in place for implementing the enforcement obligations relating to the relevant rules. And such demonstrations of course both require and create a sufficient transparency in the process.[74] This position on transparency and accountability is further supported by the ICRC and a number of other relevant international institutions.[75]

There are similar specific obligations of accountability in relation to IHRL, particularly with respect to the right to life. Nils Melzer, in a report to the European Parliament, advised that 'all major human rights bodies have held that the obligations flowing from the right to life necessarily entail a duty of States to investigate the use of lethal force by their agents, and that failure to comply with this duty may, as such, amount to a violation of the right to life'.[76] This obligation does not arise from treaty alone, but is a central and integral component of the customary international law right to life, and the state obligation not to arbitrarily deprive anyone thereof.[77]

Transparency, in turn, is similarly necessary, since these obligations of accountability cannot be meaningfully fulfilled without some level of transparency.[78] A fundamental component of accountability is the requirement to provide public demonstrations that policies, procedures, and mechanisms exist, and are operating sufficiently, so as to ensure compliance with the underlying legal regime. That requirement simply cannot be fulfilled if there is limited transparency as to what legal rules and principles are governing conduct, the extent to which such conduct is in fact consistent with the governing legal regime, and how mechanisms of investigation and enforcement are operating in the event of suspected non-compliance.

As Alston argues, accountability imposes a two-fold duty. On one level the national procedures and mechanisms designed to ensure compliance with international law regimes must meet certain standards of transparency and accountability in order to satisfy the state's international legal obligations to implement, assess, and enforce the underlying law. On a second level, however, the national procedures and mechanisms must be sufficiently transparent to permit international organisations and institutions to in turn assess the extent to which the state is, in fact, complying with both its substantive international legal obligations, and its obligations to address violations of that underlying law.[79] The US itself effectively made a similar argument in relation to Sri Lanka's position on compliance with IHL in the last stages of its conflict with the Tamils.[80]

IV. Compliance with the law

Having reviewed the data on the killing of civilians in drone strikes in Afghanistan, and examined the legal regimes that apply to those drone strikes in a traditionally defined non-international armed conflict, the inquiry now turns to examine in more detail whether the drone strike operations are being conducted in compliance with international law. In particular, this part examines whether there is a basis for arguing that there may be violations of the relevant legal principles, and explores whether such potential violations are primarily attributable to aspects of the weapon system itself, or whether they are more likely attributable to the methods of its use.

Potential violations of international law

Compliance with the principles of distinction and precautions

It is difficult to reach firm conclusions as to whether there are systemic and ongoing violations of international law obligations arising from drone strikes in Afghanistan, apart from obligations regarding transparency and accountability, given the limited data available. Yet there is sufficient evidence of civilian casualties, and evidence that there are some features relating to targeting errors that are common to many of these incidents, to at least raise serious questions about compliance with legal obligations.

There are numerous strikes, as in two of the examples discussed earlier (the Zhawar Kili strike and the Uruzgan incident), in which the civilians killed were not 'collateral damage' in relation to the targeting of a legitimate military objective, but were actually the primary target. It can be safely presumed that these are instances of accidental targeting rather than any deliberate targeting of civilians as such, and thus not examples of wilful violation of the principle of distinction. Nonetheless, these incidents clearly raise questions about compliance with the principle of precautions in attack: In accordance with what criteria are targeting decisions being made, on the basis of what intelligence, and pursuant to what standards of proof for determining whether there is sufficient evidence to satisfy the criteria? This relates in particular to so-called 'signature strikes', in which people are targeted based on inferences drawn from their behaviour, actions, location, and other such criteria, leading to the conclusion that they are fighters or civilians taking direct part in hostilities. The features of these signature strikes will be examined in more detail below, but the repeated errors in targeting civilians suggests that either the criteria, or the sufficiency of evidence required to satisfy the criteria, may not meet the obligation to take all feasible measures to ensure that targets are military objectives.

There are other examples in which the civilian casualties are collateral to strikes that are legitimately targeting military objectives. In such cases, as in the one example cited earlier (the Watapur district strike), both the principles of proportionality and precautions in attack are implicated. There are questions as to whether the operators met their obligations to take all feasible measures to ensure that the means and methods of attack were selected with a view to minimising incidental harm to civilians, and to assess whether the attack may cause excessive harm relative to the importance of the military objective, in violation of the principle of proportionality. And there are questions as to whether the actual harm caused to civilians was, in the final analysis, excessive in relation to the importance of the military objective being targeted. It has been reported that the Air Force rules of engagement (ROE) in place for Afghanistan, for instance, restrict the number of civilian casualties acceptable (known as collateral damage estimates or CDEs) in targeting operations to far fewer than the principle of proportionality might require under IHL.[81] But the ROE are

LEGAL AND ETHICAL IMPLICATIONS OF DRONE WARFARE

not publically available, and as will be discussed below, they are likely not uniform across all agencies engaged in drone strikes in Afghanistan. Moreover, the calculation of acceptable civilian casualties under the principle of proportionality is relative to an assessment of military advantage, and it is entirely unknown how that is assessed – all of which brings us back to the absence of transparency and accountability.

Transparency and accountability – the CIA and JSOC

As mentioned earlier, there are increasing claims that the lack of transparency and accountability in relation to the drone strikes is a feature of the programme that by itself constitutes a separate violation of legal obligations. Moreover, it makes it impossible to properly assess the extent to which the strikes are being otherwise conducted in compliance with international law. The example of the 2010 Uruzgan strike, which resulted in an investigation and the public disclosure of a summary of the investigation findings and resulting sanctions, is an exception that highlights the norm. Many of the cases reported by UNAMA and others working in the field reveal a pattern of behaviour in which US forces initially deny the existence or extent of civilian casualties after strikes, and even, in some cases, engage in deliberate efforts to conceal or supress facts relating to incidents.[82] There is little indication that investigations are routinely conducted in cases of alleged civilian casualties, from which lessons could be learned, and in cases of IHL violations, actions taken to enforce the legal obligations. Even when some inquiry has been undertaken, there is typically very little in the way of subsequent disclosure of information regarding the findings.[83] This is particularly so when the CIA or JSOC are involved. Indeed, all of these issues regarding both transparency and accountability, and compliance with IHL and IHRL, are vastly complicated by the fact that some of the strikes are being conducted by the CIA and some by JSOC, and sometimes by both operating together.

There tends to be a widely held view in both the scholarly and the media treatment of the targeted killing programme that while the CIA is the main operator in Yemen and Pakistan, the Air Force, or at least the regular US armed forces more generally, are the sole operators in Afghanistan.[84] But there is good reason to believe that both the CIA and JSOC forces are involved in the conduct of lethal drone strikes in Afghanistan.[85] The CIA is not, as a matter of both domestic US law and international law, part of the armed forces engaged in hostilities in Afghanistan. This raises a couple of significant issues. The first question is whether CIA operators conducting drone strikes consider themselves bound by IHL and IHRL. The regular forces of the US military are, of course, formally committed to compliance with IHL.[86] Drone strikes undertaken by the Air Force, for instance, are subject to the Air Force's well-developed targeting rules and principles, and the specific rule of engagement (ROE) that are in place at the time.[87] While specific ROE are classified, and, as will be discussed in more detail below, the criteria used for signature strikes are both opaque and questionable, there is nonetheless a body of well-known targeting doctrine grounded in principles of IHL to which the organisation is formally committed.

In contrast, little is known about what rules or targeting principles are applied by the CIA. There is evidence that the CIA operates under less stringent and more flexible rules, and it is unknown whether these rules are entirely compliant with the demands of IHL.[88] It is not at all clear whether the CIA even understands itself to be governed by IHL in particular, or international law in general.[89] Indeed, there is evidence that the CIA interprets certain provisions of its domestic enabling legislation to mean that it is not bound or limited by principles of international law.[90] Even if it did consider itself so bound, it does not have an institutional history of interpreting, operationalising, and

51

internalising principles of international law.[91] On the contrary, there are famous episodes in its history, such as its involvement in the Phoenix Program in Vietnam, in which it participated in armed conflict in ways that entirely flouted the principles of IHL and IHRL.[92]

The operations of JSOC also raise some of the same issues. While JSOC is part of the US Special Operations Command (USSCOM), it is quite unlike other elements of the regular military forces, including the other branches of Special Operations Forces. While JSOC was established after the failed Iran rescue mission in 1979, its role has expanded significantly since 9/11, and its primary mission is 'believed to be' the identification and destruction of terrorist organisations worldwide.[93] USSCOM has legal authority to engage in anti-terrorist activity abroad that is separate from the traditional Title 10 legal authority for the regular forces.[94] JSOC is notoriously secretive, and is not subject to the same level of oversight and supervision as the regular military in some aspects of its operations.[95] While many of the studies of JSOC and its operations note the dearth of publically available information, and thus the difficulty of making definitive statements about its operations and protocols, there is evidence that JSOC often operates outside of the regular regional command structure, and that it does not adhere to the normal ROE and standard operating procedures of the regular forces.[96] There is considerable evidence that JSOC has conducted operations in violation of IHL in Iraq and elsewhere, and there are allegations that it may not believe itself bound by IHL.[97]

These issues regarding transparency and accountability, and other aspects of compliance with international law, are compounded by the manner in which the CIA and JSOC have operated together in Afghanistan and elsewhere, in what has come to be referred to as 'double-hatting'.[98] This refers to combined operations undertaken by the CIA and JSOC in circumstances that exploit differences in the domestic legal authority and the distinct Congressional reporting requirements that govern the two agencies, as well as the different legal status of the two organisations under international law. There is a growing debate over the significance and extent of this 'blurring' of domestic legal authority and international legal status by this practice,[99] the details of which we need not dwell on here. For our purposes, the upshot is that such joint operations in the conduct of drone strikes may serve to avoid the normal lines of reporting, oversight, and accountability that would normally apply to the CIA and the regular military forces, thus further reducing the transparency, accountability, and possibly, the felt need to comply with IHL and IHRL in any given operation.[100]

CIA operators as civilians taking direct part in hostilities

It would be remiss not to mention one final issue raised by CIA involvement in drone strikes, which relates to the legal consequences of civilians engaging in lethal operations in an armed conflict. Some have argued that this conduct by the CIA constitutes a violation of IHL, and the US has itself prosecuted detainees under the theory that killing by unprivileged combatants in an armed conflict constitutes a war crime.[101] The better view, however, is that while such involvement in hostilities is not authorised or privileged under IHL, it is not a violation of IHL either. Thus, such civilians do not enjoy the protections and privileges of combatants under IHL, and so are themselves targetable (for such time as they are taking direct part in hostilities), and they could theoretically be prosecuted for murder for their actions.[102] The CIA operators of drones would, of course, fall into this category.

While not a violation of IHL, this is not to say that the killing of individuals in Afghanistan by CIA operatives is lawful. If the killing is in circumstances that do not satisfy the law enforcement paradigm for using deadly force, then it may constitute a violation of the IHRL obligations of the US to respect (if not to enforce) the right to life of the victims, and thus may well attract state responsibility for that violation of international law.[103] But this issue need not be fully explored here, and is best left for another day, as it is somewhat tangential to the central inquiry into the lawfulness of drones in a defined armed conflict.

In sum, there is limited information on the drone strikes in Afghanistan, but there is sufficient evidence to at least raise the possibility that there may be systemic targeting errors in violation of the principles of proportionality and precautions in attack. The next question to address then, is whether the cause for such potential violations is primarily in the nature of the weapon system itself, or in the methods by which it used.

Nature of the armed drone as weapons system – means of warfare

We turn next to examine the nature of drones as a weapons system, to assess whether there is something inherent to drones that is likely to cause violations of international law. Drones are not, of course, the only weapons system used in targeted killing operations. Cruise missiles, airstrikes with traditional manned aircraft, and even hunter-killer teams have all been used by the US for the targeting of identified individuals, in Afghanistan and elsewhere. But one of the primary questions addressed in this article is whether there are unique features of the drone that contributes to illegality. It is important to thus begin by examining the attributes of the armed drone as a weapons system. Drones have a number of features that combine in ways that reinforce one another so as to confer a significant comparative advantage over both cruise missiles and manned fixed-wing aircraft, not only in terms of military tactical advantage, but arguably also in terms of enabling optimal compliance with IHL. On the other hand, perhaps somewhat paradoxically, some of these same features may facilitate, or make more likely, certain violations of IHL.

Positive features of drones

To begin, drones such as the MQ-1 Predator and the MQ-9 Reaper can be deployed over a target for comparatively long periods of time – for as long as 22 hours at a time, as compared with perhaps 90 minutes for an F-16 – for observation and intelligence acquisition, thus providing operators with a longer evaluation and decision-making period before lethal force is employed.[104] This feature of 'persistence' is reinforced by stealth, arising from the size and low sound of the drone at altitude – up to 50,000 feet – making it difficult to detect in the absence of sophisticated air-defence systems.[105] As well, since they are typically on-site directly over the target during the decision-making process, they provide for more rapid implementation of a strike once the decision is made, as compared with, for instance, a combined use of drones for surveillance but manned air-strikes or cruise missiles for the final attack.

In addition to this persistence and stealth, a defining feature of the drones is the intelligence gathering and targeting system, which includes ever more sophisticated sensors and video feeds. The most recent innovation is called the 'Gorgon Stare', a system of cameras that will deliver video of a five-mile-diameter area at one time, while allowing operators to zoom into any one segment, or multiple segments at a time.[106] What is more, a signal advantage of the drone, relative to a manned aircraft such as an F-16, is how the intelligence from such sensors and videos are analysed. Each Air Force drone has a team of at least three operators, including a pilot, a sensor operator, and a mission intelligence coordinator.[107] Moreover, while the mission intelligence coordinator is responsible for overseeing the collection and immediate analysis of the intelligence being gathered, there are other individuals, including intelligence analysts, who may participate in the assessment of incoming data from other remote locations, and be part of the decision-making process via dedicated voice-line or on-line 'chat rooms'.[108] As compared to a pilot in a manned aircraft, the decision-making process involves more people, assessing far greater volumes of sensor information and intelligence, operating under fewer time constraints and without the stress caused by imminent personal risk to themselves. It has been argued, therefore, that this decision-making process is sounder, less prone to errors, and far more likely to comply with legal obligations.[109]

The defining feature of drones, as compared to traditional aircraft, to state the obvious, is that they are remotely controlled and thus unmanned (but not fully autonomous, which is a different kind of weapon that raises a whole host of different issues). It is this essential characteristic that gives rise to so many of the other features, such as persistence and stealth, collective decision-making and the reduction of risk to the operators to virtually zero. Being unmanned also allows for an extension of operational reach, permitting the deployment of the drone in regions where not only actual risk to the crew but also political and strategic risks would make the deployment of manned aircraft untenable.[110]

It is also argued by the defenders of drone strikes that the weapons employed by drones are both highly accurate, and characterised by relatively tight blast areas, thus making the drones a high-precision weapon system.[111] The Predator carries laser-guided Hellfire missiles, while the Reaper can carry, in addition to Hellfire missiles, GPS-guided bombs. The laser-guided missiles can be guided by the drone's own laser system, or by a laser directed at the target by forces on the ground.[112] All of these features may be said to combine in ways that make the armed drone weapons system, as it currently exists and is deployed, one that is likely to enhance compliance with IHL and IHRL, and indeed is much more so than other weapons systems used for targeted killing and air strikes.[113]

One last point should be made regarding the features of drones in the context of IHL. There is another possible consequence of all these features combining to provide the drone with a unique capacity to adhere tightly to the principles of proportionality and precautions in attack.[114] These features may also operate to raise the standard that the US forces must satisfy in order to comply with the obligation to do 'everything feasible' to avoid causing harm to civilians and civilian objects.[115] The more precise the weapons systems that are at a country's disposal for any given attack, the less justifiable will be any harm caused to civilians.

Negative features of drones

There are, however, also some corresponding weaknesses or disadvantages flowing from these very same features. Operators and decision-makers, sitting somewhere thousands of miles away, are limited in large measure to the video and other sensory intelligence being provided by the drone itself. It has been suggested that decision-makers are prone to a so-called 'soda-straw effect' – meaning that operators tend to 'zoom in' to focus on an increasingly narrow area around the target, with a resulting loss of information regarding the surrounding context – particularly during the final stages prior to firing.[116]

It has been similarly suggested that as the video and sensor feeds become ever more sophisticated and extensive – as evidenced by the new Gorgon Stare system – the operators are prone to suffer from a 'data crush', in which there is simply so much data streaming in during the targeting process, with too little time and too few people to analyse it, that crucial evidence regarding civilian presence, to take one example, is more likely to be missed.[117] There have also been concerns expressed that the operator's distance and detachment from the conflict zone and their targets, together with the complete absence of reciprocal risk, may somehow increase the likelihood of targeting errors. This is often expressed and explained in different ways. Thus there is the so-called 'PlayStation' effect, in which the concern is that the distance and detachment of operators who are killing by video-feed in the afternoon and are home for a BBQ with their families by evening, may simply not have a sufficiently grave appreciation for the moral consequences of their actions.[118]

Many of these concerns tend to get brushed aside by defenders of drones. Thus, the 'PlayStation' effect is argued to be somewhat speculative, and in any event can be addressed by strict adherence to IHL and compliant ROE.[119] Similarly, the distance and detachment concern is given short shrift on the grounds that it is actually more of a strength than a weakness, given that it creates conditions for more stress-free decision-making.[120] Moreover, these concerns can be seen as being with the operators as much as with the nature of the drone system itself. But the concerns may lack salience in part because they have not been developed in a systematic fashion, organised within a theoretical framework. We will return to them below when we examine these features through the lens of psychological theory, and assess whether they may not contribute to systemic misperception.

Nature of the drone strike policy – methods of warfare

Having considered the nature of the armed drone as a weapons system, and its inherent legality as a 'means of warfare', it remains to examine more closely certain aspects of the policy governing its use. In other words, to assess whether there are features of the 'methods of warfare' associated with the drone strikes that may contribute to systemic violations of IHL or IHRL. We have already explored some aspects of the policy relating to its use, and the issues surrounding the lack of transparency and accountability discussed above would also fall within this category. But at the centre of any inquiry into methods has to be an examination of the varying targeting policies employed in drone strikes. The targeting policies have not been publicly disclosed, but the essential elements of the policies have been inferred from the different kinds of strikes reported.

Personality strikes

Drone strikes can be broadly categorised into two types – the so-called 'personality strikes' and the 'signature strikes'. Personality strikes are premeditated attacks mounted against identified individuals, usually having been designated as a target on one of several 'kill lists' maintained by different agencies. Little is known about the decision-making process for placing individuals on such a list, but presumably it is based on the accumulation of some required level of intelligence.[121] In order to be lawful under IHL, that intelligence would have to establish that the individual is a combatant, a fighter engaged in a continuous combat function, or a civilian who routinely takes direct part in hostilities. Once on the list or otherwise selected for targeting, the agency planning the strike will typically have intelligence obtained in advance regarding the identity, conduct, and location of the target. The accuracy of that intelligence, be it signals intelligence, human intelligence, or other combinations of sources, will of course have a significant impact on the possibility of targeting errors. Moreover, if the target is a civilian who takes direct part in hostilities, the intelligence must accurately indicate that the target is actually taking direct part in hostilities at the time of the strike.[122]

There are said to be as many as six different 'kill lists' in existence for Afghanistan alone, with thousands of names among them, maintained by different agencies.[123] Mistakes can occur in designating persons as targets when they do not in fact satisfy the criteria for identifying them as members of an organised armed group fulfilling a continuous combat function, or a civilian taking direct part in hostilities. Other errors may occur through incidents of mistaken identity, in which a person other than the designated target is killed. In 2010, for instance, a man named Zabet Amanulluh, along with nine other civilians in his company, were killed due to mistaken intelligence that suggested he was a Taliban deputy governor named Muhammad Amin who was using Amanullah's name as an alias.[124]

Within the context of personality strikes there is also a distinction between the clearly premeditated strikes that are undertaken methodically according to careful planning based on considerable intelligence, and 'dynamic targeting' operations in which there is little time between the receipt of intelligence placing a designated target in a certain location, analysis of that intelligence, decision-making, and implementation of the strike.[125] Targeting errors can occur in either case due to flaws in the original intelligence, or with the sensory, video, or signals intelligence being relied on in the final targeting process, but errors are clearly more likely in dynamic targeting scenarios. In either case, all feasible efforts must be made in the implementation of the strike to minimise collateral or accidental injury to civilians, in accordance with the principles of precautions in attack and proportionality.

Signature strikes

In contrast to personality strikes, signature strikes are attacks against people whose identity is unknown, and who are targeted on the basis of a number of indicia or criteria that comprise a 'signature', which is considered sufficient for an inference that the individuals are combatants (in the context of an international armed conflict), members of armed groups who are fulfilling a continuous combat function (in non-international armed conflict, and assuming this standard is accepted), or are civilians taking a direct part in hostilities (in either form of armed conflict). These strikes are typically the result of decisions based entirely on real-time observation of the persons targeted rather than intelligence about them obtained prior to the operation. The probability of error, and indeed the legality of such strikes, will depend in large measure on the criteria being applied – that is, the nature of the conduct, behaviour, or other indicia that comprise the 'signature ' – in making targeting decisions, as well as the sufficiency of the evidence used to establish that the criteria were satisfied in the circumstances.[126]

The US government has not made public the criteria used in signature strikes, but inferences can be made from an analysis of known strikes, and a number of different sets of criteria are said to be employed in Afghanistan and elsewhere.[127] A recent legal analysis of signature strikes by Kevin Heller identifies these various criteria. Heller argues that several of these criteria will almost always conform with the requirements of IHL or be 'legally adequate' (assuming that there is sufficient evidence to satisfy them in any given circumstance), while some will almost always be 'legally inadequate' under IHL, and the legality of a third group will depend on the precise interpretation placed upon the signature criteria by the decision-makers.[128] The signatures that are legally adequate include indicia that the individuals are, at the time of the strike: (i) planning attacks; (ii) transporting weapons (which is to be distinguished from merely being armed); (iii) handling explosives; or (iv) present in the compound or training camp of an organised armed group that is a party to the conflict. Assuming the sufficiency and reliability of the evidence establishing them, all of these signature criteria are sufficient indications that the individuals in question are, at a minimum, taking direct part in hostilities, and thus are targetable.[129]

LEGAL AND ETHICAL IMPLICATIONS OF DRONE WARFARE

Legally *inadequate* signature criteria, which the US has on at least some occasions applied, include indicia that individuals are: (i) military-age males in an area of known terrorist or insurgent activity, or 'strike zones'[130]; (ii) consorting with known militants, or organised armed groups party to the conflict[131]; (iii) among an armed group travelling in enemy-controlled territory ('armed group' here merely referring to a group of people with weapons, as distinguished from an 'organized armed group party to the conflict')[132]; and (iv) present in a 'suspicious camp' in enemy controlled territory.[133] These signature criteria may tend to be more often employed in Yemen, Pakistan, and other such regions that do not constitute a hot battlefield, but there is evidence that they are also used in Afghanistan. Indeed, both the 2002 Zhawar Kili strike by the CIA and the 2010 Uruzgan strike by the Air Force, discussed above, appear to have involved targeting based on a combination of indicia that included several of these 'inadequate' criteria. Moreover, it was arguably reliance upon these criteria that contributed to what was the likely unlawful killing of civilians.

Finally, there are signature criteria that may or may not be legally adequate, depending on how they are interpreted by decision-makers. These include: (i) groups of armed men travelling towards a combat zone (which will be adequate if there is other evidence to corroborate that there is actual intent to take direct part in hostilities); (ii) persons operating in the training camps of an organised armed group party to the conflict (which may be adequate if there is evidence that the targeted individuals are training for specific operations or attacks); (iii) persons training to join the Taliban or al-Qaeda in Afghanistan (which may be adequate if there is sufficient evidence that the individuals are indeed training for a specific operation or to take up a continuous combat function within the armed group); and (v) persons deemed to be 'facilitators' (which could only be adequate if it involved action that comes within the scope of taking direct part in hostilities, but would be inadequate if it involved such actions as financing, recruiting, propagandising, feeding, and so forth, all of which could constitute 'facilitation' but does not constitute taking direct part in hostilities).[134] Again, the Uruzgan strike reflected reliance on the criteria of armed men travelling in the general direction of a combat zone (and the even more problematic 'military-age male' criteria), without sufficient corroboration of whether they were in fact armed, or whether there were other indicia to establish that they intended to join the hostilities.

Having reviewed the features relating to the nature of drones, and features of the policy and practice surrounding their use, we turn to examine in a little more detail the relationship between the two – and address more specifically the question of attributing between them the responsibility for any systemic violations of international law.

V. The means-method paradox

The foregoing examination would tend to suggest that it is the manner in which drone strikes are conducted, with policies such as those governing signature strikes, that is more conducive to IHL violations than anything in the nature of the drone itself. Thus, to the extent there are systemic violations of IHL in the conduct of the drone strikes in Afghanistan, this examination would seem to indicate that the problem lies with the methods of warfare, not the means. And yet, having said that, a more careful examination of the causes of the errors in such strikes as the Uruzgan incident, raises interesting questions as to whether there may be a more complex relationship between the means and methods of warfare. Indeed, a consideration of the relationship through the lens of psychological theory raises the prospect that some of the features of the armed drone that were identified above as making it particularly conducive to compliance with IHL may paradoxically facilitate or make more likely the employment of methods that could lead to systematic violations of IHL.

We begin this exploration with a concern that has been raised regarding a specific feature of armed drones, namely that the drone team is operating at great distances from the target and often in a completely detached environment. As was mentioned briefly above, the criticism is that drone crews will lack the same kind of nuanced understanding of the typical cultural behaviour and patterns of life of the target population, as compared to the understanding that forces on the ground normally would develop – and thus drone operators will be more prone to misinterpreting the situations and behaviour they are observing.[135] But while this argument has been made frequently before, and indeed has been summarily dismissed by others,[136] some of its deeper implications have not been fully explored. An absence of such deeper familiarity with the theatre of conflict will not only lead to direct and more obvious errors in the interpretation of this or that behaviour pattern. Considered from the perspective of psychological theory, this detachment and lack of familiarity may actually create the foundation for more systemic and systematic errors. Moreover, once we begin to examine the drone operations through the lens of psychological theory, it becomes apparent that other features of the drone, features that are considered among its strengths, may feed into misperceptions that could help explain systemic targeting errors.

Cognitive consistency theory and misperception

It is well-established in cognitive consistency theory and certain aspects of attribution theory that our perceptions, and in particular our interpretation of the posture, behaviour, and intentions of others, is heavily influenced by our expectations or assumptions about them.[137] We tend to interpret information about others in ways that are consistent with our long-held theories and attitudes about them (commonly referred to as our 'perceptual set'), and with our more immediate short-term hypothesis, assumptions, and expectations about their likely behaviour (known as our 'evoked sets').[138] While this predisposition of people to interpret information in ways that are consistent with their views and expectations is actually quite important to their ability to efficiently and effectively make sense of the world around us, it can also be the cause of misperception and misinterpretation. This happens because people tend to interpret ambiguous information in a manner that is consistent with pre-existing assumptions and hypotheses, and to discount or ignore possible alternative interpretations, and even worse, they will often reject or supress inconsistent information as being false, flawed, or irrelevant.[139] Indeed, misperceptions can be increasingly entrenched by recurring feedback loops, in which ambiguous information is assimilated to existing hypotheses, thus confirming and reinforcing them, making it ever more difficult for inconsistent information to get through to dislodge or change the perceptions in question.

The likelihood of such misperception can be increased by a number of factors. The first of these is overconfidence. Where decision-makers are overly confident in their information about a situation and their understanding of it, they are more likely to develop the view that the event or situation supports obvious inferences, and will be blind to the very real possibility that the inferences are actually being shaped by the pre-existing assumptions or hypotheses. This in turn will lead to over-confidence in the soundness of the inferences, and exclusion or discounting of alternative options.[140]

A second factor, related to the first, is what is called premature cognitive closure. This refers to situations in which decision-makers become excessively bound to pre-existing views, assumptions, or hypotheses, and consequently become too prone to discount or reject information that cannot be reconciled with those views. This is caused in part by the sheer psychological difficulty of escaping the influence of a perceptual set or evoked set once it has been established in one's mind, and by the person being insufficiently aware of the extent to which such perspectives are influencing their analysis. But this problem is also most likely to arise when actors prematurely form hypotheses or working assumptions. Most people do not sufficiently understand that the very formation of such working assumptions or preliminary hypotheses can then operate to skew their perception through premature cognitive closure.[141] The results are illustrated in the realm of criminal justice, in cases where investigators are said to have developed 'tunnel vision' once they have identified a suspect, and been victims of 'confirmation bias' in their subsequent analysis of evidence in the course of the investigation.[142]

A third factor that can operate to skew perceptions is the extent to which decision-makers often interpret the behaviour of others through an unrealistically egocentric lens – that is, they tend to exaggerate the significance of themselves or their institution in the decision-making and behaviour of others. Indeed, in some contexts, the decision-maker may perceive themselves as being central to other actors' behaviour, when in fact there may be no such relationship at all.[143]

The tendencies that flow from these factors can be further exacerbated by another but separate psychological phenomenon, which is the influence of group dynamics on collective decision-making. Famous studies in psychology have demonstrated that people can be influenced into making flawed judgments about the simplest and most obvious of tasks (such as indicating which of two lines on a piece of paper is longer), when surrounded by others expressing support for the wrong answer.[144] The opinions of those around a person engaged in a decision-making process exert pressure to a surprising degree, and can cause the mediation and distortion of judgment in the wrong direction. This could quite conceivably operate in the context of drone crew deliberations, as will be seen when we examine the Uruzgan strike more closely below.

We return to the context of drone strikes, and the question of whether the operators' distance from the theatre of conflict could lead to misinterpretation. The consequences of this detachment are not only that the operators lack familiarity with the target culture and environment, such that they might make straightforward mistakes in interpreting behaviour due to ignorance of local conditions. Rather, it may contribute to more systemic problems of misperception. As a result of the detachment, the drone crew are entirely immersed in their own particular institutional sub-culture back home, as well as living and operating within the home culture far from the front. Quite apart from the possibility that this may interfere with their understanding of the moral implications of their work – the so-called 'PlayStation effect' criticism discussed earlier – there is the prospect that it may be highly conducive to the development of inappropriate and premature assumptions or hypotheses about potential target populations. That will in turn lead to operators misinterpreting ambiguous information and ignoring contrary evidence in a manner that is consistent with and reinforcing the assumptions, with resulting targeting errors.[145] Moreover, this tendency would likely be further exacerbated by the 'data crush' and 'soda straw' concerns that were discussed earlier, providing a more sound theoretical foundation for those criticisms of the drone operations.

A study of the 2010 Uruzgan targeting incident suggests that the tragic targeting error may be explained at least in part by precisely this kind of pattern of misperception. The findings of the formal investigation noted that the drone operations team received evidence that was inconsistent with the hypothesis that the group was a Taliban force, but that this evidence had been 'ignored or downplayed' by the operators.[146] Portions of the dialogue among the pilot, the sensor operator, and the intelligence coordinator who were operating in Nevada, and the screeners who were reviewing intelligence at a location in Florida, and the ground force in Afghanistan that the drone was supposed to be protecting, have been publicly disclosed.[147] It suggests shared attitudes, mind-sets, and perspectives about the local population (perceptual sets), and reveals that they held assumptions, hypotheses, and mutually reinforcing mind-sets (evoked sets) about the group of men under observation from virtually the moment they came under observation.

The team's dialogue from the beginning exhibits a collective desire to find evidence of hostility. There were several instances in which information that was ambiguous or even inconsistent with the team's starting assumption – that the group under observation comprised insurgent fighters – was incongruously interpreted to actually confirm the presumption. For instance, when the trucks stopped and passengers disembarked to pray at one point early in the operation, the camera operator commented 'this is their force ... Praying? I mean, seriously, this is what they do.'[148] Praying became evidence of belligerence. At other times, there was frustration when the operators were unable to find more conclusive confirmation, or when evidence that was clearly inconsistent with the presumption was suggested by the intelligence screeners in Florida. Thus the pilot at one stage states, during a discussion of whether the screeners could see any evidence of weapons: 'I was hoping we could make a rifle out ... never mind'. A little later, when one of the screeners raised the possibility of a child having been spotted among the group, the pilot protests: 'why didn't he say "possible" child? Why are they so quick to call kids but not to call rifle?'[149] Here we see the potential for the group pressure being brought to bear, with the possible modification and distortion of judgment.[150]

The suggestion that there might be children present was then quickly reinterpreted as being evidence of possible adolescents. That in turn morphed into 'possibly military age males'. Military age males is, as we have seen, one of the 'legally inadequate' criteria for signature strikes which is thought to have been employed by US forces in Afghanistan (it has been reported that as a result of this incident General McChrystal issued an order banning the use of the criteria).[151] Information indicating the presence of protected persons was thus assimilated to existing assumptions and hypotheses, and thereby incrementally transformed to become information confirming the presence of targetable fighters. This was, arguably, due in large measure to flawed initial and potentially prematurely established assumptions, resulting in cognitive closure. As one of the team later recounted: 'we all had it in our head, "Hey, why do you have 20 military age males at 5 a.m. collecting each other?" There can only be one reason, and that's because we've put [U.S. troops] in the area.'[152] Here laid bare are indications of the premature formation of assumptions and consequent cognitive closure, bolstered by classic egocentric interpretation of the actions of others. It was only after the strike, when over 20 people lay dead and dying, that the operators finally recognised the presence of women and children, several of whom were younger than six years old.[153] It may be that a more rigorous adherence to legally valid criteria for signature strikes could have helped prevent this tragedy, but as we will explore next, it may be that features of the armed drone weapon system facilitate misperception that makes such errors more likely.

The features of drones and misperception

To the extent that the above account may reflect an example of a more systemic problem of misinterpretation and misperception, it would not appear to be caused by features of the armed drone itself, but rather of the operators and the targeting criteria being employed.

Indeed, once we are talking about the psychology of operators we would seem to be, by definition, out of the realm of the weapon itself. In other words, the problems would appear to relate to the 'methods of warfare' according to which the weapon is being used, rather than to anything apparently inherent to the 'means of warfare' comprising the weapons system. And yet upon closer consideration this may not be the case. To the extent that systemic targeting errors are being caused by misperception and other cognitive problems, these may be caused or facilitated by a combination of features that relate to both the nature of the operators and the policy they operate under, on the one hand, and features of the drone as a weapon system that may systematically influence how the operators behave. The misperception is, in the final analysis, a function of the operators. And it may be enabled and exacerbated by the policies and rules of engagement they are operating under. But the proposition that requires further study is whether features of the drone itself feed into and facilitate such misperception as well. These features may be interwoven in ways that can be difficult to disentangle and assess individually.

Some of these features may seem more clearly related to the operators, even though the features in question may be made possible by those of the weapons system. Thus, for instance, we have already observed in examination of the Uruzgan strike that the distance and detachment of the operations team may have been a factor in their susceptibility to forming premature and mistaken hypotheses and assumptions. That is at once a feature of how the drone is operated, but also perhaps of the drone itself. The distance and detachment may not be necessary or required by the nature of the drone, but it is a feature of the overall system, and is indeed viewed as one of the advantages of the weapon system.

Similarly, we have seen above how overconfidence is one of the factors identified in cognitive consistency theory that can contribute to the problem of misinterpretation and misperception. Such overconfidence has also been identified as a feature of the drone operators. As one senior officer who oversaw the investigation into the Uruzgan incident noted, '[t]echnology can occasionally give you a false sense of security that you can see everything, that you can hear everything, that you know everything'.[154] An exaggerated confidence in the infallibility of the assumptions the team is operating under and the intelligence the team is receiving from the drone and other sources, may contribute to systemic misperception. And such overconfidence flows in part from a confidence in the technology of the weapons system itself.

Other features implicated in the problem of misperception may be more uniquely tied to the nature of drones, and be a necessary aspect of how they operate. Or, if not necessary, be integral to the advantages attributed to the armed drone as a means of warfare. This would include the combination of features identified earlier as being central to effectiveness and indeed the precision of the drone: namely, being able to linger for prolonged periods, silently and undetected, at low cost and low risk, all the while feeding its team of operators with volumes of real-time video and other sensory intelligence. The upshot of this combination of features is that the drone will enable the protracted observation of individuals who might otherwise not have come under close observation at all if they had been spotted, for instance, by an F-16 or other manned aircraft. The pilot of a manned aircraft will have to make relatively quick decisions, typically within minutes, as to whether the individuals are hostile and targetable, and then move on if no such evidence presents itself. The drone operators can linger for tens of hours. As discussed earlier, this should be a key advantage. The team of operators and support screeners can take their time in a low-stress environment making a careful determination as to whether the individuals are hostile and legitimately targetable under IHL principles.

It would not be an advantage, however, if operators prematurely develop assumptions and hypotheses about the individuals at the very outset of observation. As illustrated in the Uruzgan incident, the protracted observation may then facilitate a process in which drone crew members misinterpret the incremental inputs of ambiguous information, assimilating the data in ways that simply conform with and confirm pre-existing assumptions, accumulating to support a conclusion that they are hostile and targetable. The process in that case, in combination with insufficiently clear and prudent targeting criteria, arguably contributed to the crew reaching an entirely erroneous conclusion regarding the status of the individuals, resulting in the tragic killing of some 20 civilians including children. In short, this combination of features that are central to the advantage of drones as a weapons system may operate to create an environment that is more conducive to systemic targeting errors due to this process of misperception.

This would indeed be consistent with, and perhaps help explain, the Air Force's own surprising and counterintuitive finding, published in the JCOA study referenced earlier, which reported that:

> [d]rone strikes in Afghanistan were seen to have close to the same number of civilian casualties per incident as manned aircraft, and were an order of magnitude more likely to result in civilian casualties per engagement.[155]

If we can safely assume that not all civilian casualties are within the anticipated and acceptable range for collateral damage estimates, this would seem to suggest that drone strikes are causing greater rates of accidental and impermissible killing per strike than manned air strikes. In other words, notwithstanding every reason to believe that as a weapons system it would be more precise, the improved intelligence, and longer stress-free targeting process that characterises the drone's operations are actually leading to greater rates of targeting error than those suffered by manned air strikes.

The paradox

I should stress that this argument – that features of the drone and its operations may combine in ways that facilitate misperception that in turn increases the risk of systemic targeting errors – must be rather tentative at this stage. In order to confirm the proposition, far more detailed data on other incidents of targeting error, and for that matter on the likely many more instances of both successful strikes and the appropriate identification of civilians leading to decisions *not* to strike, would have to be obtained and analysed. That is not possible for legal scholars working in the public domain, given the dearth of information that is currently available. But it may indeed be possible for policymakers within the Department of Defense and other branches of government to pursue such inquiries. In addition to requiring further data, more empirical and field work would be required to explore and test the psychological theory propositions advanced here. That too would be work that those within the relevant agencies could undertake.

If there is some validity to the proposition, however, an important issue to explore would be to identify the features of the drones system that are most central to the facilitation of systemic targeting errors, and how precisely they are combining to contribute to such effects. This would be key to understanding the phenomenon and, where possible, correcting the problem through changes in training, operating procedures, and the like. It would seem likely that some of the preconditions for the operation of cognitive consistency leading to misperception could clearly be ameliorated through such steps – for instance by developing training modules aimed at sensitising operators to the dangers of formulating assumptions and hypotheses prematurely. But as part of the process of identifying the features central to the problem, and thinking about how to resolve the issues, we would be returning to the question of whether the problem is primarily with the method of using the drones, or whether it is related to something inherent to the weapon itself. That is, whether it is a problem with the drone as a means of warfare, an issue of weapons law, or a problem with the method of warfare, and an issue of targeting law.

Herein lies the nature of the paradox referred to at the outset. For as we have explained, the very features that make the drone highly conducive to compliance with IHL, could also, paradoxically, indirectly contribute to not only more targeting errors and failures in relation to precautions in attack once a legitimate target has been identified, thus leading to higher and perhaps impermissible rates of 'collateral damage'; but also, and much more significantly, to more strikes being undertaken against civilians mistakenly identified as being fighters or taking direct part in hostilities. It is possible to conceive of scenarios in which groups of civilians who would not have attracted the attention of manned aircraft or other weapons systems are erroneously being killed precisely because of the drone's capacity for low-risk, low-cost lingering over the target to provide pattern-of-life observation, combined with the problem of the data not being interpreted correctly and being fed into a targeting decision matrix based on overly broad criteria.[156] And this is not simply to say that the weapon is being misused. Rather, the essential point is that it is not just that the methods, the manner of use that is causing potentially non-compliance, but that the means, the weapon system itself, may be facilitating and enabling those questionable methods.[157]

VI. Conclusions

The examination in this article has focused on the legality of drone strikes within a traditionally defined armed conflict for the purpose of simplifying the inquiry into whether there are features inherent to the remotely controlled armed drone as a weapons system, which may make it more susceptible to potential violations of IHL and IHRL. While the lack of transparency and accountability poses problems in reaching definitive conclusions, our analysis of the record of civilian deaths caused by drone strikes suggests that the drone strike operations may indeed be characterised by systemic violations of IHL and IHRL. In examining the reasons for such violations, the article has explored the features of drones as a means of warfare, and the features of the policy and practices that underlie the methods of warfare related to drone strikes.

On the one hand, the features of the drone as a weapons systems would appear to make it more conducive to compliance with IHL than other competing aerial weapons systems, while such aspects of policy as the criteria for signature strikes would be most likely responsible for possible violations of international law. On the other hand, however, an examination of these features in the context of a specific notorious drone strike, and conducted through the lens of cognitive consistency theory and misperception, suggests that the picture may be more complicated. The very features that are most likely to make drones compliant with IHL – their ability to linger undetected and at little risk and low cost for protracted periods over potential targets, feeding large volumes of intelligence back to an operations team that can engage in decision-making in a relatively stress-free environment – may paradoxically facilitate and make more likely targeting errors caused by misperception and misinterpretation of the target data. This proposition requires further empirical and theoretical study to be confirmed, but it is advanced here as an intriguing possibility deserving of further examination.

Acknowledgements

I would like to thank Michael Boyle for inviting me to contribute to this special volume of the journal, on what is an important issue. I would also like to thank, for their thoughts and comments at various stages of the development of this article: Michael Boyle, Lois Chiang, Benson Cowan, Will Foster, Alex Glashausser, Emily Grant, Jericho Hockett, Rebecca Hollender-Blumoff, Sarah Holewinski Matt Lamkin, Daniel Morales, Susannah Pollvogt, Margaret Ryznar, David Rubenstein, Laurent Sacharoff, Michael Schmitt, Nicholas Stephanopoulos, and the anonymous referees for the Journal. I am also grateful for the help provided by my research assistants: Norah Avellan, David Derochick, and Megan Williams.

Disclosure statement

No potential conflict of interest was reported by the author.

Notes

1. It should also be made perfectly clear here that the weapons system under discussion here is the remotely controlled armed drones such as the MQ-1 Predator and MQ-9 Reaper, as distinguished from a truly autonomous weapons systems that makes its own targeting decisions, about which there is growing debate. It is because of this distinction that the United States (US) Air Force now refers to the current generation of drones as remotely piloted aircraft, or RPAs, rather than UAVs. See Aaron M. Drake, 'Current U.S. Air Force Drone Operations and their Conduct in Compliance with International Humanitarian Law – An Overview', *Denver Journal of International Law & Policy* 39, no. 4 (2011): 630, n.1.
2. Targeted killing has been defined as when 'lethal force is intentionally and deliberately used, with a degree of pre-meditation, against an individual or individuals specifically identified in advance by the perpetrator'. Philip Alston, 'Report of the Special Rapporteur on Extrajudicial, Summary or Arbitrary Executions', United Nations Human Rights Council, 28 May 2010, Doc. A/HRC/14/24/Add.6, 5, citing Nils Melzer, *Targeted Killing in International Law* (Oxford: Oxford University Press, 2008), 4–5. In this article, however, it is taken to have a broader meaning that includes so-called 'signature strikes', in which otherwise unidentified individuals are targeted based on behaviour and other indicia that are taken to mean that the individuals are members of organised armed groups or are civilians taking direct part in hostilities.
3. Whether or not drone strikes in Yemen, Somalia and even Pakistan are conducted within an armed conflict as that term is understood in international law is itself a hotly debated issue, which we need not explore here.
4. For my own analysis of the *jus ad bellum* implications of targeted killing operations in countries such as Yemen, Somalia, and Pakistan, see Craig Martin, *Going Medieval: Targeted Killing, Self-Defense and the* Jus ad Bellum *Regime*, in *Targeted Killings: Law and Morality in an Asymmetrical World*, ed. Claire Finkelstein et al. (2012), http://papers.ssrn.com/sol3/papers.cfm?abstract_id=1956141.
5. See infra, note 34, and accompanying text.
6. See infra, note 36, and accompanying text.
7. See infra, note 68 et seq., and accompanying text.
8. Alston, 'Report of the Special Rapporteur', 4.
9. John Sifton, 'A Brief History of Drones', *The Nation*, 7 February 2012.
10. John F. Burns, 'Villagers Say U.S. Should Have Looked, Not Leapt', *The New York Times*, 17 February 2002.
11. Sifton, 'A Brief History of Drones'.
12. Burns, 'Villagers Say U.S. Should Have Looked, Not Leapt'; see also, Sifton, 'A Brief History of Drones'.

13. United Nations Assistance Mission in Afghanistan (UNAMA), *Annual Report 2013: Protection of Civilians in Armed Conflict* (Kabul: United Nations, 2014), 46–7.
14. Drake, 'Current U.S. Air Force Drone Operations', 658; Center for Civilians in Conflict, *The Civilian Impact of Drones: Unexamined Costs, Unanswered Questions* (2012), 42; Maj. Gen. Timothy P. McHale, 'Memorandum for Commander, United States Force-Afghanistan/International Security Assistance Force, Afghanistan – Subject: Executive Summary for AR 15–6 Investigation, 21 February 2010 CIVCA Incident in Uruzgan Province'; Gen. Stanley A. McChrystal, 'Memorandum for Record – Subject: AR 15–6 Investigation, 21 February 2010 U.S. Air-to-Ground Engagement in the Vicinity of Shahidi Hassas, Uruzgan Province, Afghanistan', http://www.isaf.nato.int/images/stories/File/April2010-Dari/May2010Revised/Uruzgan%20investigation%20findings.pdf.
15. Philip Alston, 'The CIA and Targeted Killing Beyond Borders', *Harvard National Security Journal* 2 (2011), 299; Alice K. Ross, 'Who is Dying in Afghanistan's 1,000-plus Drone Strikes?', *The Bureau of Investigative Journalism*, 24 July 2014, http://www.thebureauinvestigates.com/2014/07/24/who-is-dying-in-afghanistans-1000-plus-drone-strikes/.
16. Alston, 'CIA and Drones Beyond Borders', 331, citing David Kilcullen and Andrew Mcdonald Exum, 'Death From Above, Outrage from Below', *The New York Times*, 16 May 2009, http://www.nytimes.com/2009/05/17/opinion/17exum.html.
17. UNAMA, Annual Report (2012), 31; see also, Ben Emmerson, Report of the Special Rapporteur on the Promotion and Protection of Human Rights and Fundamental Freedoms While Countering Terrorism (Third Annual Report to the General Assembly), United Nations, Doc. A/68/389, 18 September 2013, 7.
18. Emmerson, *Third Annual Report to the General Assembly*, 7 (reporting a steady rise up to 2012); UNAMA, *Annual Report* (2013), *Interim Report* (2014) (reflecting the continued increase in 2013 and 2014).
19. UNAMA, *Annual Report* (2012), 33.
20. UNAMA, *Annual Report* (2013), 8.
21. Ross, 'Who is Dying in Afghanistan's 1,000-plus Drone Strikes?'
22. The 2014 report states the number as over 1,000 since 2001, but a prior report with more detailed annual numbers reflects 1,015 strikes between 2008 and 2012. See Chris Woods and Alice K. Ross, 'Revealed: US and Britain Launched 1,200 Drone Strikes in Recent Wars', Bureau of Investigative Journalism, 4 December 2012, http://www.thebureauinvestigates.com/2012/12/04/revealed-us-and-britain-launched-1200-drone-strikes-in-recent-wars/.
23. Ross, 'Who is Dying in Afghanistan's 1,000-plus Drone Strikes?'
24. Ibid.
25. Lawrence Lewis, 'Drone Strikes: Civilian Casualty Considerations', *Joint Coalition Operational Analysis*, 18 June 2013, http://cna.org/research/2013/drone-strikes-civilian-casualty-considerations.
26. Lewis, 'Drone Strikes'.
27. For analysis of the entire regime, see Yorum Dinstein, *The Conduct of Hostilities Under the Law of International Armed Conflict*, 2nd ed. (Cambridge: Cambridge University Press, 2010); Andrew Clapham and Paola Gaeta, eds, *The Oxford Handbook of International Law in Armed Conflict* (Oxford: Oxford University Press, 2014); Dieter Fleck, *The Handbook of International Humanitarian Law* (Oxford: Oxford University Press, 2013).
28. The Hague Convention (II): Laws and Customs of War on Land, 32 Stat. 1803, 29 July 1899; The Hague Convention (IV) Respecting the Laws and Customs of War on Land and its Annex: Regulation Concerning the Laws and Customs of War on Land, 187 CTS 227, 18 October 1907.
29. See, in particular, Geneva Convention Relative to the Treatment of Prisoners of War, 12 August 1949, 75 UNTS 135 (1950)(Geneva Convention III); Convention Relative to the Protection of Civilian Persons in Time of War, 12 August 1949, 75 UNTS 287 (1950)(Geneva Convention IV).
30. Protocol Additional to the Geneva Conventions of 12 August 1949, and Relating to the Protection of Victims of International Armed Conflicts, (Protocol I), 1125 UNTS 3 (1979), 8 June 1977.
31. Dinstein, *Conduct of Hostilities*, loc-862 et seq. (Kindle edition).
32. For analysis of the regime as it applies to non-international armed conflict, see Lindsay Moir, *The Law of Internal Armed Conflict* (Cambridge: Cambridge University Press, 2002); Michael

LEGAL AND ETHICAL IMPLICATIONS OF DRONE WARFARE

N. Schmitt et al., *The Manual on the Law of Non-International Armed Conflict with Commentary* (Sanremo: International Institute of Humanitarian Law, 2006); Yorum Dinstein, *Non-International Armed Conflicts in International Law* (Cambridge: Cambridge University Press, 2014); for the definition of non-international armed conflict, the so-called Tadic test elaborated by the Appeal Chamber of the International Criminal Tribunal for the Former Yugoslavia, see *Prosecutor* v. *Dusko Tadic (Defense motion for interlocutory appeal on jurisdiction)*, 2 October 1995, para. 70, http://www.icty.org/x/cases/tadic/acdec/en/51002.htm.

33. Schmitt et al., *Manual on the Law of Non-International Armed Conflict*, 8–10; Mary Ellen O'Connell, 'Unlawful Killing with Combat Drones: A Case Study of Pakistan, 2004–2009', Notre Dame Law School Legal Studies Research Paper No. 09-43 (unpublished), 21; Dinstein, *Non-International Armed Conflicts in International Law*, 257–8; Laurie R. Blank, 'After "Top Gun": How Drone Strikes Impact the Law of War', *University of Pennsylvania Journal of International Law* 33 (2012): 681 et seq., 690–1.

34. Hague Convention (IV), 1907, Art. 22. See also, Steven Haines, 'The Developing Law of Weapons: Humanity, Distinction, and Precautions in Attack', in *The Oxford Handbook of International Law in Armed Conflict*, ed. Andrew Clapham and Paola Gaeta (Oxford: Oxford University Press, 2014), 281–2.

35. Haines, 'The Developing Law of Weapons', 277, 281.

36. Ibid. See also, Willam H. Boothby, *The Law of Targeting* (Oxford: Oxford University Press, 2012), 57–8; Stefan Oeter, 'Methods and Means of Combat', in *The Handbook of International Humanitarian Law*, ed. Dieter Fleck, 3rd ed. (Oxford: Oxford University Press, 2013), 401–88.

37. Haines, 'The Developing Law of Weapons', 277.

38. Ibid., 312, 331.

39. Dinstein, *Conduct of Hostilities*, loc-756 et seq. (Kindle edition); Gary D. Solis, *The Law of Armed Conflict* (Cambridge: Cambridge University Press, 2010), 257–65; Boothby, *The Law of Targeting*, 58.

40. *Additional Protocol I*, Art. 48, Art. 44, Art. 51. It should be noted that the principle of distinction is referred to in Additional Protocol II as well: *Protocol Additional to the Geneva Conventions of 12 August 1949, and Relating to the Protection of Victims of International Armed Conflicts, (Protocol II)*, 1125 UNTS 609 (1979), 8 June 1977, Art. 13(1); see also, International Committee of the Red Cross, *Customary International Humanitarian Law – Vol. 1: Rules* (Cambridge: Cambridge University Press, 2005), 3–6, 25–9.

41. *Geneva Conventions*, Common Article 3; AP II, Art. 13(3). ICRC, *Customary International Humanitarian Law – Vol. 1: Rules*, 12–13, 19.

42. International Committee of the Red Cross, *Direct Participation in Hostilities Under International Humanitarian Law* (Geneva: ICRC, 2009), 41–68.

43. International Committee of the Red Cross, Direct Participation in Hostilities Under International Humanitarian Law, 59, 72–3; Dinstein, Non-International Armed Conflicts in International Law, 61–3.

44. The ICRC notes that this is less than satisfactory, since in some languages the word 'fighter' would be translated with the same term as used for 'combatant' in any event: ICRC, *Customary International Humanitarian Law – Vol. 1: Rules*, Rule 3, 13; but see Schmitt et al., *Manual on the Law of Non-International Armed Conflict*, 4 (classifying both members of armed forces and members of organised armed groups as fighters).

45. AP I., Art. 51. See also ICRC, *Customary International Humanitarian Law – Vol. 1: Rules*, Rule 11, 37. While explicit language articulating the rule was not included in AP II, the ICRC considers it to be customary international law as applicable to non-international armed conflict. Ibid., 38–9.

46. Boothby, *The Law of Targeting*, 99; Solis, *The Law of Armed Conflict*, 269.

47. AP I, Art. 51(5)(b) and Art. 57(2)(a)(iii); ICRC, *Customary International Humanitarian Law – Vol. 1: Rules*, Rule 14, 46–50.

48. Dinstein, *Conduct of Hostilities*, loc-5379-5421 (Kindle edition); Boothby, *The Law of Targeting*, 95–7.

49. AP I, Art. 57(1); ICRC, Customary International Humanitarian Law – Vol. 1: Rules, Rule 15, 51.

50. AP I, Art. 57(2)(a)(i)–(iii), (b); ICRC, *Customary International Humanitarian Law – Vol. 1: Rules*, Rules 16–19, 55–61.

LEGAL AND ETHICAL IMPLICATIONS OF DRONE WARFARE

51. Michael N. Schmitt, 'Drone Attacks Under *Jus ad Bellum* and *Jus in Bello*: Clearing the "Fog of Law"', *Yearbook of International Humanitarian Law – 2010* (The Hague: T.M.C. Asser Press, 2011), 321; Michael N. Schmitt, 'Extraterritorial Lethal Targeting: Deconstructing the Logic of International Law', *Columbia Journal of Transnational Law* 52 (2013): 92 et seq.

52. See, for example, Alston, 'The CIA and Targeted Killing Beyond Borders', 283, 301.

53. Dinstein, *Conduct of Hostilities*, loc-1170 (Kindle edition).

54. David Kretzmer, 'Targeted Killing of Suspected Terrorists: Extra-Judicial Executions or Legitimate Means of Defence?', *The European Journal of International Law* 6, no. 2 (2005): 181 (providing examples of such confusion on the part of the Inter-American Commission for Human Rights).

55. Ibid., 185; Advisory Opinion on the Legality of the Threat or Use of Nuclear Weapons [1996] I.C.J. Rep. 226; Advisory Opinion on the Legal Consequences of the Construction of a Wall in the Occupied Palestinian Territory [2004] I.C.J. 136, para. 106.

56. Kretzmer, 'Targeted Killing of Suspected Terrorists', 186, 201–4; and see infra, note 66, and accompanying text.

57. *International Covenant on Civil and Political Rights*, 23 March 1976, 999 U.N.T.S. 171, Art. 6 (ICCPR).

58. ICCPR, Art. 2.

59. See Jon Heller, 'Does the ICCPR Apply Extraterritorially?', *Opinio Juris*, 18 July 2006, http://opiniojuris.org/2006/07/18/does-the-iccpr-apply-extraterritorially/ (including text of the US Statement to the Human Rights Committee on its interpretation). Harold Koh, as legal counsel to the State Department, wrote an extensive memo arguing for a change of position (http://justsecurity.org/wp-content/uploads/2014/03/state-department-iccpr-memo.pdf), but the Obama administration reiterated the US interpretation in early 2013; see Charlie Savage, 'U.S., Rebuffing U.N., Maintains Stance that Rights Treaty Does Not Apply Abroad', *The New York Times*, 13 March 2014, A12.

60. See, for example, United Nations Human Rights Committee, *Concluding Observations on the Fourth Periodic Report of the United States of America*, 23 April 2014, CCPR/C/USA/CO/4, 2–3; though the actual position of the U.S. was more ambiguous in the actual report: *Fourth Periodic Report of the United States of America*, 22 May 2012, CCPR/C/USA/4, 142.

61. Legal Consequences of the Construction of a Wall in the Occupied Palestinian Territory, Advisory Opinion [2004] I.C.J. 136, para. 108–11.

62. See note 59, supra.

63. Kretzmer, 'Targeted Killing of Suspected Terrorists', 186; Alston, 'CIA and Targeted Killing Beyond Borders', 23, citing Nigel S. Rodely and Matt Pollard, *The Treatment of Prisoners Under International Law*, 3rd ed. (Oxford: Oxford University Press, 2009), 250.

64. *Armed Activities on the Territory of the Congo (Democratic Republic of Congo (DRC) v. Uganda)* [2005] I.C.J. 168, 179–80, 205–12, 216–19. As with the *Al-Skeini* case, infra, the finding that Uganda was an occupying power at the relevant times was a significant aspect of the decision, which does cast some doubt on how persuasive an authority this may be as a general principle.

65. *Al-Skeini and others* v. *The United Kingdom*, ECtHR 7 July 2011, 40–1. It should be noted that while the court held that the convention applied, and that the UK had violated the right to life of several of the applicants, the decision was based on the language of the European convention relating to jurisdiction. Moreover, the fact that the killings were conducted in the context of belligerent occupation by occupation forces was relevant to the decision. Ibid., 59–61.

66. Ben Emmerson, *Third Annual Report to the General Assembly.* See also, Christof Heyns, *Report of the Special Rapporteur on Extrajudicial, Summary or Arbitrary Executions*, United Nations General Assembly, Doc. A/68/382, 13 September 2013, 7–9 (describing the right against the arbitrary deprivation of life as not only a principle of customary international law attaining the status of *jus cogens*, but also a general principle of international law, and that it is 'now a well established principle of international law that international human rights law continues to apply during armed conflict, as a complement to international humanitarian law').

67. 'Obama's Speech on Drone Policy', *The New York Times*, 23 May 2013, http://www.nytimes.com/2013/05/24/us/politics/transcript-of-obamas-speech-on-drone-policy.html?pagewanted=all.

68. Alston, 'Report of the Special Rapporteur', 26; Emmerson, 'Interim-Report of the Special Rapporteur', 12; Emmerson, 'Report of the Special Rapporteur', 9; Hayes, 'Report of the Special Rapporteur', 20–2.

LEGAL AND ETHICAL IMPLICATIONS OF DRONE WARFARE

69. Nils Melzer, *Human Rights Implications of the Usage of Drones and Unmanned Robots in Warfare* (European Parliament, Policy Department – Directorate-General for External Policies, May 2013), 37 et seq.; Gen. John P. Abizaid and Rosa Brooks, *Recommendations and Report of the Task Force on US Drone Policy* (Washington, DC: The Stimson Center, 2014), 34. On a review of different theories of the rule of law more generally, see Brian Z. Tamanaha, *On the Rule of Law: History, Politics, Theory* (Cambridge: Cambridge University Press, 2004).

70. *Report of the Secretary-General's Panel of Experts on Accountability in Sri Lanka*, March 31, 2011, 115, http://www.un.org/News/dh/infocus/Sri_Lanka/POE_Report_Full.pdf.

71. Alston, 'CIA and Targeted Killing Beyond Borders', 310 (citing common Article 1 of the Geneva Conventions); Alston, 'Report of the Special Rapporteur', 26.

72. Alston, 'The CIA and Targeted Killing Beyond Borders', 310–11.

73. Emmerson, 'Report of the Special Rapporteur on the Promotion of Human Rights', 12. Emmerson relied in part on the report of the 2013 Public Commission to Examine the Maritime Incident of 31 May 2010 (the Turkel Commission, which investigated the Israeli killing of several individuals while boarding a Turkish vessel bound for Gaza), which itself conducted an 'analysis of a broad range of sources'.

74. Alston. 'The CIA and Targeted Killing Beyond Borders', 310–11.

75. Ibid., 22, citing ICRC Rules, Vol. 1, 608–9, and a range of cases and institutional reports – see note 87; but see Michael N. Schmitt, 'Investigating Violations of International Law in Armed Conflict', *Harvard National Security Journal* 2 (2011): 35 et seq, 77–82.

76. Melzer, *Human Rights Implications*, 40, See note 186 for authorities referred to.

77. Alston, 'The CIA and Targeted Killing Beyond Borders', 312.

78. Ibid.

79. Ibid., 317.

80. Amantha Perera, 'Sri Lanka Ducks International Probe', *Interpress Service*, 20 August 2011.

81. Center for Civilians in Conflict, *The Civilian Impact of Drones*, 54; see also, Gregory S. McNeal, 'Are Targeted Killings Unlawful? A Case Study in Empirical Claims Without Empirical Evidence', in *Targeted Killing: Law and Morality in an Asymmetrical World*, ed. Claire Finkelstein et al. (Oxford: Oxford University Press, 2012), 328–33.

82. One of the best documented and egregious examples of this followed a Special Forces night raid on a civilian household in Gardez, on 12 February 2010, in which five civilians, including three women, were killed. ISAF initially claimed that the women had been stabbed to death by the Taliban, and there were reports that Special Forces personnel involved in the raid had dug the bullets out of the dead bodies with knives to destroy the evidence of how they had died. ISAF only changed its version of events almost two months later after numerous media stories about a possible cover up. See Jeremy Scahill, *Dirty Wars: The World is a Battlefield* (New York: Nation Books, 2013), 333–46.

83. Alston, 'CIA and Targeted Killing Beyond Borders', 364; Center for Civilians in Conflict, *The Civilian Impact of Drones*, 44–6; UNAMA, *Annual Report* (2013), 48.

84. Alston, 'CIA and Targeted Killing Beyond Borders', 355, citing Afsheen Radsan and Richard Murphy, 'Measure Twice, Shoot Once: Higher Care for CIA Targeted Killing, *University of Illinois Law Review*, no. 4 (2011).

85. Alston, 'CIA and Targeted Killing Beyond Borders', 355; Abizaid, *Task Force on US Drone Policy*, 39.

86. Department of Defense Directive, Number 2311.01E, 9 May 2006 (certified current as of 22 February 2011), http://www.dtic.mil/whs/directives/corres/pdf/231101e.pdf.

87. Drake, 'Current U.S. Air Force Drone Operations', 641–5; Abizaid, *Task Force on US Drone Policy*, 33.

88. Alston, 'CIA and Targeted Killing Beyond Borders', 357–66; see also, Radsen and Murphy, 'Measure Twice, Shoot Once', 1217–20 (exploring CIA practice, but in the absence of concrete information, recognising that 'in fashioning its own standards and procedures, [the CIA] has presumably relied on the military'); and Tara McKelvey, 'Inside the Killing Machine', *Newsweek*, 13 February 2011, http://www.newsweek.com/inside-killing-machine-68771.

89. Centers for Civilians in Conflict *The Civilian Impact of Drones*, 57–8; Murphy and Radsan, 'Measure Twice, Shoot Once' (arguing that the CIA *should* be so governed by IHL).

90. Centers for Civilians in Conflict, *The Civilian Impact of Drones*, 57. Though, see Robert Chesney, 'Military-Intelligence Convergence and the Law of the Title 10/Title 50 Debate',

LEGAL AND ETHICAL IMPLICATIONS OF DRONE WARFARE

Journal of National Security Law & Policy 5 (2012): 617 et seq. (arguing that Title 50 does not provide any domestic law justification for violation of international law).

91. Centers for Civilians in Conflict *The Civilian Impact of Drones*, 57, citing W. Hayes Parks, 'The United States and the Law of War: Inculcating an Ethos', *Social Research* 69, no. 4 (2002): 981; and Laurie Blank and Amos Guiora, 'Teaching an Old Dog New Tricks: Operationalizing the Law of Armed Conflict in New Warfare', *Harvard National Security Journal* 1 (2010).

92. See for example, Douglas Valentine, *The Phoenix Program* (New York: William Morrow Co., 1990).

93. Andrew Feickert and Thomas K. Livingston, 'U.S. Special Operations (SOF): Background and Issues for Congress', *Congressional Research Service*, 3 December 2010, 10.

94. Andrew Feickert, 'U.S. Special Forces (SOF): Background and Issues for Congress', *Congressional Research Service*, 18 September 2013; Feickert and Livingston, 'U.S. Special Operations (SOF): Background and Issues for Congress'; Schahill, *Dirty Wars*, Chapter 3; Marshal Curtis Erwin, 'Covert Action: Legislative Background and Possible Policy Questions', *Congressional Research Service*, 10 April 2013.

95. Chesney, 'Military-Intelligence Convergence', 573; Jennifer D. Kibbe, 'Covert Action and the Pentagon', *Intelligence and National Security* 22, no. 1; Centers for Civilians in Conflict, *The Civilian Impact of Drones*, 64; Alston, 'CIA and Targeted Killing Beyond Borders, 346–7.

96. Centers for Civilians in Conflict, *The Civilian Impact of Drones*, 63; Kibbe, 'Covert Action and the Pentagon'.

97. Centers for Civilians in Conflict, *The Civilian Impact of Drones*, 63; on details of JSOC conduct at Camp Nama in Iraq, see Scahill, *Dirty Wars*, Chapter 13, and Jane Mayer, *The Dark Side: The Inside Story of how the War on Terror Turned Into a War on American Ideals* (New York: Doubleday, 2008), loc. 4913–25 (Kindle edition).

98. P.W. Singer, 'Double Hatting Around the Law: The Problem with Morphing Warrior, Spy and Civilian Roles', *Armed Forces Journal*, 1 June 2010.

99. See, for example, Chesney, 'Military Intelligence Convergence'; Kibbe, 'Covert Action and the Pentagon'; Andru E. Wall, 'Demystifying the Title 10-Title 50 Debate: Distinguishing Military Operations, Intelligence Activities & Covert Action', *Harvard National Security Journal* 3 (2011); Alston, 'CIA and Targeted Killing Beyond Borders'; Abizaid, *Task Force on US Drone Policy*.

100. Chesney, 'Military Intelligence Convergence', 540–1; Kibbe, 'Covert Action and the Pentagon', 65–8; Alston, 'CIA and Targeted Killing Beyond Borders', 348–50; Centers for Civilians in Conflict, *The Civilian Impact of Drones*, 64–5; but see Wall, 'Demystifying the Title 10-Title 50 Debate' (arguing generally that the blurring of accountability is exaggerated and misunderstood).

101. See Scott Horton, 'The Khadr Boomerang', *Harper's Magazine*, 25 May 2010.

102. Schmitt, 'Clearing the "Fog of Law"', 324; Blank, 'After "Top Gun"', 708.

103. On the law enforcement paradigm, see Melzer, *Targeted Killing*, Chapter 5.

104. Abizaid, *The Task Force on US Drone Policy*, 21; Lynn E. Davis et al., *Armed and Dangerous? UAVs and U.S. Security* (Washington, DC: RAND Corporation, 2014), 11; Drake, 'Current U. S. Air Force Drone Operations', 637.

105. Drake, 'Current U.S. Air Force Drone Operations', 637.

106. Ibid., 637–8.

107. Ibid., 639.

108. Ibid.

109. Ibid., 640; Blank, 'After "Top Gun"', 686–8.

110. Abizaid, *Task Force on US Drone Policy*, 18; Davis et al., *Armed and Dangerous?*, 11–12.

111. Schmitt, 'Clearing the "Fog of Law"', 314; Drake, 'Current U.S. Air Force Drone Operations', 645; Blank, 'After "Top Gun"', 687.

112. Drake, 'Current U.S. Air Force Drone Operations', 645.

113. Schmitt, 'Clearing the "Fog of Law"', 322; Drake, 'Current U.S. Air Force Drone Operations', 645; Blank, 'After "Top Gun"', 688–702.

114. Schmitt, 'Clearing the "Fog of Law"', 315.

115. Drake, 'Current U.S. Air Force Drone Operations', 645; Blank, 'After "Top Gun"', 713–14.

116. Centers for Civilians in Conflict, *The Civilian Impact of Drones*, 37.

LEGAL AND ETHICAL IMPLICATIONS OF DRONE WARFARE

117. Ibid., 41; see also, Wayne Chappelle et al., 'Assessment of Occupational Burnout in United States Air Force Predator/Reaper "Drone" Operators', *Military Psychology* 26:5–6 (2014): 376–385.
118. Alston, 'Report of the Special Rapporteur', 317.
119. Schmitt, 'Clearing the "Fog of Law"', 321; Blank, 'After "Top Gun"', 680.
120. Schmitt, 'Clearing the "Fog of Law"', 319–20.
121. One of the most often-cited authorities for how the 'kill lists' are compiled and maintained is a series of articles in *The New York Times*, particularly Jo Becker and Scott Shane, 'Secret "Kill List" Proves a Test of Obama's Principles and Will', *The New York Times*, 29 May 2012, A1.
122. As indicated earlier, the temporal window during which such a civilian is targetable is hotly debated, and has been the subject of judicial analysis: See, for example, Nils Melzer, *Direct Participation in Hostilities Under International Humanitarian Law* (Geneva: ICRC, 2009), 65–8; *Public Committee Against Torture in Israel* v. *Israel*, HCJ 762/2 [2005], paras 38–40.
123. Alston, 'CIA and Targeted Killing Beyond Borders', 285.
124. Kate Clark, "The Takhar Attack: Targeted Killings and the Parallel Worlds of US Intelligence and Afghanistan", Afghan Analysts Network, May 2011, http://aan-afghanistan.com/uploads/20110511KClark_Takhar-attack_final.pdf; Centers for Civilians in Conflict, *The Civilian Impact of Drones*, 38.
125. Centers for Civilians in Conflict, *The Civilian Impact of Drones*, 11.
126. Kevin Jon Heller, '"One Hell of a Killing Machine": Signature Strikes and International Law', *Journal of International Criminal Justice* 11, no. 1 (2013): 94.
127. On the efforts within the government to formalise the criteria, see Scott Shane, 'Election Spurred a Move to Codify U.S. Drone Policy', *The New York Times*, 24 November 2012, A1.
128. Heller, 'One Hell of a Killing Machine', 94–103.
129. Ibid., 94–7.
130. Ibid., 97, citing for evidence of the use of such signatures, Stanford Law School International Human Rights and Conflict Resolution Clinic & NYU School of Law Global Justice Clinic, *Living Under Drones: Death, Injury and Trauma to Civilians from US Drone Practices in Pakistan*, September 2012, 31.
131. Heller, '"One Hell of a Killing Machine"', 97–8, citing D. Filkins, 'The Journalist and the Spies', *New Yorker*, 19 September 2011, http://www.newyorker.com/reporting/2011/09/19/110919fa_fact_filkins.
132. Heller, '"One Hell of a Killing Machine"', 98–9, citing B. Roggio, 'US Predators Strike Again in Southern Yemen', *Long War Journal*, 16 April 2012, http://www.longwarjournal.org/archives/2012/04/us_predators_strike_35.php.
133. Heller, '"One Hell of a Killing Machine"', 99–100, citing 'Munter Found Drone Strikes Unacceptable', *DAWN*, 30 May 2012, http://dawn.com/2012/05/30/munter-found-drone-strikes-unacceptable/.
134. Heller, '"One Hell of a Killing Machine"', 100–3, citing for the adequacy of such criteria, ICRC, 'Interpretative Guidance on the Notion of Direct Participation in Hostilities Under International Humanitarian Law', *International Review of the Red Cross* 90 (2008), 1002.
135. Centers for Civilians in Conflict, *The Civilian Impact of Drones*, 41–2.
136. Schmitt, 'Clearing the "Fog of Law"', 319.
137. Cognitive consistency theory developed in the area of social psychology in the 1940s through to the 1960s, with such work on balance theory by Fritz Heider, cognitive dissonance by Festinger, and cognitive consistency by Robert Abelsohn – see, Fritz Heider, *The Psychology of Interpersonal Relations* (New York: Wiley, 1958); Leon Festinger, *A Theory of Cognitive Dissonance* (Stanford, CA: Stanford University Press, 1957); Robert Abelsohn and Milton Rosenberg, 'Symbolic Psycho-Logic', *Behavioral Science* 3 (1958); Robert Abelsohn et al., eds, *Theories of Cognitive Consistency* (Chicago: Rand McNally, 1968). It worked its way into other fields over the next several decades, such as its brilliant application in international relations in Robert Jervis, *Perception and Misperception in International Politics* (Princeton, NJ: Princeton University Press, 1976). It has had a resurgence in the last couple of decades. For a short review of the more recent theoretical development see Dan Simon et al., 'The Redux of Cognitive Consistency Theories: Evidence Judgments by Constraint Satisfaction', *Journal of Personality and Social Psychology* 86, no. 6 (2004), 814–37; and Raymond S. Nickerson, 'Confirmation Bias: A Ubiquitous Phenomenon in Many Guises', *Review of General Psychology* 2 (1998), 175–220. For recent applications in the context of law, see for example,

LEGAL AND ETHICAL IMPLICATIONS OF DRONE WARFARE

Stephanie Stern, 'Cognitive Consistency: Theory Maintenance and Administrative Rulemaking', *University of Pittsburgh Law Review* 63 (2002): 589; and in police work, Karl Ask and Par Anders Granhag, 'Motivational Sources of Confirmation Bias in Criminal Investigations: The Need for Cognitive Closure', *Journal of Investigative Psychology and Offender Profiling* 2 (2005): 43–63; on attribution theory, see John H. Harvey and Gifford Weary, 'Current Theories in Attribution Theory and Research', *Annual Review of Psychology* 35 (1984): 427–59.

138. Jervis, *Perception and Misperception*, 203–6; Stern, 'Cognitive Consistency', 603–4.

139. Jervis, *Perception and Misperception*, 143–54; Stern, 'Cognitive Consistency', 603–5, 608–11.

140. Simon, 'The Redux of Cognitive Consistency Theories', 817; Jervis, *Perception and Misperception*, 195–202;

141. Jervis, *Perception and Misperception*, 187; Ask, 'Motivational Sources of Confirmation Bias', 45–8.

142. Ask, 'Motivational Sources of Confirmation Bias'; Carole Hill et al., 'The Role of Confirmation Bias in Suspect Interviews: A Systemic Evaluation', *Legal and Criminological Psychology* 13 (2008), 357–71.

143. Jervis, Perception and Misperception, 211–16.

144. Solomon Asch, 'Effects of Group Pressure Upon the Modification and Distortion of Judgments', in *Groups, Leadership and Men: Research in Human Relations*, ed. Harold Guetzkow (New York: Russell & Russell, 1963), 177–90.

145. See notes 137–40, supra.

146. Centers for Civilians in Conflict, *The Civilian Impact of Drones*, 41; David S. Cloud, 'Anatomy of an Afghan War Tragedy', *Los Angeles Times*, 10 April 2011. See also McChrystal, 'Memorandum for Record'.

147. Cloud, 'Anatomy of an Afghan War Tragedy'.

148. Ibid.

149. Ibid.

150. See note 141, supra.

151. Heller, '"One Hell of a Killing Machine"', 97; Centers for Civilian in Conflict, *The Civilian Impact of Drones*, 75. On the order of Gen. McChrystal banning the use of the criteria, see Cloud, 'Anatomy of an Afghan War Tragedy'.

152. Cloud, 'Anatomy of an Afghan War Tragedy'.

153. Ibid.

154. Ibid., quoting Air Force Maj. Gen. James O. Poss, who oversaw the Air Force investigation.

155. Lewis, 'Drone Strikes'.

156. But see Schmitt, 'Clearing the "Fog of Law"', 320, stating that 'compared to attack by manned aircraft or ground-based systems, the result is often a significantly reduced risk of misidentifying the target or causing collateral damage to civilians'. Hence the paradox if this is in fact not always the case.

157. Laurie Blank hints at this, writing: 'Furthermore, given that proportionality rests on a reasonable commander's determination based on the information available to him at the time of the attack, we must consider whether drones at some point will no longer add to that process but could actually impede that process simply because of the flood of information.' Blank, 'After "Top Gun"', 714.

Clashing over drones: the legal and normative gap between the United States and the human rights community

Daniel R. Brunstetter and Arturo Jimenez-Bacardi

Department of Political Science, UC Irvine, USA

The use of lethal drones by the United States (US) marks a paradox insofar as the US government claims that these strikes respect human rights, while the human rights community – including Human Rights Watch and Amnesty International – raise serious concerns that challenge this claim. Would reconciling these seemingly mutually exclusive human rights narratives regarding drone use lead to the formation of a more robust regime that would provide greater respect for human rights than in the current state of legal and moral ambiguity? In order to explore this question, we examine the evolution of these conflicting discourses through three key frames of legitimation – strategic, legal and normative. We argue that the US government has moved from a strategic-legal framework characterised by a focus on strategic objectives and a permissive view of international humanitarian law to a legal-normative discourse that, by incorporating the principles of just war theory, has restrained the strategic scope of the drone programme while reinforcing the legitimacy of international humanitarian law as the paradigm of choice. Comparatively, we assert that the human rights community has pursued a human rights-centric approach that rejects the more permissive standards of an international humanitarian law-centric legal paradigm, while pushing a normative agenda that seeks to enhance respect for human rights under both international humanitarian law and international human rights law. This includes rejecting the US interpretation of just war principles and appealing to a broader understanding of the right to life norm. Taking these 'right to life' considerations seriously raises concerns about whether drones can ever satisfy human rights. In the conclusion, we explore how combining certain elements of these narratives may contribute to an emerging norm on drone use.

Introduction

The enhanced ability of drones to enable the US to kill at a distance without serious risk to its soldiers – what some have called the 'silver bullet of democracy' – has accentuated the ambiguous space between law enforcement (where attempting to apprehend suspected criminals is the legal obligation) and war (where killing of the enemy is legal) that characterises the struggle against non-state terrorist actors in the post 9/11 era.[1] The use of drones to combat Al-Qaeda and its affiliates impacts the respect of human rights of perceived enemies and the civilian population in the areas in which they operate and reside. The former have de facto become subject to lethal force outside the traditional battlefield, which marks a major shift – problematic for some – in international humanitarian law (IHL). The latter are, by consequence, forced to live under the ubiquitous threat of drone strikes which, while legally permissible in a state of war (assuming civilians are not directly targeted), places these civilians under significant duress that some argue raises serious challenges for respecting human rights under international human rights law (IHRL).[2] While both IHL and IHRL aim at respecting some level of human rights, they form the basis of two very different narratives – that of the US government and that of the human rights community (HRC) – regarding the legitimacy of drone use.

On the one hand, the US claims to be a defender and promoter of human rights across the globe. As stated in the 2010 National Security Strategy, 'America's commitment to democracy, human rights, and the rule of law are essential sources of our strength and influence in the world'.[3] At the same time, the US claims that strategic concerns in the post 9/11 era require a more permissive view of international law that allows for preventive self-defence – including drone strikes outside the recognised battlefield. Rather than a violation of human rights, the use of lethal drones in the struggle against al-Qaeda and affiliates has been characterised as part of a war in which the killing of militants is claimed to be in conformity with US domestic law and IHL, two legal regimes that place a premium on the rights of individuals. While drone strikes have caused civilian casualties, US officials claim that respect for human rights has been enhanced by drone use because they are better than other weapons at respecting the *jus in bello* criteria of proportionality and distinction.[4] Moreover, proponents also claim that the US drone campaign has a far better track record compared to the militaries of other nations, such as Pakistan, when it comes to respecting civilian immunity during military operations.[5]

On the other hand, the HRC – broadly defined to include inter-governmental organisations (IGOs; such as the United Nations Human Rights Office of the High Commissioner), non-governmental organisations (NGOs; including Amnesty International, Human Rights Watch, and the International Committee of the Red Cross), and academic institutes (including New York University's Global Justice Clinic, Stanford University's International Human Rights and Conflict Resolution Clinic, and the Columbia Law School's Human Rights Clinic) – have converged on a broad consensus that directly challenges the US legal and moral claims on the use of lethal drones. While the HRC as we define it consists of a wide variety of institutions with disparate influence in the realm of international relations, we group them together for this study in order to reveal the basis of a common front against US drone use. The HRC, first and foremost, disagrees with the IHL-centric approach, insisting that the more restrictive legal framework of IHRL applies. In addition, even when they concur that IHL could apply, the HRC challenges what they deem a robust security rationale advocated by the US that expands the *jus in bello* principles of distinction, military necessity and proportionality. Finally, while they agree with the US that there are conflicting laws, legal ambiguities and a lacuna in the legal structure, they present a normative frame that pushes the law in a human rights direction, emphasising the greater protection of civilians.[6]

These conflicting discourses elicit a host of important questions: What impact has the concept of human rights had on the way drones are used? Has the use of drones altered the way human rights are understood? Would reconciling these seemingly mutually exclusive human rights narratives regarding drone use lead to the formation of a norm that would provide greater respect for human rights than in the current state of legal and moral ambiguity?

In order to explore these questions, we trace the rhetoric used by US government officials and the HRC to address the human rights challenges of drone use. To tease out the significance of human rights concerns within these discourses, we examine their evolution through three key frames of legitimation – strategic, legal and normative. The strategic lens captures the notion that the fight against terrorist groups obliges states to think differently about traditional norms of sovereignty and human rights, the legal framework contrasts the saliences of two competing discourses of international law (IHL and IHRL), and the normative framework incorporates 'universalist' notions of just war to provide moral gloss to fill the gaps in legal discourse. We argue that the US government has moved from a strategic-legal framework to a legal-normative discourse. The former is characterised by a focus on strategic objectives and a permissive view of IHL, with respect of human rights subject to strategic necessity (and thus minimal). The latter incorporates the principles of just war theory, thus restraining the strategic scope of the drone programme while reinforcing the legitimacy of IHL as the paradigm of choice. This provides enhanced respect of human rights, albeit that of IHL (which is far more permissive than IHRL). Comparatively, we assert that the HRC has pursued a human rights-centric approach that rejects the more permissive standards of IHL, while pushing a normative agenda that seeks to enhance respect for human rights under both IHL and IHRL. This includes rejecting the US interpretation of just war principles and appealing to a broader understanding of the right to life norm. Taking right to life considerations seriously raises concerns about whether lethal drones can ever satisfy human rights. In the conclusion, we explore how combining certain elements of these narratives may be contributing to an emerging norm on drone use, and explore the human rights tradeoffs of alternatives to drones in order to push the debate on their use in new directions.

Three frames of legitimation

For the past decade, the US government and the human rights community have presented quite disparate understandings of the legal and moral norms governing drone use outside the traditional battlefield, and in doing so they have used different frames to legitimise their positions. We build on Krebs and Jackson's 'rhetorical coercion' model, in which the authors contend that 'rhetorical coercion is a political strategy that seeks to twist arms by twisting tongues'.[7] Here, speech acts, broadly defined to include public speeches, white papers, legal memorandums, reports, declarations and recommendations, represent an exercise of power with two aims: persuading the public at large of the legitimacy of certain preferences, while leaving one's 'opponents without access to the rhetorical materials needed to craft a socially sustainable rebuttal … [because] the claimant's opponents have been talked into a corner, compelled to endorse a stance they would otherwise reject'.[8] Successful rhetorical coercion is achieved through skillful framing. In the case of drone use, human rights have been a key part of this framing strategy. The US government and the HRC have employed three overlapping frames of reference to legitimise their preferences, while also discounting those of their critics: a strategic frame, a legalistic frame and a normative frame.

As an ideal type, the strategic frame is guided by utility-maximisation. An actor rationalises his or her actions based on what is perceived to yield the highest probability of success – i.e. maximising security – regardless of legal or moral considerations. In the international realm, this frame is often associated with the realist paradigm, whereby a state will take whatever actions necessary to ensure its security. States usually have to frame their actions at least in part on strategic grounds because a government needs to signal to its population that it is doing everything in its power to guarantee the security of its citizens and ensure maximum protection of its soldiers.[9] The HRC, on the other hand, minimises the salience of the strategic frame because its cardinal preference – maximising human rights for everyone – is undermined if the security concerns of one party are allowed to dominate. To quote a UN report on drones:

> Although drones are not illegal weapons, they can make it easier for States to deploy deadly and targeted force on the territories of other States. As such, they risk undermining the protection of life in the immediate and longer terms. If the right to life is to be secured, it is imperative that the limitations posed by international law on the use of force are not weakened by broad justifications of drone strikes.[10]

On the ground, however, states sometimes find that security concerns conflict with their international legal obligations, including respect of human rights. Reliance on a purely strategic frame tends to suppress human rights because if states can do whatever they need to preserve their security, then they can violate the sovereignty of other states and kill the civilians residing there whenever this is deemed necessary. However, in a world where international law imposes some checks on state behaviour (even if ultimately unenforceable), states suffer costs – in reputation and perhaps security – if they openly and frequently transgress international law. As we will explore in depth below, the US has taken a permissive view of self-defence to use drones to kill suspected militants and/or deny safe havens for terrorist groups outside of defined warzones. This has been perceived as a violation of state sovereignty and has led to civilian casualties. In light of this, the US, left with a choice between either abandoning a controversial military tactic, or trying to legitimise its actions using legal and/or normative frames, opted for the latter.

The legalistic frame attempts to legitimise an actor's preferences and actions based on a supposedly objective assessment of the facts interpreted through the lens of applicable international laws, regardless of strategic or normative concerns. International law is designed to protect the human rights of all people in the world, both in times of peace and in times of war. As with any legal structure, the applicability and interpretation of the law is contestable – especially concerning customary international law – though actors rarely admit this. Instead, when actors justify their preferences in a legalistic frame, they present it as an objective reflection of agreed upon norms. Both the US and the HRC turn to international law to justify preferences. Citing international law provides a sense of global legitimacy – either by affirming that state actions are in conformity with recognised behavioural norms (i.e. non-aggressive behaviour) or in exerting pressure on states to conform to such norms.[11]

Regarding drones, the challenge lies in discerning which paradigm of international law is most appropriate to targeted killings. The US government has claimed, since the first drone strike in 2002 outside of the Afghanistan warzone, that it is at war with al-Qaeda, meaning IHL should be the legal regime governing the conflict. The key IHL documents in this context include the 1899 and 1907 Hague Conventions; the 1949 Geneva Conventions; and the 1977 Additional Protocols I and II to the Geneva Conventions, which the US has not ratified, although several of its provisions have become part of customary law. The HRC, on the other hand, emphasises that US targeted killings are taking place outside a declared zone of war, meaning that IHRL should be the governing framework. The key international human rights legal documents here include the 1947 Universal Declaration of Human Rights, where several of its provisions have attained a customary character; the 1966 International Covenant on Civil and Political Rights; the 1966 International Covenant on Economic, Social and Cultural Rights; and the 1989 Convention on the Rights of the Child. Depending on which framework is used, the required level of respect for human rights is different. During war, IHL applies against combatants of the adversary's forces, while in a state of conflict short of war or not reaching a high level of violence, the constraints of law enforcement and IHRL shape the extent to which a state can use lethal force against a suspected criminal. The distinction is important because the level of respect of human rights required in a situation of law enforcement is much greater than what is required in the context of war. By claiming the US is at war, the government can suppress, to a certain extent, the human rights of suspected terrorists and the civilians living around them, in so far as operations that increase the risk of civilian harm become more permissive. This means that the enemy can be killed without being afforded the chance to surrender or being brought to trial. Furthermore, civilian death can, under certain circumstances, be permissible. Contrast this with the law enforcement paradigm where the right to life and trial by jury are paramount, and the justification for the use of force is severely curtailed in order to limit civilian casualties, including those who are presumed suspects.

In the normative frame, actors seek to justify their preferences based on their identity as members of a larger community organised under an agreed understanding of what is true, reasonable, natural, just, and good.[12] While the law provides strong guidance, often there are legal ambiguities, conflicting laws or a genuine lacuna in the legal structure. In addition, actors may disagree with the law or find it obsolete given changing conditions in the international arena. To justify a preference or action that is legally disputed, a normative frame can be used that emphasises a larger set of meta-norms with the hope that controversial actions will be perceived as morally right despite legal ambiguities.[13] Concerning targeted killings, for example, the US has begun to justify its policy by using principles of just war theory as its normative frame to respond to critics who say drones are wantonly killing civilians.

The principles of just war have consistently influenced the way statesmen think about the relationship between war and ethics in the post-Cold War era. For example, all US presidents since the end of the Cold War have referenced the language of just war in some form or another, albeit in different ways.[14] The principles can be divided into the *jus ad bellum* (how one determines the justice of *going to* war) and *jus in bello* (how one determines what one can do *in* war). The *jus ad bellum* includes the criteria of just cause, right authority, right intention, proportionality, last resort and reasonable hope of success, while the *jus in bello* is defined by the criteria of necessity, distinction and proportionality of means. President Obama's reference to the concept of just war as a means 'to regulate the destructive power of war' in his Nobel Peace prize acceptance speech in 2009 points to the salience of this moral framework, spanning several thousand years of philosophical reflection, as a guide to assist statesman in adjudicating the challenges linked to the use of force in the world today.[15]

Obama's interpretation of just war ethics marks a stark rejection of Bush's ethics of war in that it revalorises the notion of last resort (whose significance had been diluted in Bush's thinking); however, Obama actually continued the drone policies implemented by the Bush administration.[16] In particular, he has adopted the same diluted notion of imminence, which led him to expand the drone programme significantly in the first two years of his presidency, while largely remaining silent on the morality of drone strikes. We raise this point to show that the shift towards applying just war principles to drones occurred not simply because Obama was interested in just war thinking.[17] Rather, the turn to the just war framework in early 2012 coincides with the increased pressure from the HRC to define the moral principles by which the drone programmes were being governed.[18]

The turn to just war rhetoric has important human rights implications. On the one hand, incorporating just war principles restricts targeting practices (thus protecting human rights compared to the strategic paradigm). This bows to the criticisms of the HRC, who have vehemently criticised the targeting practices of the US government. On the other hand, just war rhetoric provides moral gloss that portrays drone strikes as being governed by universal principles, implicitly reinforcing the legal paradigm of war as the legitimate framework (thus diminishing human rights compared to the law enforcement paradigm). As we will argue below, appealing to just war principles as part of a rhetorical strategy paints human rights groups into a corner by using the goal of maximising protection of human rights in a time of war as a rhetorical frame to disarm criticism.

Taking advantage of the legal ambiguities, the US can claim it is doing everything morally required to assure civilians are not harmed, while affirming the right to use such lethal force to achieve strategic goals.[19] The HRC's response has been to challenge the US understanding of both the *jus ad bellum* and especially, the *jus in bello* principles, and focus on the negative impact constant drone use has on the right to life norm.

US drone discourse: from the strategic-legal to legal-normative frame

It is important to acknowledge that drone use by the US government is circumscribed by the real-world challenges of statecraft. While the US accepts human rights in the abstract, as evidenced by key government documents and policy speeches, the ideal of human rights compliance is limited by difficult decisions political leaders have to make. This is done in a context of legal ambiguity as the legitimate regime of international law to combat non-state actors – the prime target of US Special Operations Forces and CIA drone strikes – remains a matter of debate. As Obama articulated in a 2013 speech: 'This new technology raises profound questions – about who is targeted, and why; about civilian casualties, and the risk of creating new enemies; about the legality of such strikes under U.S. and international law; about accountability and morality'.[20] Drone use is thus defined by the tension between upholding the ideal of human rights and providing for national security, that is to say, between ensuring strategic goals and normative preferences while maintaining some level of adherence to legal norms. The Obama administration in particular has used a strategy of rhetorical coercion to navigate this tension in the public sphere.

Drones and the US government's strategic-legal frame

The first reported US drone strike outside an official warzone came in 2002. Abu Ali al-Harethi, a senior al-Qaeda leader and suspect in the bombing of the *U.S.S. Cole*, was killed by a predator drone in Yemen, along with five other purported militants. Deputy Secretary of Defense Paul Wolfowitz described the strike in purely strategic terms. As part of a larger war, the drone operation was

> [A] very successful tactical operation, and one hopes each time you get a success like that, not only to have gotten rid of somebody dangerous, but to have imposed changes in their tactics and operations and procedures. And sometimes when people are changing, they expose themselves in new ways.[21]

Despite the mission's success, backlash from the HRC was immediate. Amnesty International wrote in a communication to President Bush: 'If this was the deliberate killing of suspects in lieu of arrest, in circumstances in which they did not pose an immediate threat, the killings would be extrajudicial executions in violation of international human-rights law'.[22] While the criticism employed a legalistic frame, the US responded using a counter-legal frame, arguing that the strike was permitted under the international laws of war because the target was an enemy combatant. The Senate Intelligence Committee, which is responsible for overseeing CIA covert operations, defended the strike in such legal terms as well. The committee chairman, Senator Robert Graham, asserted that 'having defined this as an act against a military adversary and applying the standards of international law, this was within the legal rights of a nation at war'.[23] National Security Advisor Condoleezza Rice added that that the strategic outlook had changed, implying that the legal understanding of self-defence had changed as well: 'We're in a new kind of war, and we've made very clear that it is important that this new kind of war be fought on different battlefields'.[24]

The exchange between Amnesty International and the Bush administration captures the legal contest over the ambiguity that came to characterise the drone debate: human rights groups argued that targeted killings violate IHRL, including the most important human right of all, the right to life, while US officials argued that such killings were legitimate under IHL, and thus not a violation of human rights because killing combatants in war is permitted. In each legal frame, human rights has a place, but with very different repercussions for those being targeted and the civilians around them. While the HRC position placed a premium on the right to life (even of suspected militants), and a fair trial, the US government's position was driven by a strong strategic element.

The strategic frame was expressed by deed, as rhetorical rationales were not articulated. Following the 2002 strike, the US began operating under the cloak of plausible deniability by refraining from publicly acknowledging suspected drone operations so that Washington, and potentially its allies, could deny US involvement. This stance persisted through the rest of the Bush administration's tenure in the White House and through most of Obama's first term. Because the US did not acknowledge alleged strikes, it therefore did not need to publically offer legal or normative justifications. This allowed the administration to pursue strategic directives, such as targeting terrorist threats and denying safe havens, and ignore the concerns and critiques of the HRC.

By insulating the administration from public responsibility, a clear precedent regarding targeted killing came to be solidified within the US government and the main bodies that operate drones outside declared warzones (the CIA and Joint Special Operations Command (JSOC)). This marked a clear shift in the political mindset of the key parties involved. Prior to 9/11, CIA Director George Tenet was 'skeptical about whether a military weapon should be fired outside of the military chain of command', insisting that during peacetime, no one at the CIA, including the director, had the legal authority to fire a missile.[25] After 9/11, the situation changed as the CIA was granted wide-sweeping authorities to target members of al-Qaeda under the Authorized Use of Military Force (AUMF). Following the approval of the AUMF, the senior leadership at the CIA and in the US government believed that the more permissive IHL regime governed all operations against al-Qaeda, meaning its members were considered militants who could be justly targeted with lethal force. Al-Harethi's death thus marked the culmination of a protracted debate about the legality of targeted killing outside a hot battlefield. As one former CIA official noted, 'There was discussion about this for years in the CIA. The discussion is now over, and the operations have begun'.[26] This precedent was extended to JSOC who now also employ drones for targeted killings outside traditional warzones.

The choice of legal frames – that of IHL – conformed to the strategic concerns of the US. The problem, however, was that in pursuing the use of force under the more permissive rules of IHL (compared to IHRL), the US expanded the drone programme in such a way that made the strategic-legal frame unsustainable. Between 2002 and 2007, drones were a small part of the 'global war on terror', never exceeding more than four lethal strikes per year outside of Iraq and Afghanistan. However, beginning in 2008, their use skyrocketed. According to the New America Foundation, there were 36 strikes in Pakistan in 2008, 54 strikes in 2009 and 122 strikes in 2010.[27] Had drones remained a very limited tool with only a few strikes per year, the human rights impact would have been much smaller. But with more frequent strikes, the stance of plausible deniability became untenable because reports of significant civilian casualties mobilised the HRC to put pressure on the US. Given that the US was silent on drones, the HRC was able to control the discourse. Through its campaign criticising US lethal drone strikes and its emphasis on the need to take IHRL seriously, the HRC backed the US into a rhetorical corner, as it were, and began to delegitimise its actions. This, in turn, forced the US to begin a public campaign to counter the HRC narrative on drones.

The initial period of plausible deniability served to create the space for new norms regarding the use of force to emerge, which impacted the way in which human rights came to be understood. As Kegley and Raymond argue, when a set of new norms is endorsed by a powerful state, this can set the foundation for a more permissive normative world order with regard to the use of force because custom is key in international law.[28] The strategic-legal frame reflects the emergence of an expanded concept of anticipatory self-defence that included what would be termed, 'preventive self-defense', or the right to attack an adversary even when there is no clear evidence of an imminent attack.[29]

The norm of preventive self-defence has its roots in the Bush Doctrine. Under the Bush administration, the US used a legal-strategic frame that argued that international law was inadequate for combating transnational terrorist groups, and that an expanded notion of anticipatory self-defence was required.[30] One of the clearest articulations of this perspective is found in the 2002 National Security Strategy:

> For centuries, international law recognized that nations need not suffer an attack before they can lawfully take action to defend themselves against forces that present an imminent danger of attack. Legal scholars and international jurists often conditioned the legitimacy of preemption on the existence of an imminent threat – most often a visible mobilization of armies, navies, and air forces preparing to attack. *We must adapt the concept of imminent threat to the capabilities and objectives of today's adversaries.*[31]

While the administration used the language of preemption, which has historical legal precedents dating back to the *Caroline affair* in the nineteenth century, the thrust of the argument pressed for a different kind of force. The distinction between preemption and prevention is that the former is self-defence against an imminent threat, while the latter is against a potential future or emerging threat.[32] While George W. Bush spoke the language of preemptive war, his doctrine was considered by many as one of preventive war. Although preemptive war is widely considered just, the Bush doctrine, as Matthew Flynn explains, 'expanded US power to the point where it had moved the country away from self-preservation. Preemption in this broader sense suddenly becomes much more frequent. It also becomes a justification for aggression'.[33] Neta Crawford argued that the bar for anticipatory war was set 'too low in the Bush administration's National Security Strategy'. She thus warned that 'the consequences of lowering the threshold may be increased instability and the premature use of force', and that such a doctrine 'short-circuits nonmilitary means of solving problems'.[34]

Even though the Bush Doctrine was largely repudiated because it was seen as enabling the use of force in dangerous ways, this expanded interpretation of anticipatory self-defence would form the basis of the US targeted killing policy enabled by drones.[35] Despite significant differences between Bush and Obama with regard to the use of force, the US drone programme fit into the scope of an emerging norm, what Fisk and Ramos describe as the norm of preventive self-defence that emerged in the post 9/11 era: 'states' cost–benefit calculations regarding the options available for this purpose certainly lean toward drones as the weapon of choice, as they offer a trifecta of capabilities: precision, reconnaissance, and surveillance'.[36] While the first strike in 2002 was an isolated incident in taking the fight to al-Qaeda wherever its members resided, it was part of a larger strategy that had significant human rights implications as it expanded the geographic scope of the war to a global battlefield. As Wolfowitz explained: 'So we have just got to keep the pressure on everywhere we're able to, and we've got to deny the sanctuaries everywhere we're able to, and we've got to put pressure on every government that is giving these people support to get out of that business'.[37] Drones would come to fill this role in a much wider sense as they became the weapon of choice towards the end of Bush's second term and throughout Obama's first term, especially in the region along the Afghanistan-Pakistan border.

There are significant human rights implications that emerge as a consequence of accepting preventive self-defence as a strategic and legal norm for both those deemed combatants as well as non-combatants. In claiming the legal right to wage preventive war against terrorists groups, the US assumes a wider latitude to use lethal force compared to criminal law enforcement. And while the laws of war specify minimum human rights, these are, as David Luban notes, 'far less robust than rights in peacetime'. Luban goes on to argue that such a view 'depresses human rights from their peacetime standard to the war-time standard'.[38]

Regarding perceived combatants, applying IHL allows for a very wide target list, one that might include top leaders, low-level militants, and perhaps civilians aiding combatants in various ways. The initial use of drones focused on key leaders to decapitate the chain of command; as the fight progressed, the strategy evolved to deny safe havens, which increased the target list to include potentially anyone associated with or inspired by al-Qaeda. At the peak of the strategic-legal phase of the drone campaign in Pakistan in 2010, there was a drone strike every three days on average, pursuing a wide range of targets. Even within the IHL paradigm, this vision of the global battlefield posed multiple human rights concerns. A major concern, of course, is that of identifying who is an actual member of al-Qaeda. Killing people whose identity is uncertain can be a violation even under IHL. Several reputable news agencies published stories on the convoluted 'Kill List' protocol employed by the Obama administration, and the way it identified non-combatants as any man of military age.[39]

Regarding non-combatants, an increased number of strikes and a wider range of targets augments the probability of greater civilian deaths due to error or over-aggressive targeting. But more generally, the application of IHL places civilian populations where terrorists reside under the legal regimes governing war. The protection of human rights in such a context permits more collateral damage compared to a zone of peace where law-enforcement is used, thus subjecting civilians' human rights to the strategic calculations of the US. This shift has led to what some scholars have called 'risk transfer', or relying on technology to decrease the risk to US soldiers and transferring that risk to non-combatants during conflict.[40] By prioritising the lives of its soldiers, the US effectively increased the

LEGAL AND ETHICAL IMPLICATIONS OF DRONE WARFARE

potential harm to non-combatants who might be in the vicinity of drone strikes (although sending in a team to capture a suspected individual may also pose risks).

If the suppression of human rights that Luban describes had been temporary and for a limited duration during an exceptional crisis (something akin to Walzer's notion of supreme emergency) the impact on human rights may have been circumscribed.[41] However, as Luban argues, the war on terror appears as though it will go on perpetually, which means 'the suspension of human rights ... is not temporary but permanent'.[42] The use of drones as the tool of choice in the US fight against terrorism has led to a perpetual war and with it a permanent re-interpretation and devaluing of what human rights mean in the contemporary world. As we argue below, this has even deeper implications when the nefarious consequences of drones, detailed by the HRC, are taken into account.

Although the strategic-legal frame did not provide enough moral clout to fill the space of legal ambiguity, when the Obama administration chose to publicly justify its drone use, the foundation for a more permissive world order was already in place. To publically legitimise its drone programme, government officials employed the language of just war.

Drones and the US government's legal-normative frame

The US publicly defended its lethal drones programme through a shift towards a legal-normative frame. Beginning with President Obama's first public acknowledgment of drone operations in January 2012, and followed by a series of speeches by government officials – including General Counsel for the Department of Defense Jeh Johnson, State Department Legal Adviser Harold Koh, Attorney General Eric Holder, and CIA General Counsel Stephen Preston – the US reaffirmed the legitimacy of the IHL framework, but buttressed this defence by turning to the principles of just war. In so far as just war principles are inscribed into IHL, their use clearly overlaps with the legal frame. However, these principles also serve a powerful rhetorical purpose. By appealing to universalist principles, or meta norms that have emerged from the authority of history, the use of just war principles distanced the US from the strategic-centric approach of the period of plausible deniability, appearing to fill the gaps in legal ambiguity by showing the US was waging not just a legal war, but also a *moral* one, indeed the most 'moral' war in human history as some proponents argued.[43]

The use of just war language by the Obama administration should come as no surprise. Obama referenced the principles of just war in his 2009 Nobel Prize acceptance speech as a means 'to regulate the destructive power of war', and its principles are integrated into the 2010 National Security Strategy. While the principles were applied initially to describe interstate war, they have now become standard for framing the use of drones against al-Qaeda. As Obama stated in his 2013 speech at the National Defense University, in which he outlines the legal and moral reasoning behind drone use: 'We are at war with an organization that right now would kill as many Americans as they could if we did not stop them first. So this is a just war – a war waged proportionally, in last resort, and in self-defense'.[44]

The speech that set the tone for the legal-normative frame was given by John Brennan, who was deputy National Security Adviser and Obama's primary counsellor on counterterrorism, on April 2012 at the Wilson Center. The context for the speech was a discussion of the Obama administration's counter-terrorism strategy, and in particular, its 'ethics and efficacy' which had been the subject of both domestic and international concern given the ever-increasing controversy surrounding drone use. Brennan's speech sought to define drone use as legal (the IHL frame), ethical (the just war frame) and wise (the strategic frame). While the legal and strategic frames remained the same, the major novelty in his speech was the incorporation of just war language into the government's rhetoric. Departing from the strategic-legal view that the US does not have to try to capture terrorists because they can simply be targeted as enemy combatants in a war, Brennan argues that 'our unqualified preference is to only undertake lethal force when we believe that capturing the individual is not feasible... It is our preference to capture suspected terrorists whenever and wherever feasible'.[45] This claim sought to counter accusations that the US was killing anyone at will by suggesting drone strikes must adhere to the *jus ad bellum* principle of last resort. This means every reasonable alternative must be explored before resorting to a lethal strike. Following such a view preserves, in theory, two principles key to upholding human rights, the right to life and to a fair and public trial. Adhering to last resort would thus mark a more restrained view of the use of lethal force compared to the strategic-legal framing discussed above.

Yet, Brennan admitted that opportunities for capture are rare, and that at times, drone strikes become a military necessity in the war against al-Qaeda. As he explains in the question and answer session: 'But if it's not feasible, either because it's too risky from the standpoint of forces or the government doesn't have the will or the ability to do it, then we make a determination whether or not the significance of the threat that the person poses requires us to take action, so that we're able to mitigate the threat that they pose'.[46] In such instances, Brennan claimed that the US is adhering to the *jus in bello* principles, which are incorporated into IHL, to protect the human rights of civilians. Brennan makes explicit reference to the *jus in bello*

> principle of necessity, the requirement that the target have definite military value ... the principle of distinction, the idea that only military objectives may be intentionally targeted and that civilians are protected from being intentionally targeted ... [and] the principle of proportionality, the notion that the anticipated collateral damage of an action cannot be excessive in relation to the anticipated military advantage.[47]

In essence, Brennan explained that the US was taking core IHL principles and imbuing them with greater moral restraint somehow implicit in just war theory.[48] The new rhetoric marked a stark shift from a strategic-legal to a legal-normative frame to legitimise drone strikes. Under the former, the administration was able to strike widely, without having to publically take responsibility. The legal constraints contained in IHL – such as distinction and proportionality – were interpreted in such a way to ensure mission success, leaving respect for human rights prey to the strategic necessities of the war on terror. Thus, one could err on the side of uncertainty when pursuing suspected militants by targeting them even if there was doubt about their identity or whether civilians might be unduly harmed.

Turning to just war principles, however, reintroduces the notion of public responsibility to uphold certain norms. As a deep moral discourse, just war standards emphasised a re-interpretation of core IHL concepts including, distinction, proportionality, military necessity and imminence. This is reflected in Obama's 2013 speech at the National Defense University:

> As our fight enters a new phase, America's legitimate claim of self-defense cannot be the end of the discussion. *To say a military tactic is legal, or even effective, is not to say it is wise or moral in every instance.* For the same human progress that gives us the technology to strike half a world away also demands the discipline to constrain that power – or risk abusing it. And that's why, over the last four years, my administration has worked vigorously to establish a framework that governs our use of force against terrorists – insisting upon clear guidelines, oversight and accountability.[49]

LEGAL AND ETHICAL IMPLICATIONS OF DRONE WARFARE

Infusing IHL with the deep moral discourse of just war has led the US to take greater pains before approving a drone strike than what is required under IHL. Under IHL, it is legally permissible for civilians to be killed when targeting the enemy, but as the US has learned, even the unintentional killing of one civilian can create considerable backlash from the affected civilian population, the HRC and world opinion at large. Consequently, the US has shifted from viewing its lethal operations from an IHL centric strategic-legal context to a more moral legal-normative one that prioritises just war principles. This shift is reflected in the Obama administration's attempts to persuade the public that it is waging a moral war, which in turn has led to greater restraint as a matter of policy. As Obama explained in 2014, 'Before any strike is taken, there must be near-certainty that no civilians will be killed or injured – the highest standard we can set'.[50] The introduction of this 'near certainty standard', where lethal strikes will only be carried out when the probability that civilians will not be harmed is very, very low, goes well beyond what is required under IHL.

While calls for greater public transparency have fallen largely on deaf ears, the empirically available data on drone strikes suggests that the US turn to just war principles parallels two trends related to drone use. According to the New America Foundation, the number of drone strikes in Pakistan has plummeted since 2012, when there were 48 strikes. In 2013, there were 27 strikes, and at the time of writing (October 2014), there have been 17 strikes (Compared to 122 strikes in 2010, the peak of the strategic-legal frame).[51]

The number of civilian casualties has also decreased, both in absolute numbers and in proportion to the total number of strikes. In a study on drone strikes in Pakistan from 2007–2012, Braun and Brunstetter demonstrate that 23% of CIA strikes (80 out of 343) during that period caused civilian deaths (estimated between 462 and 676 civilians and unknowns), which is a far higher percentage than what the US military tolerates as a permissible ratio of combatant kills/collateral damage. They argue that the data raise serious concerns about the CIA's targeting protocol concerning the principles of distinction and proportionality, and the concern for human rights.[52] The end of their study, however, coincides with the beginning of the shift in rhetorical framing by the US government and the use of just war discourse to defend drone strikes. Presumably, the government has partially reformed its targeting policy to reflect its rhetoric. The numbers suggest such a shift as they have accordingly decreased in 2013 and 2014; in a total of 44 strikes through October 2014, only two strikes (4.5% of total strikes) have killed between three and five civilians and three and four unknowns, while all others have killed only militants.[53]

We are not suggesting that there is a monocausal relationship between the HRC, the US just war turn and the decrease in US drone strikes. Clearly other factors have also contributed to the decreased use of strikes and the more restrictive rules of engagement. For example, the escalating political costs of the signature strikes campaign led to strained relations between Washington and Islamabad, which may have limited US military options and helped the US to realise drones are not the only option available for dealing with suspected militants in Pakistan. Furthermore, the US has encouraged Islamabad to take a greater role in diminishing threats emanating from the region. The Pakistani government has done so by asking for a lull in strikes to negotiate with the Taliban, while also taking a greater role in pursuing militants through military means, though it is unclear how effective this has been.[54] This shift in policy represents a new US security, political and economic strategy called the 'New Silk Road', a plan that US government officials see as the long-term alternative to a perpetual drone war, the ethical implications of which we discuss in the conclusion.

However, what we are suggesting is that regardless of whether just war thinking is the most important cause of this trend, the turn to just war principles has created an ethical structure that arguably reduces the temptation to use drones; and when they are used, such strikes are also governed by a more restrictive legal-moral frame. While strikes have increased in Yemen during the same period (albeit with open consent of that government), an optimistic interpretation of this trend would suggest that the legal-normative frame imposes an inherent restraining mechanism by limiting the individuals who can be targeted to those who pose a clear threat, thus reducing the range of permissible targets. Despite persisting ambiguity regarding who is a clear threat and what imminence means, adherence to just war principles appears to have delegitimised signature strikes – drone strikes carried out based on merely suspicious patterns of behavior – which were considered legitimate under the strategic-legal frame. This shift in policy and discourse was a reaction to the challenge posed by the HRC's consensual condemnation of US signature strikes.[55] Moreover, such a framework makes other alternatives – those encouraged by New Silk Road strategy for example – look more attractive.[56]

It is important to highlight that while the constraints of just war principles on US drone strikes have had a positive effect on human rights (when compared to the strategic-legal frame) in so far as fewer strikes are permissible and greater care must be taken regarding who is targeted and whether civilians are at risk, this legal-normative turn has also introduced a normative gloss that reinforces the IHL-centric legal paradigm that the US prefers, as opposed to the IHRL regime that the HRC advocates. Therefore, the new legal-normative discourse still preserves a key element of its strategic-legal precursor, namely the controversial view that the US claims the right to use lethal force against suspected terrorists residing anywhere in the world. Here, the discourse of just war contributes to the further solidification of the norm of preventive self-defence that perpetually diminishes the human rights of suspected terrorists and those civilians living under drones. We now turn to the HRC challenge of the US legal-normative justification of lethal drones to shed light on an important counter-narrative about the relationship between drones and human rights.

Drones and the human rights community: defending IHRL and expanding human rights protections

The HRC position on drones challenges the underpinnings of both the strategic-legal and legal-normative frames employed by the US. Since Amnesty International's initial criticism of the 2002 drone strike in Yemen, a series of important official reports from the UN, Amnesty International, Human Rights Watch and other NGOs and academic clinics have consistently challenged the evolving US position. In reading these documents, three overarching lines of critique relevant to our argument regarding how the US understands the relation between drone use and human rights emerge.

First, the HRC rejects the IHL-centric framework guiding US drone strikes. The HRC emphasises that context (whether the strike is carried out within an armed conflict, or outside of an armed conflict) is key for assessing which legal structure (IHL or IHRL) applies.[57] As Philip Alston explains in a 2010 report commissioned by the Office of the United Nations High Commission for Human Rights: 'In the legitimate struggle against terrorism, too many criminal acts have been re-characterized so as to justify addressing them within the framework of the law of armed conflict'.[58] According to the HRC, the US has failed to provide enough evidence to clearly indicate that, outside of the warzones in Iraq and Afghanistan, drone strikes against al-Qaeda, the Taliban, and 'affiliated forces' such as Yemen's al-Qaeda in the Arabian Peninsula, and Somalia's al-Shabab, should be governed by IHL.[59] A 2013 Amnesty International report describes this challenge when reporting the death of an elderly woman in Pakistan:

> If the drone attack took place as part of an armed conflict, then international humanitarian law would apply alongside international human rights law. Under international humanitarian law, not all civilian deaths that occur as a result of armed attacks are unlawful ... If the attack took place outside an actual situation of armed conflict, then only international human rights law would apply to this case, rather than the more permissive rules of international humanitarian law. The law enforcement standards that uphold the right to life prohibit the use of intentional lethal force except when strictly unavoidable to protect life.[60]

Ultimately however, for the HRC, the default legal paradigm is that of IHRL:

> The most immediate protection for the right to life is provided by the international human rights law framework. This is the default legal regime from which deviations are permissible only when, and for as long as, those who justify the more permissive use of force under international humanitarian law can show that the requisite conditions have been fulfilled.[61]

The main problem with the US position is that it has failed to show that al-Qaeda, the Taliban and 'affiliated forces' constitute a centralised and organised 'party' under the laws of war, or that their violent acts reach the quantity and severity thresholds to be declared an armed conflict.[62] Although the HRC acknowledges that the 9/11 terrorist attacks carried out by al-Qaeda did meet the severity threshold, they question, as the current UN Special Rapporteur on extrajudicial, summary or arbitrary executions, Christof Heyns, has suggested, whether, 'killings carried out in 2012 can be justified as in response to [events] in 2001'.[63] Consequently, the HRC views targeted killings outside of a clear warzone as illegal, claiming they should be characterised as extra-judicial executions, given that human rights law prohibits the premeditated and intentional use of lethal force.[64] As Fernando Tesón argues in his critical analysis of targeted killing, 'during peacetime, the state can use lethal force only in very limited circumstances, mostly in self-defense or to protect persons from deadly threats. Beyond that, a suspected criminal is entitled to due process and may not be killed except in execution of a lawful sentence pronounced by a court of law after a finding of guilt'.[65] In other words, for a drone strike to be legitimate according to the HRC, the US would need to provide, in a transparent fashion and under some court's supervision, clear and incontrovertible proof that the suspected individual is directly involved in hostilities, cannot be apprehended, and represents a serious and imminent threat.

Second, even when the HRC agrees that IHL could apply to US targeted killings (in Iraq and Afghanistan, or in the event that more evidence is put forth by the US showing that IHL indeed applies to strikes in Pakistan, Yemen and Somalia), they nonetheless challenge what they see as inadequate attention paid to the *jus ad bellum* principle of last resort as it might apply to a particular drone strike (i.e. serious attempt to capture), as well as the 'robust', 'expanded' and overly permissive interpretations of the *jus in bello* principles of distinction, military necessity and proportionality.

Regarding last resort, the HRC challenges the US view, explained in a leaked Department of Justice (DoJ) White Paper, that imminence in the context of terrorism often comes before all reasonable non-violent options can be tried. As argued in a 2013 joint letter to President Obama on drones and targeted killings written by the American Civil Liberties Union, Amnesty International, Center for Human Rights & Global Justice, NYU School of Law, Human Rights First, Human Rights Watch and other members of the HRC:

> Administration officials have in the past defined an 'imminent threat' in ways that emphasize the opportunity to attack a target rather than the immediacy of the threat posed. Justifying the use of lethal force against a 'continuing' threat seems to similarly endorse the use of lethal force in response to fear of an unspecified adverse action at an undefined point in the future. These interpretations of imminence are inconsistent with international law.[66]

Rather, the HRC falls back on the level of force permitted in IHRL, purporting the view that 'outside of actual armed conflict, lethal force may only be used when strictly unavoidable to protect against an imminent threat to life'.[67]

In terms of the principles of distinction and military necessity, the HRC defers to the position outlined in the 'Interpretive Guidance on the Notion of Direct Participation in Hostilities under International Humanitarian Law', adopted by the International Committee of the Red Cross (ICRC).[68] Claiming the US is in a conflict with organised non-state armed groups, the HRC asserts that the laws of a non-international armed conflict should apply. Under such a legal framework, there are no 'combatants', only civilians who 'directly participate in hostilities'. Drone strikes are thus legal when carried out against these individuals, but who these legitimate targets are is contested.

This position contrasts directly with the IHL-centric legal paradigm espoused by the US in that it challenges what constitutes 'membership' in an organised armed group, what establishes 'direct participation' in hostilities, and how long direct participation – i.e. continuing threat – lasts.[69] In contrast to the broad targeting principles that could be justified under IHL, the HRC offers a more restrictive rendering of who constitutes a legitimate target by claiming that individuals who indirectly assist a non-state armed group's war effort through financing, recruitment, training, propaganda, political advocacy, capacity building (including the production of weapons), or by providing food and shelter, are not legitimate targets for attack.[70] Targeting these individuals cannot be considered an act of military necessity. Rather, in a zone outside the traditional battlefield, for a civilian to be considered as directly participating in hostilities he or she needs to be either carrying out an attack, directly helping in the planning of an imminent attack, loading a weapon, or spotting for artillery.[71]

With regard to proportionality, the main challenge in satisfying this principle is that it is difficult to measure. To further complicate matters, while one can count civilian causalities and the numbers of buildings or weapons destroyed, the psychological impact of living under drones does not neatly fit into the standard legal definitions or normative ideals. One human rights report describes the difficulties of living in a state of perpetual fear of a drone strike, the repercussions to family and social structures caused by the killing of innocent community members, and the threat of reprisals from local militants.[72] These outcomes clearly impact the way civilians go about their daily lives, diminishing their quality of life. The US government views such consequences as an inevitable part of even a 'moral' war. Drone proponents thus argue that as long as drones satisfy the proportionality requirement, then the US is acting within its legal and moral obligations.

However, as Braun and Brunstetter illustrate, the US government's claim that drones are proportionate suffers from what they call 'proportionality relativism – the use of impertinent comparisons to argue that drones are proportionate because they cause less collateral damage than other uses of force'. Such comparisons not only misrepresent the true meaning of proportionality 'as an independent assessment of the balance between the anticipated civilian harm and military gain associated with each act of force' but also ignore human rights concerns of civilians not technically considered in the proportionality calculus, including 'post-traumatic stress disorder and social disruption caused by the persistent threat of drones'.[73] In their study of US drone strikes in Pakistan from 2007–2012, they show that nearly one in four CIA drone strikes in Pakistan led to civilian deaths, while also causing harms that are overlooked if one only focuses on the numbers. They conclude that 'the anticipated military advantage of the average strike is found more in denying safe haven to suspected militants than in targeting the leadership. A proportionality balancing calculus that permits civilian deaths for such goals raises serious concerns about the effects of such a long-term campaign on civilian human rights, the U.S. global image, and on the probability of success in the struggle against al Qaeda'.[74] Their conclusion, reflecting the harrowing stories from HRC reports, points to the need to move beyond the IHL-centric paradigm of proportionality the US applies to drone strikes. The notion of harm, which is key to determining proportionality, they argue, needs to be considered not just in terms of death and destruction, but also by considering the 'human rights concerns that deeply and negatively affect civilian lives'.[75]

Third, by emplacing psychological trauma into the discourse, the HRC employs a legal-normative frame that highlights human rights concerns that are currently not protected by IHL, and possibly not even IHRL. The criticisms emanating from the HRC point to where legal and normative conventions fall short and where existing treaties do not cover certain conceptions of human rights, particularly the right to life. While the US government has arguably been able to exploit such lacunae in the law through its legal-normative just war justifications, the HRC has countered with its own legal-normative discourse emphasising the meta-norm of the 'right to life'. Several qualitative studies that illustrate the impact of drones on individual lives attempt to raise awareness of the deeper impact drones have beyond ambiguous legal precedents and *jus in bello* ideals. The implication is that sustained drone presence, even if a particular strike might be justified under the rare conditions of IHRL, nevertheless has a vast and negative human rights impact on civilians. The stories communicate a vision of the right to life that includes not only freedom from arbitrary killing by drones, but also a life without the psychological duress that civilians face when living constantly under drones. Ben Emmerson's recent report to the UN made the following conclusion:

> If used in strict compliance with the principles of international humanitarian law, remotely piloted aircraft are capable of reducing the risk of civilian casualties in armed conflict by significantly improving the situational awareness of military commanders.[76]

However, given the trauma that comes from the constant threat of a strike 'out of the blue' made possible by drones' constant presence in the skies, the question becomes whether drones can ever adequately satisfy human rights requirements outside a warzone. Although none of the reports go as far as to say that drones could never satisfy human rights requirements under IHRL, pushing such an expanded view of the right to life might lead to such a conclusion. Because the precedent set by overly permissive US drone use during the period of strategic-legal framing has instilled a fear that 'I might be next even if I am innocent', drone use even under the restrictive conditions of IHRL becomes suspect. If drones under even the most restrictive applications of international law become unconvincing, then morally (and perhaps legally) speaking, one of the main strategic advantages of drones – to provide omnipresent strike capability that denies terrorist safe havens – is effectively denied. This is because their mere presence would violate the expanded view of the right to life. The HRC does not go this far, resting instead on the restrictions imposed by IHRL and calls for greater transparency. However, the concerns caused by drones raise important questions about what the right to life, and thus the very notion of human rights will come to mean, as drone technology and legal and moral norms evolve.

Conclusion: towards an imperfect norm regarding lethal drone use

In this article we have argued that the US government has shifted from a strategic-legal frame for legitimising drones to a legal-normative one. This shift both restricts the types of drone strikes that can be legitimated by incorporating just war principles, and maintains the strategic advantages of drones by validating the IHL paradigm that perpetually suspends the human rights of those caught in the crosshairs of the 'forever war'. The HRC, on the other hand, has rejected the IHL frame while employing a legal-normative frame grounded in IHRL that expands what is meant by the right to life, thus potentially denying some of the strategic advantages of drones. In so far as these shifting and contrasting discourses set the contours for the debate about what norms should govern lethal drones in the future, we conclude with a few observations that might help us understand what a plausible norm might look like that emphasises greater respect for human rights.

First, at the time of writing, the US appears to be moving in the direction of the HRC – that of greater respect of human rights. However, greater respect of human rights does not mean the same thing for the US government as it does for the HRC. For the US, this means following a less strategic and more normative version of IHL, in lieu of IHRL. In so far as the US sees the need to take advantage of the tactical advantages afforded by drones to pursue strategic ends, then the IHL paradigm will be favoured by presidents because it is more permissive than IHRL. While the incorporation of just war principles curtails drone use and leads to greater respect of human rights than under the strategic-legal paradigm, US actions and discourses nevertheless contribute to a permissive legal and normative regime legitimising targeted killings that could set a problematic global precedent. For the HRC, greater respect of human rights means a continued rejection of the IHL paradigm in cases of lethal strikes outside a warzone, and a greater focus on respect for the right to life to include the duress caused by living under drones.

Second, despite agreement that the strategic-legal framework of the early years of the US drone programme is morally problematic, there continues to be a gap between how human rights are understood in a world of drones. The HRC seems unlikely to accept IHL as applicable to ubiquitous drone strikes outside the battlefield because this would acquiesce to the strategic demands of powerful states and depress the human rights of suspected terrorists as well as civilians living under the spectre of drones. On the other hand, the US seems unwilling to accept IHRL as the sole means in the fight against al-Qaeda and like-minded groups across the globe. The result is that the human rights of populations living under drones will continue to be suppressed under wartime standards. Given this gridlock, perhaps one could surmise that in a world of lethal drones and growing terrorist threats, the norm that will come to govern drones lies somewhere within this space.

If this were the case, two further observations merit our attention as we think about the future. Drones have, in some ways, altered how human rights are understood. Drones have enabled the US to de facto extend in unprecedented ways the wartime human rights standard to non-war zones. As several HRC reports reveal, what is unique to drones is that they bring the 'death from out of the blue' element to everyday life because of their ability to loiter on an almost permanent basis. Human rights are not only diminished because civilians are killed, but because there is a ubiquitous threat of death from the skies that severely disrupts the social fabric of local communities. As norms regarding drone use evolve this impact should come to be reflected in future targeting policies. If this were the case, the US (and other states) would not necessarily have to abandon the IHL-centric approach, but they would have to recognise the nefarious consequences that IHRL highlights when populations live under an aerial drone occupation. A deeper understanding of just war principles would restrict drone use to isolated cases, perhaps contributing to a norm that would permit a few strikes per year against identified individuals with the explicit consent of other states who cannot employ law enforcement mechanisms with the same accuracy that drones can provide.

There are obvious issues with such a norm that further research would need to explore. For one, it does not fully satisfy the main HRC concerns, namely that even limited drone use circumvents the right to life. Second, it makes drones a projection of the power of (strong) states that diminishes human rights of peoples residing in weak states. Third, it is open to abuse unless it is transparent and connected to clear legal precedents. Nonetheless, such a norm would significantly limit drone use, especially when compared to the strategic-legal phase which some feared would become the norm, as well as the current legal-normative phase. The result would be greater respect for human rights than the current IHL framework, albeit falling short of an IHRL-centric regime.

If such a norm were to emerge, one final observation that puts the relationship between drones and human rights into a broader context deserves attention. As norms governing drone use evolve it is important to recognise the tension between pursuing security and respecting human rights. This means resisting the temptation to view omnipresent drones as the only solution to the problem of al-Qaeda and like-minded threats, but also recognising that restricting (or eliminating) drone strikes will lead to significant human rights tradeoffs as alternative coercive actions inevitably replace drones.

Indeed, we can catch a glimpse of some of these moral tradeoffs already. The US has begun to realise that drones cannot be the solution to ending the struggle against al-Qaeda and affiliates. As a result, it has begun exploring other solutions that have less blowback than the perpetual drone campaign. As Harold Koh acknowledged in a 2013 speech on 'How to End the Forever War?', he explained that, 'We need a security transition, a political transition, and an economic transition, particularly implementation of an economic plan now known as "The New Silk Road."'[77]

We highlight the 'New Silk Road' because doing so illustrates the potential human rights tradeoffs that the norm we described above – and perhaps any norm that restricts drone use – will engender. Understanding the moral tradeoffs of such alternatives is key to grasping the full scope of solidifying drone norms. It allows us to anticipate the need to theorise about how to incentivise states – both strong states who have armed drones and weak states whose territorial integrity is compromised by terrorist groups within their borders – to pursue alternatives aimed at eliminating terrorist safe havens through alternative means while also upholding human rights standards that would meet the HRC's view of IHRL.

The idea of a 'New Silk Road' as the vision for a region where drones have frequently been used (Afghanistan and Pakistan) is deeply rooted in history, namely the 'sprawling trading network that crisscrossed Asia – connecting East to West, and North to South' – spanning several millennia and connecting diverse peoples and economies.[78] It is an idea that is quietly being implemented as a non-interventionist way to deal, long-term, with the threat from terrorist groups. To the extent that this effort can succeed in ending the 'forever war' by helping to reestablish the rule of law in these ungoverned spaces and eliminate the need for drone strikes, then the geographic sphere where drones can be justifiably used under IHL will be greatly diminished. In principle, this is a good thing for human rights. However, it does not necessarily mean that human rights under IHRL will be adequately protected or enforced. Rather, it is important to realise that each of the transitions referenced in Koh's speech will have human rights tradeoffs that could lead to serious human rights violations.

For example, the security transition called for by Koh involves reducing the US military footprint by placing the burden on local governments to provide security and uphold the law. Given the records of these local regimes (including Pakistan and Yemen) it is likely that they will not place a premium on respecting the human rights of their populations to the extent expected by the HRC under IHRL. In other words, fewer drone strikes (or eliminating them altogether) will not necessarily improve the human rights of those populations currently living under drones, since the security burden, and hence control over operations, will be transferred to regimes that might also disregard IHRL.[79]

Furthermore, pushing for democratic reforms in countries where US drone strikes currently occur should also be met with some scepticism, given the results of past attempts by the US to do so (including Iraq and Afghanistan). Unfortunately, although not acknowledged publicly, the most likely scenario is that the US will continue to support regimes that are willing and able to take on the threat of terrorist groups by whatever means necessary, regardless of idealistic democratic reforms and respect for human rights.

Finally, calls for economic reform are founded on the belief that lasting stability and security go hand in hand with increased economic opportunity. By increasing the free-flow of goods in the region, the belief is that the insurgency-driven economic isolationism that has enabled pockets of terrorist safe havens will be greatly diminished. However, it is unclear how US-led economic integration in Central Asia would address regional and local economic inequalities (especially given past US campaigns of economic-restructuring elsewhere). Moreover, to be successful, it would have to invite regional powers such as China and Russia, who have dubious human rights records, to hold more soft power over the region in the future. This brings us full circle back to the issue of drones because China has lethal drones, and Russia is close to acquiring them.

One worries that these states will follow the initial precedent of US drone use, namely that of the strategic-legal framework. However, were a norm that solidifies the shift towards a legal-normative frame in addition to include the HRC's expanded view of the right to life to encompass living free from the fear of a drone 'strike out of the blue' to emerge, this would provide customary precedent to condemn such behaviour. In addition, it may even be the catalyst for a shift in international law that would allay some, albeit not all, of the unique dangers drones pose to respecting human rights in a time of terror.

Acknowledgements

The authors would like to thank the following centres at the University of California, Irvine for their support of this research: the Center for Citizen Peacebuilding, the Center for Global Peace and Research Studies, and the Academic Council on Research, Computing and Library Resources.

Disclosure statement

No potential conflict of interest was reported by the author.

LEGAL AND ETHICAL IMPLICATIONS OF DRONE WARFARE

Notes

1. The literature on the ethics of drones is vast. For a good overview, see Frank Sauer and Niklas Schörnig, 'Killer Drones: The "Silver Bullet" of Democratic Warfare?', *Security Dialogue* 43, no. 4 (2012): 363–80; Daniel Brunstetter and Megan Braun, 'The Implications of Drones on the Just War Tradition', *Ethics & International Affairs* 25, no. 3 (2011): 337–58; Christian Enemark, *Armed Drones and the Ethics of War: Military Virtue in a Post-Heroic Age* (New York: Routledge, 2013); James DeShaw Rae, *Analyzing the Drone Debates: Targeted Killings, Remote Warfare, and Military Technology* (New York: Palgrave Macmillan, 2014).
2. Rosa Brooks, 'Drones and the International Rule of Law', *Ethics & International Affairs* 28, no. 1 (2014): 83–103.
3. Barack Obama, 'The National Security Strategy of the United States of America', Washington DC, The White House, May 2010, 22. http://www.whitehouse.gov/sites/default/files/rss_viewer/national_security_strategy.pdf (accessed 4 November 2014).
4. Megan Braun and Daniel R Brunstetter, 'Rethinking the Criterion for Assessing CIA-Targeted Killings: Drones, Proportionality and Jus Ad Vim', *Journal of Military Ethics* 12, no. 4 (2013): 304–24.
5. Avery Plaw, 'Counting the Dead: The Proportionality of Predation in Pakistan', in *Killing by Remote Control: The Ethics of an Unmanned Military*, ed. Bradley. J. Strawser (New York: Oxford University Press, 2013), 126–53.
6. For the purposes of our analysis, we focused mainly on the following reports: Philip Alston, 'Report of the Special Rapporteur on Extrajudicial, Summary or Arbitrary Executions', *Human Rights Council* (New York: United Nations General Assembly, 2010). http://www2.ohchr.org/english/bodies/hrcouncil/docs/14session/A.HRC.14.24.Add6.pdf; Christopher Heyns, 'Report of the Special Rapporteur on Extrajudicial, Summary or Arbitrary Executions' *Human Rights Council* (New York: United Nations, 2013). http://justsecurity.org/wp-content/uploads/2013/10/UN-Special-Rapporteur-Extrajudicial-Christof-Heyns-Report-Drones.pdf; Ben Emmerson, 'Report of the Special Rapporteur on the Promotion and Protection of Human Rights and Fundamental Freedoms while Countering Terrorism', *General Assembly* (New York: United Nations, 2013). http://justsecurity.org/wp-content/uploads/2013/10/2013EmmersonSpecialRapporteurReportDrones.pdf; Human Rights Watch, 'Between a Drone and Al-Qaeda' (New York: HRW, 2013). http://www.hrw.org/node/119909/section/7; Amnesty International, 'Will I be Next? US Drone Strikes in Pakistan' (London: Amnesty International, 2013). http://www.amnestyusa.org/sites/default /files/asa330132013en.pdf; Human Rights Watch, 'A Wedding that Became a Funeral: Us Drone Attack on Marriage Procession in Yemen' (New York: HRW, 2014). http://www.hrw.org/reports/2014/02/19/wedding-became-funeral; Amnesty International, 'USA: The Devil in the (Still Undisclosed) Detail. Department of Justice "White Paper" on Use of Lethal Force against US Citizens Made Public' (Amnesty International, 2013). http://www.amnestyusa.org/sites/default/files/the_devil_in_the_still_undisclosed_detail.pdf; International Human Rights and Conflict Resolution Clinic (Stanford Law School), and Global Justice Clinic (NYU School of Law), 'Living under Drones: Death, Injury, and Trauma to Civilians from US Drone Practices in Pakistan'. http://www.livingunderdrones.org/wp-content/uploads/2013/10/Stanford-NYU-Living-Under-Drones.pdf. All reports accessed on 4 November 2014. The HRC documents also highlighted many other issues related to human rights that are beyond the scope of this article. These include the lack of: transparency of the US drone programme, a formal process for victims of drone strikes to seek justice, and access to reparations for survivors.
7. Ronald R. Krebs and Patrick Thaddeus Jackson, 'Twisting Tongues and Twisting Arms: The Power of Political Rhetoric', *European Journal of International Relations* 13, no. 1 (2007): 35–66.
8. Ibid., 36.

LEGAL AND ETHICAL IMPLICATIONS OF DRONE WARFARE

9. Neta C. Crawford, *Accountability for Killing: Moral Responsibility for Collateral Damage in America's Post-9/11 Wars* (Oxford: Oxford University Press, 2013).
10. Heynes, 'Report', 2.
11. Beth Simmons, *Mobilizing for Human Rights: International Law in Domestic Politics* (New York: Cambridge University Press, 2009).
12. James G. March and Johan P. Olsen, 'The Logic of Appropriateness', in *The Oxford Handbook of Public Policy*, ed. Michael Moran, Martin Rein, and Robert E. Goodin (New York: Oxford University Press, 2008), 689–90.
13. Anthea Roberts, 'Legality vs. Legitimacy: Can Uses of Force Be Illegal but Justified?', in *Human Rights, Intervention, and the Use of Force*, ed. Philip Alston and Euan Macdonald (New York: Oxford University Press, 2008), 179–213.
14. Presidents were aware of a moral framework – sometimes called just war theory, other times referred to as the concept of just war. For a discussion, see Daniel R. Brunstetter, 'Trends in Just War Thinking During the U.S. Presidential Debates 2000–12: Genocide Prevention and the Renewed Salience of Last Resort', *Review of International Studies* 40, no. 1 (2014): 77–99.
15. Barack Obama, 'Obama's Nobel Remarks', *The New York Times*, 11 December 2009.
16. For a discussion, see Megan Braun, 'Predator Effect: A Phenomenon Unique to the War on Terror', in *Drone Wars: Transforming Conflict, Law and Policy*, ed. Peter Bergen and Daniel Rothenberg (Cambridge: Cambridge University Press, 2014), 253–84.
17. For a discussion of Obama's use of just war principles, see Brunstetter, 'Trends in Just War Thinking', 11–16.
18. BBC Staff, 'Obama Defends US Drone Strikes in Pakistan', *BBC*, 31 January 2012. http://www.bbc.co.uk/news/world-us-canada-16804247?print=true (accessed 15 March 2012).
19. Braun and Brunstetter, 'Rethinking the Criterion', 306–10.
20. Barack Obama, 'Remarks by the President at National Defense University', 23 May 2013. http://www.whitehouse.gov/the-pressoffice/2013/05/23/remarks-president-national-defense-university (accessed 7 May 2014).
21. CNN, *Live Today*, interview with Paul Wolfowitz, 5 November 2002. http://www.defense.gov/transcripts/transcript.aspx?transcriptid=3264 (accessed 5 July 2014).
22. Howard Witt, 'U.S.: Killing of Al Qaeda Suspects Was Lawful'. http://articles.chicagotribune.com/2002-11-24/news/0211240446_1_al-qaeda-killings-terrorist (accessed 5 July 2014).
23. Doyle McManus, 'A U.S. License to Kill', *The LA Times*, 11 January 2003. http://articles.latimes.com/2003/jan/11/world/fg-predator11 (accessed 5 July 2014).
24. McManus, 'A U.S. License to Kill'.
25. George Tenet and Bill Harlow, *At the Center of the Storm: My Years at the CIA* (New York: Harper Collins, 2007), 160.
26. Greg Miller, 'Despite Apparent Success in Yemen, Risks Remain', *The LA Times*, 6 November 2002. http://articles.latimes.com/2002/nov/06/world/fg-yemen6 (accessed 5 July 2014).
27. New America Foundation, 'Drone Wars Pakistan: Analysis'. http://securitydata.newamerica.net/drones/pakistan/analysis (accessed 30 June 2014). For a discussion of the pros and cons of alternative sources for data on drone strikes, see Plaw, 'Counting the Dead', 136–7.
28. Charles W. Kegley Jr, and Gregory A. Raymond, 'Preventive War and Permissive Normative Order', *International Studies Perspectives* 4, no. 4 (2003): 390–1.
29. Michael P. Scharf, *Customary International Law in Times of Fundamental Change* (New York: Cambridge University Press, 2013), 200.
30. Ibid., 199.
31. Emphasis added, George W. Bush, 'The National Security Strategy of the United States of America' (Washington, DC: The White House, September 2002), 15.
32. Whitley Kaufman, 'What's Wrong With Preventive War? The Moral and Legal Basis for the Preventive Use of Force,' *Ethics & International Affairs* 19, no. 3 (2005): 23–38.
33. Matthew J. Flynn, *First Strike: Preemptive War in Modern History* (New York: Routledge, 2008), 3.
34. Neta C. Crawford, 'The Slippery Slope of Preventive War', *Ethics & International Affairs* 17, no. 1 (2003).
35. Not all states reject the preventive force doctrine. Other states, including Russia and Israel, have their own versions. See, for example, Ariel Colonomos, *The Gamble of War: Is it Possible to Justify Preventive War?* (New York: Palgrave Macmillan, 2013).

36. Kerstin Fisk and Jennifer M. Ramos, 'Actions Speak Louder Than Words: Preventive Self-Defense as a Cascading Norm', *International Studies Perspectives* 15, no. 2 (2014): 163–85.
37. McManus, 'A U.S. License to Kill'.
38. David Luban, 'The War on Terrorism and the End of Human Rights', *Philosophy and Public Policy Quarterly* 22, no. 3 (2002): 9–14.
39. Scott Shane, 'Secret "Kill List" Tests Obama's Principles', *The New York Times*, 29 May 2012.
40. For example, see Martin Shaw, 'Risk-Transfer Militarism, Small Massacres and the Historical Legitimacy of War', *International Relations* 16, no. 3 (2002): 343–59.
41. Michael Walzer, *Just and Unjust Wars: A Moral Argument with Historical Illustrations* (New York: Basic Books, 2006), 251–68.
42. Luban, 'War on Terrorism', 13–14.
43. Kenneth Anderson, 'Efficiency *in Bello* and *ad Bellum*: Making the Use of Force Too Easy?', in *Targeted Killings: Law and Morality in an Asymmetrical World*, ed. Claire Finkelstein, Jens David Ohlin, and Andrew Altman (Oxford: Oxford University Press, 2012), 283–4.
44. Obama, 'Remarks by the President at National Defense University'.
45. John O. Brennan, 'The Ethics and Efficacy of the President's Counterterrorism Strategy', *Wilson Center*, 30 April 2012. http://www.wilsoncenter.org/event/the efficacy-and-ethics-us-counterterrorism-strategy (accessed 15 July 2012).
46. Brennan, 'Ethics and Efficacy'; Brunstetter and Braun warn that such an argument may nullify the last resort criterion if 'the targeted killing of (alleged) terrorists becomes the default tactic', see Brunstetter and Braun, 'The Implications of Drones', 345–6; Brooks takes issue with the way the US defines 'feasibility' and 'imminence', arguing that the US understanding of these terms is very problematic. For a thorough discussion, see 'Drones and the International Rule of Law', 94–5.
47. Brennan, 'Ethics and Efficacy'.
48. There are, of course, intense scholarly debates about what the principles mean and the level of restraint they should imply. See for example the various viewpoints in Davi Rodin and Henry Shue, eds, *Just and Unjust Warriors: The Moral and Legal Status of Soldiers* (Oxford: Oxford University Press, 2008).
49. Emphasis added, Obama, 'Remarks by the President at National Defense University'.
50. Obama, 'Remarks by the President at National Defense University'; this is different from early – and patently false – claims that there had been zero civilian casualties because it speaks to future strikes, not to past strikes for which dubious counting methods were used; See Scott Shane, 'CIA is Disputed in Civilian Toll on Drone Strikes'. http://www.nytimes.com/2011/08/12/world/asia/12drones.html?pagewanted=all (accessed 2 November 2014).
51. New America Foundation, 'Drone Wars Pakistan: Analysis'.
52. Braun and Brunstetter, 'Rethinking the Criteria', 315–19.
53. New America Foundation, 'Drone Wars Pakistan: Analysis'.
54. Eric Schmitt, 'Lull in Strikes by U.S. Drones Aids Militants in Pakistan'. http://www.nytimes.com/2012/01/08/world/asia/lull-in-us-drone-strikes-aids-pakistan-militants.html?pagewanted=all&_r=0 (accessed 2 November 2014).
55. See, for example, Amnesty International, 'Will I Be Next?', 28; International Human Rights and Conflict Resolution Clinic, 'Living under Drones', 114; Alston, 'Report', 24–5.
56. The real test that such changes will be solidified lies in seeing whether unmitigated drone strikes would resume should another 9/11-type attack occur, what would happen if al-Qaeda resurge in Pakistan and Islamabad balk at taking the responsibility of dealing with the threat, or if the next US president has a completely different view of just war. We thank an anonymous review for bringing these concerns to our attention. The risk of a return to the period of signature strikes could be diminished if norms restricting drone use – whether within US institutions and/or internationally – are solidified, a point that we address later in the article.
57. International Human Rights and Conflict Resolution Clinic, 'Living under Drones', 110; See also, Alston, 'Report', 55.
58. Alston, 'Report', 3.
59. Emmerson, 'Interim Report', 19; Alston, 'Report', 107–8; International Human Rights and Conflict Resolution Clinic, 'Living under Drones', 111; Amnesty International, 'Will I Be Next', 44–6; Human Rights Watch, 'A Wedding That Became a Funeral', 22.
60. Amnesty International, 'Will I be Next?', 23.

LEGAL AND ETHICAL IMPLICATIONS OF DRONE WARFARE

61. Heyns, 'Report', 6.
62. Ibid.
63. Quoted in: International Human Rights and Conflict Resolution Clinic, 'Living under Drones', 107–8.
64. Alston, 'Report', 21–2; Amnesty International, 'Will I Be Next?', 43–4.
65. Fernando R. Tesón, 'Targeted Killing in War and Peace: A Philosophical Analysis', in *Targeted Killings: Law and Morality in an Asymmetrical World*, ed. Claire Finkelstein, Jens David Ohlin, and Andrew Altman (Oxford: Oxford University Press, 2012), 403–33.
66. 'Joint Letter to President Obama on Drones and Targeted Killings', 5 December 2013. http://www.hrw.org/news/2013/12/05/joint-letter-president-obama-drone-strikes-and-targeted-killings (accessed 15 July 2014).
67. 'Joint Letter'; for a detailed discussion of the DoJ White Paper in question, see Brooks, 'Drones and the International Rule of Law'.
68. International Committee of the Red Cross, 'Interpretive Guidance on the Notion of Direct Participation in Hostilities under International Humanitarian Law', ed. Nils Melzer (Geneva, Switzerland: International Committee of the Red Cross, 2009).
69. Alston, 'Report', 19.
70. Ibid., 20.
71. Human Rights Watch, 'A Wedding That Became a Funeral', 24.
72. See also the descriptions in: International Human Rights and Conflict Resolution Clinic 'Living Under Drones', and the congressional testimonies from the various Pakistani families, http://chrgj.org/transcripts-of-testimonies-from-may-8-congressional-hearing-on-u-s-drone-policy-now-available/ (accessed 22 July 2014).
73. Braun and Brunstetter, 'Rethinking the Criteria', 319.
74. Ibid., 315.
75. Ibid., 318.
76. Emmerson, 'Report', 23.
77. Harold Koh, 'How to End the Forever War?' http://www.lawfareblog.com/wp-content/uploads/2013/05/2013-5-7-corrected-koh-oxford-union-speech-as-delivered.pdf (accessed 20 July 2014).
78. Robert M. Hormats, 'The United States' "New Silk Road" Strategy: What is it? Where is it Headed?', U.S. Department of State. http://www.state.gov/e/rls/rmk/2011/174800.htm (accessed 1 July 2014).
79. Plaw, 'Counting the Dead', 144–50; for a counter-argument, namely that certain populations in Pakistan view drones as having had a positive effect on the quality of life, see Christine C. Fair, 'Drones over Pakistan: Menace or Best Option?', *The Huffington Post*, 2 August 2010. http://www.huffingtonpost.com/c-christine-fair/drones-over-pakistan——m_b_666721.html.

Drones to protect

David Whetham

Defence Studies Department, King's College London, UK

While the more contentious use of drones to carry out targeted killings is often focused upon, very little attention has been paid to the potential benefits that their unarmed variants can offer in preventing the mass violation of human rights in conflict areas. Drones have already been employed with some success to support UN peacekeepers. This paper looks at their use in monitoring and deterring deliberate acts of harm against civilian populations in situations where the international community is unwilling or unable to deploy a peacekeeping force on the ground. With an appropriate command, control and dissemination arrangement in place, the use of surveillance drones could provide a viable option between doing nothing and committing to full-scale military intervention. Combined with clear signalling of intent to prosecute such crimes as soon as circumstances allow, knowing that one's actions might be observed and recorded could potentially curb and restrain the perpetrators of human rights atrocities.

Rightly or wrongly, much of the public discussion about drones focuses upon negative perceptions of violations of international law or excessive collateral damage.[1] There has been much written on this subject covering the multiple angles of the debate surrounding the use of drones.[2] However, while much of the debate focuses upon their alleged role in perpetrating various types of alleged atrocities in the form of Central Intelligence Agency (CIA) targeted killing operations, very little has been written about their potential use in *preventing* violations of human rights. April 2014 marked the 20th anniversary of the beginning of the genocide in Rwanda that claimed the lives of more than 800,000 innocent men, women and children. It has been rightly described by United Nations (UN) Secretary General Ban Ki-moon as 'an epic failure' of the international community. Twenty years on, mass atrocities continue unabated in Syria, and distressingly, few lessons seem to have been learnt. While up-to-date figures are difficult to uncover, as of August 2014, an estimated 200,000 people had died over the course of the three-year civil war in Syria,[3] and according to the UN, around nine million people have been forced to leave their homes and over three million refugees have fled into neighbouring countries.[4] Experiences in Chad in 2009 suggest that surveillance drones can provide significant advantages to peacekeepers once they are deployed to an area: dramatically improving information-gathering activities near populations at risk; keeping an eye on potential arms smugglers and embargo breakers that can undermine peace efforts, and, increasing situational awareness and therefore the ability to respond quickly when people are at risk of human rights abuses.[5] Clearly, however, as this article is being submitted, there are no peacekeepers in Syria. This article will look at the use of unarmed surveillance drones to monitor and deter deliberate acts of harm against civilian populations in situations where some or all of the international community may desire to act but, for whatever reason, is unable or unwilling to deploy a peacekeeping force on the ground.

Mass human rights abuses and perceptions of impunity

Human Rights Watch has documented how the Syrian government has systematically committed war crimes as part of its battle strategy.[6] The lives of civilians in opposition-held areas are quite deliberately being targeted in the hope of turning public support against the opposition and/or forcing the population to flee from these contested areas. The Syrian military has 'dropped barrel bombs on Aleppo, used chemical weapons in the Damascus suburbs and imposed harsh sieges on rebel-held enclaves'.[7] The situation is, of course, not one-sided and while once the Syrian government appeared to have a monopoly on committing outrages against humanity, the global media is now full of the atrocities also being committed by the Islamic State in Syria (ISIS) against the civilian population and anyone who defies them.[8]

The situation is, unfortunately, hardly unique. Atrocities against civilian populations appear to be an endemic feature of many conflicts around the globe, and yet it appears extraordinarily difficult to curtail such criminal activities, whether they are systematically planned, motivated through anger, or revenge, or merely opportunistic individual acts.[9] In domestic life we know that it is the chance of being caught rather than merely the severity of the punishment that affects criminal behaviour. While the fear of being caught does not affect the behaviour of those who were not likely to commit criminal acts anyway, it can have a deterrent effect on those with a propensity to commit acts of crime.[10] For example, when trying to prevent corruption, research shows that an increase in the audit rate and/or resolute penalties by governmental agencies is a highly recommended path to reduce corruption, and this is independent of the existing culture in the country.[11] In political affairs, such thinking was, at least in part, the idea behind the creation of the International Criminal Court (ICC) – a standing organisation that does not need to be specially convened for a specific conflict, but instead stands ready to hold people to account for their actions at any time – a permanent deterrent against committing the worst crimes that humanity is capable of.[12] The ICC has had some notable successes.[13] However, having the institution to hold people to account and actually bringing people before it are two very different matters. The court requires evidence of wrong-doing and the perpetrators of war crimes all around the world know this. Getting credible evidence of wrong-doing can be extremely challenging, especially during an ongoing conflict. Without the type of oversight a robust and well-equipped peacekeeping presence can provide to monitor and record activities on the ground, there can be a belief that the perpetrators of atrocities are unlikely ever to have to answer for their actions. Even if you can catch them, getting sufficient evidence can be too hard for a realistic prosecution.

For example, commercial satellite images used by non-governmental organisations (NGOs) such as Human Rights Watch can document the damage caused by illegal aerial attacks on civilian populations, but such tools, sophisticated though they are, are very unlikely to catch perpetrators in the act, document the military unit involved and therefore eventually identify the individual flight crew involved – they can record the crime but not the criminal.[14] Given the fog of war, partiality and partisanship, getting accurate eyewitness accounts can also be a profoundly difficult task and it is often easy to dismiss such evidence as merely anecdotal or unsubstantiated by any 'hard' evidence. The environment of conflict is therefore, all too often, effectively, consequence-free.

Even well-trained militaries provide evidence of the corrosive effect a lack of oversight can have for military discipline. To take just one example from recent British military history, a Royal Marine sergeant with 15 years distinguished service was jailed for life in 2013 for executing an insurgent in Afghanistan in 2011. The insurgent had been wounded by fire from an Apache helicopter gunship and, although considered *hors de combat*, was subsequently shot in the chest at close range with a 9 mm pistol. The soldier acted in the belief that no-one else was going to know what he had done and was recorded saying words to this effect: 'Obviously this doesn't go anywhere fellas. I just broke the Geneva Convention.' The only reason the charges could be brought was because the whole incident was inadvertently captured on a camera mounted on another marine's helmet and the footage was subsequently recovered from a laptop during an investigation into an entirely unrelated matter.[15]

Despite being part of an institution that prides itself on upholding and maintaining high standards of discipline, the Royal Marine sergeant was only caught by accident.[16] What type of behaviour might one see in a less professional organisation, or even a military force that has actually explicitly been ordered to carry out attacks against a civilian population in order to ethnically cleanse an area or punish non-combatants for their alleged support for the 'wrong' side in a civil conflict if there were no fear of repercussions? This, regretfully, is where we find ourselves, all too often.

Psychologist Cris Burgess argues that 'the science of behaviour modification is a complex one and the mechanisms for this are far from perfect'.[17] The best way of challenging risk-taking behaviour is to prevent such habits being established in the first place. There would be no need to observe and record criminal behaviour from a drone if effective training and education had prevented it in the first place. This fits with some of the thinking behind the conflict prevention and capacity building work being carried out by Western governments around the world under the broad umbrella of upstream engagement, for example, see the United Kingdom's international defence engagement strategy.[18] Professional military ethics education seeks to ensure that institutions and structures are in place to help develop effective and appropriate ethical decision-making in a defence setting, but also to internalise moral behaviour so that it becomes part of one's core professional (and in some cases also personal) values.[19] The author of this article has worked with the British Military Advisory Training Team in Nigeria to introduce and develop military ethics components through the various officer training and education curricula.[20] However, training, even where it can be provided, is not going to be enough on its own, as the Royal Marine example above demonstrates.

Grasmick and Green suggest that three independent variables – moral commitment, threat of social disapproval and the perceived threat of legal punishment – appear to make up an exhaustive set of factors which inhibit illegal behaviour.[21] This reflects that people who break rules, whether those rules relate to taking bribes, speeding or perpetrating war crimes, justify their behaviour in a number of different ways.[22] Sometimes they consider that the rule is simply not justifiable in the circumstances and therefore the rule is perceived to have low legitimacy – why obey a 'reduce speed now' sign when it is obvious that the traffic queue has dispersed, or why try and apply discrimination in the use of force if this entails greater risk to your own troops? Sometimes, if a rule is frequently broken by other people it generates a feeling that the norm does not really apply or the rule-breaking behaviour is either not actually viewed seriously by other people, or is even condoned by those that are aware of it – if everyone breaks the rule, why bother to adhere to it? If everyone drives after a few beers and the police are known to turn a blind eye, why not relax and stay for just one more? If there is a culture of casual violence towards detainees and this is seen as condoned by the chain of command, it becomes 'normal', doesn't it? Furthermore, if people believe that any negative consequences for their actions are either unlikely, so far in the future as to be irrelevant, or they do not believe that other people would consider them 'bad' because of their actions (perhaps even regarding them as heroes rather than villains), the rules become far easier to flout.[23]

Aside from academic studies, which tend to focus on corruption prevention or domestic law enforcement situations,[24] the most practical contribution in the area of atrocity prevention is probably the direct experience of military personnel themselves. Interviews with serving soldiers suggest that the experience of the British training teams working with the Afghan military pre-2010 accords with the explanation of rule-breaking set out above.[25] The teams found many examples of where rules would be casually broken by their mentees if there was no fear of oversight or punishment. If the rules were not enforced, they were seen as effectively optional and therefore not adhered to, whether this was because the action was not going to be found out or, if it was, if there was a belief that there were unlikely to be repercussions from the chain of command. Thus, with reference to the variables mentioned above, this experience demonstrates how, although they might be independent, they can come together and negatively reinforce each other. If people feel they are acting in a consequence-free environment, expecting adherence to the rules seems naïve in any situation, let alone wartime. At a low level, when considering things like petty theft (or 'borrowing' items), this was actually an issue for both UK and Afghani units – thus it was seen as an imperative for British forces to adhere to expected UK standards of behaviour regardless of the environment, behaviour of indigenous allies or other challenges. It was widely understood by British commanding officers that standards needed to be enforced and be seen to be enforced – there had to be visible consequences for inappropriate actions by UK troops. The normal standards needed to be upheld even while accepting that a more relaxed standard had to be accepted from the mentees during the training process, or the environment would be corrosive to discipline and, ultimately, military effectiveness.

A solution?

What have such observations to do with preventing crimes against humanity? In the chaos and confusion of a conflict environment where large-scale abuses of the civilian population are being alleged, how could such academic notions about the psychology of rule-breaking be applied by the international community, and what has this to do with drones?

One of the key independent variables discussed above relates to perceptions about being caught. To at least some extent, it is the belief pertaining to the chance of being caught rather than merely the severity of the punishment that affects criminal behaviour. In Syria at present, but also in many other parts of the world where belligerents are deliberately targeting civilian populations, there appears to be simply no accountability at all. When the perpetrators of war crimes know this, they are effectively in a consequence-free environment. If it is accepted that this perception is, at least in part, a factor in why atrocities take place, one response would be to try and change this perception and end the feeling of being able to act with impunity. Unarmed, unmanned aerial vehicles (UAVs) with surveillance capabilities – 'flying cameras' – could be deployed under a relatively uncontroversial United Nations Security Council Resolution (UNSCR) in a matter of days or even hours to nearly anywhere on the planet to stand witness and record events on the ground as they happen. If this could be done in a suitably public way, thus deploying them with as much fanfare as possible to ensure that belligerents are aware of what is going to happen, the fear of being observed may be enough to modify behaviour.[26]

All footage showing violations of human rights could then be passed to the ICC for culpable individuals to be identified, prosecution cases to be built, and indictments handed out where possible. If actually apprehending the individual is too difficult in the middle of an ongoing conflict (as will often be the case), that does not stop individuals from being named, demonstrating that the international community is watching and that there will be a reckoning at some point. The archive data from the drones will also provide a record that can be cross-referenced with later eyewitness accounts to verify the facts and piece together events on the ground. This will hugely aid in the identification and eventual prosecution of culpable individuals even after the fact. As noted above, at the moment, satellite images are being used even by NGOs to chart scorched earth policies being perpetrated on civilian populations. How much more effective would this be if the actual perpetrators could be caught in the act, identified and, eventually, punished for their actions?

What would the potential problems be with such a course of action? The hurdles can be usefully grouped together into political, legal and military practicalities, of which the biggest of these, by far, is the political one.

Political and legal concerns

The ongoing impasse over action in Syria demonstrates that the international community is rarely, if ever, non-partisan in its decision-making. Sympathies can usually be found on all sides of a conflict and even the most heinous of regimes or non-state actors will often find powerful friends due to special interests, regional or global power politics. With all of their competing interests, could the United Nations Security Council (UNSC) ever agree on providing a flying observer mission anywhere in the world?

Perhaps the first question is, would they actually need to agree? Some have argued that sending *unarmed* drones into the sovereign airspace of a state, without the intruded-upon state's permission, does not necessarily constitute an illegal action even if it does not have a UNSC Resolution as long as: there is a severe humanitarian situation; there is a reliable basis for believing that the monitored state is committing, or is manifestly failing to protect civilians against, atrocities; there is a reasonable expectation that sending UAVs to monitor will result in the collection of useful information potentially demonstrative as to the monitored state's complicity in the alleged atrocities; and there are limits on the type and use of the information collected and upon whom may carry out these monitoring missions.[27]

However, the aspiration would be to ensure that the international community was acting together if possible, as this emphasises the social disapproval element outlined above. An international community united sends a much more powerful signal than an individual state acting as a moral guardian. One of the ways that the political situation could be smoothed is by ensuring that where there are violations and atrocities being perpetrated by multiple actors involved in a conflict, the deployment of a non-invasive UN 'observer team' in the skies would not be aimed at any specific group or actor. So, for example, if the Russians feel that this would be used against their friends in Damascus, they would be free to either offer their own capabilities, or suggest that (even insist) any observation includes specific areas, activities or actors to ensure that no specific party is unduly 'favoured'. People can and should be held accountable, regardless of the side they are fighting on, so ensuring all parties are scrutinised increases the legitimacy of the action.[28] The most effective safeguard could actually be that people *do not* trust each other, thus ensuring that scrutiny can end up being applied to all parties precisely because of the partisanship of individual actors. Indeed, unless or until the UN has its own unarmed surveillance drone capability, it would be good to encourage as many different states to offer their own unarmed flying cameras to be deployed over a conflict zone.

While they are more concerned with the lethal use of drones, Buchanan and Keohane have proposed the setting up of a Drone Accountability Regime to help ensure better compliance with the existing law and to prevent the rules being undermined through an apparent lack of accountability.[29] For various reasons, states have been reluctant to publicise the specific details of their actions when using lethal drones, especially extraterritorially. However, this can understandably fuel the impression that the rules are being flouted and the law ignored. Even if the action has been carried out with the best of intentions and impeccable reasoning based on a clear self-defence rationale and the preservation of life in the face of an imminent threat, in the absence of a credible explanation, it might as well be considered an assassination or just plain murder – there is no way for the rest of the world to tell the difference.[30] Buchanan and Keohane's intention, therefore, is to build towards a situation where a trusted, impartial ombudsman can review the legal justification for an attack and has the right to hold actors to a standard and judge whether they have fulfilled their responsibilities. While conceived for a different context, such a regime, if expanded to cover observer missions of the type this article is concerned with, might address many of the political problems with deploying drones to monitor and prevent human rights abuses.

Even if the coordination of the surveillance evidence cannot be done using a central UN observer team or 'observer ombudsman' due to national asset caveats, etc., from a deterrence point of view, the potential perpetrators on the ground do not know if they are being observed at any given moment, or if they are, which national flag is 'on' the asset doing the observing. Therefore, the deterrent effect remains. Could intelligence from these unarmed observers be passed onto belligerent parties to provide military advantage? Of course this is a factor to take into account, but one would be naïve to think that activities on the ground in Syria, for example, are not currently being observed by various interested parties who may or may not be passing that information on already. This option just tries to ensure that the presence is publically acknowledged and harnessed for a more humanitarian end.

Could the violation of sovereignty demonstrated by the presence of surveillance drones ever be acceptable to the government of the country over which they were operating? It may be possible that a government who is nominally in charge of a territory and is accused of atrocities can be persuaded that such an observer mission is in their interests to permit under a Chapter Six Peacekeeping Resolution. Governments are keen to try and explain how their actions are necessary and proportionate to the risk faced by the state. Opening themselves to scrutiny by the UN would go a long way to convincing the world that they have nothing to hide and that it is indeed the 'other side' that is responsible for the atrocities that the international community is so concerned about. Such an even-handed approach would keep any observer mission true to the core ideas of the UN. However, if the government cannot be persuaded by their remaining friends that this would be in their own interests, precisely because the observation would be impartial and very limited in the sense that it is purely an unarmed observation presence, it might be possible to get sufficient support on the Security Council to secure a Resolution under Chapter Seven, providing authority to deploy the surveillance mission even without host government support. In the case of a failed state, the political situation is less problematic as there are already precedents where the Security Council's permanent members, who are normally wary of perceived threats to sovereignty, have been persuaded to act. For example, in the case of Somalia, the wording of UNSCR 794 referring to the 'unique character of the present situation', meant that China could support the international action due to the absence of a functioning government at the time.[31]

One of the problems of international action in the face of a humanitarian crisis is the perception of the cost for those wanting to help. As the UN does not have a standing force, it is always up to member states to offer assets, personnel and material as well as financial support if the UN is ever to do more than talk about problems. The political cost of action is seen by some analysts to have been significantly lowered by the new stand-off capabilities offered by drones.[32] There is no risk of friendly troops coming home in body bags, undermining public support for the mission, so politicians can more freely commit to interventions. While this has been referred to as a problem in terms of lowering the bar to the resort to force in international affairs, in the case of unarmed humanitarian missions, the lowering of such political costs can be seen as a huge positive.

Information gathering itself is clearly a sensitive issue, and fears about aerial surveillance have contributed (along with the general negative connotations about the way their armed variants have been employed) to an apparent reluctance to consider observation drones as part of humanitarian missions. Indeed, one can imagine that rather than reducing anxiety, a civilian population may become even more anxious if they are unable to tell the difference between an observation drone sent to protect them and a hostile, armed platform sent to kill them. One solution may be to ensure that civilian UAVs could be painted in 'bright colours to distinguish them from military vehicles'.[33] Clearly, different types of harm need to be carefully balanced. However, at a time when Western governments find themselves having to justify surveillance policies upon their own populations, intercepting and analysing the communications of millions of people not suspected of any wrongdoing around the world,[34] it seems ironic that it might be difficult to get a political consensus on using a far less contentious form of surveillance to monitor and prevent gross human rights abuses around the world.

Military practicalities

What about the military practicalities? The risk of losing platforms is obviously high. Unmanned flying cameras may be vulnerable to anti-aircraft fire, air-to-air systems and ground-based missiles. However, precisely because these platforms would be unmanned, most of the problems associated with a military deployment are removed. One of the objections to deploying UN observation teams on the ground is that their safety in such situations cannot be secured – they are simply at too much risk. However, an unmanned aerial camera does not need protecting in the same way. It is possible to deploy systems with increased survivability (from stealth characteristics, ultra-high flight paths through to anti-missile protection systems), but these high-end capabilities are expensive and often jealously guarded assets by governments who do not wish to tip their hand to other parties about their potential capabilities. An alternative path (or indeed, parallel one) is to deploy cheap systems with little protection apart from their very numbers. When viewed in terms of military budgets, while there are extremely expensive unmanned platforms that rival their manned alternatives for cost and sophistication, unmanned platforms can be extremely cheap, almost disposable. No-one is going to mourn the loss of a flying camera, so there is no sapping of political will if they are lost, and in financial terms, for the cost of one cruise-missile, any state could buy a large number of basic flying cameras as an off-the-shelf capability. Indeed, for around $1000, the North Koreans have demonstrated that they can build a drone with a functioning (though limited) camera and fly it through some of the most heavily monitored airspace in the world between two countries that are still technically at war.[35] Imagine what a slightly larger budget per asset with real-time transmitting cameras, deployed *en mass* could achieve over the skies of Syria or any other area in which crimes against the civilian population are being alleged. Apart from buying cheap, off-the-shelf equipment, states can also suddenly find a use for otherwise obsolete kit that has been superseded by more impressive technology in a state's inventory.

If there is a geographic area in which the flying cameras are apparently suffering a particularly high attrition rate, this is precisely where more cameras should be sent. Obviously this represents a place that people on the ground do not wish to have scrutinised. Thus, trying to counter the aerial observers may well backfire on the perpetrators of war crimes. This could obviously be backed-up with footage from spy satellites or higher-end unarmed drone capabilities with better survivability by those states with this option at their disposal. The balance between what capabilities were deployed would be up to the international community and those who were willing to offer their capabilities.

One of the objections to this policy suggestion is that having aerial observation might simply displace activity to areas that cannot be monitored, driving atrocities underground. This is a valid point, but is also one that is hardly unique to using drones to monitor and deter atrocities. Observers on the ground are much easier to keep track of and avoid than an unseen aerial presence. Moving large-scale human rights abuses 'indoors' to where they cannot be recorded is not necessarily easy. Even where such facilities do exist, it should still be possible to cross-reference and match large-scale movements of vehicles or even specific individuals entering or leaving covered buildings to eye-witness accounts that may emerge later on, making it easier to document, build cases and eventually hold people accountable. The capabilities of surveillance drones can also be very impressive. For example, in 2013 the UNSC granted the Department of Peacekeeping Operations (DPKO) permission to bring in surveillance drones to support United Nations Organization Stabilization Mission in the Democratic Republic of the Congo (MONUSCO) in the Democratic Republic of Congo. These drones were 'equipped with infrared technology that can detect troops hidden beneath forest canopy or operating at night, allowing them to track movements of armed militias, assist patrols heading into hostile territory, and document atrocities'.[36] Making people aware that they can be seen wherever they are goes against normal surveillance practice where the idea is to watch without the subject being aware. In this case, for deterrence of criminal behaviour to occur, it is necessary to make people aware of the potential capabilities of those doing the watching so they understand that they can be caught.[37]

The capabilities of observation drones are not limited to just aerial video surveillance either. For example, the technology already exists so that they can be fitted with sensors to detect when chemical or biological agents are being deployed in an area. A long-wave infrared hyperspectral sensor, fitted to an unmanned platform, would be able to monitor a large area and identify threatening substances or gasses even before they are used in anger.[38] Real-time analysis of the data would mean that those who deploy illegal weapons could potentially be traced very quickly, allowing other assets to be deployed and evidence to be collected and cross-referenced. If deemed prudent, warnings can be issued if the international community becomes aware of the movement of such weapons before they are actually deployed so those responsible understand that they are being monitored and will not be able to act with impunity.

Of course, it is possible that things can go wrong. For example, in 2006, Belgian peacekeepers deployed reconnaissance drones in Congo as part of the 1500-strong European Union deployment supporting the 17,500 UN presence there. One drone was shot down, but another crashed on take-off killing one person and injuring two others.[39] This tragic accident led to the end of that particular drone deployment, but it also highlights the unintended effects of operating very large pieces of military hardware over the heads of a local population – a Reaper (an armed drone – therefore not the type of platform being advocated here but indicative of the potential size) has a 20-metre wingspan and weighs several thousand kilogrammes whether armed or not – clearly a significant amount of damage can occur if one is brought down into a civilian area, whether through accident or design. Much like the problem of unintended casualties on the ground when aid is being delivered from the air, it is obviously extremely distressing when an action intended to save life results in harming it instead. However, as long as appropriate safeguards and procedures are in place, such as carefully considering flight paths, etc., wherever possible, the benefits of trying to help surely outweigh the potential harm that such help may end up unintentionally causing. Unless one can demonstrate negligence or malicious intent, it does not seem appropriate to sue the doctor over the bruises sustained during life-saving CPR treatment. Transparency when something goes wrong is probably one of the best mitigation strategies that can be adopted.

Conclusion

At the moment, in too many parts of the world, there is simply no adverse consequences for those carrying out deliberate attacks against civilian populations. Deterrence is a simple concept – human decision-making is driven by an awareness of the consequence of our actions. We refrain from taking actions that we believe will have adverse consequences outweighing any potential gains. Deterrence is about exploiting this to influence others, in this case, to prevent the carrying out of atrocities. Deploying surveillance drones to monitor and deter atrocities is only ever going to be a small part of any solution. The best way to prevent militaries from carrying out mass atrocities is to concentrate on maintaining peace and making sure that conflict remains in the political rather than military sphere of activity. When this fails, developing and promoting professional behaviours – the capacity building that Western states involve themselves in around the world – can be seen as part of just such a prevention strategy. If all of that fails, we are left with deterrence of bad behaviour. Instilling a belief that people can be held accountable for their actions is part of that deterrence.

Making it clear from the start that holding people to account for serious abuses (on whatever side they occur) must be central to any transition plan towards a post-conflict settlement and is a key ingredient for a meaningful and durable peace wherever interethnic, political or religious conflict is endemic. In Syria and elsewhere, the ICC will investigate crimes on all sides. Rather than waiting for observers on the ground to be committed to begin the case-building process, evidence gathering by the international community can and should be started at the earliest opportunity – this will no doubt be happening anyway, but committing drones to the task sends a powerful and visible message. Such a public, international response would also put commanders and political leaders on notice that they can be held responsible for the atrocities that they commit.

With eyes now firmly moving towards events in the Ukraine and the UN Security Council likely to be deadlocked over any concerted action where there is a national interest involved, the chances of any new peacekeeping missions being authorised right now are slim. This also makes it highly unlikely in the current political climate that even a relatively uncontroversial deployment of unarmed 'flying cameras' could be deployed to stand witness and record events on the ground. However, the political situation will inevitably change, making such actions possible again. If there are no obvious vital interests at stake for the UN's veto-wielding powers, this could be sooner rather than later. In such circumstances, this option could and should be considered at a much earlier stage of a future conflict. The fact that for such an option to be most effective, multiple countries would need to offer up the capability and be involved with the monitoring of all parties to a conflict might even offer the type of collaborative enterprise that builds badly needed diplomatic bridges.

If a person or group is in a consequence-free environment, they are likely to act in a different way than if there is a chance of being seen and punished for their crimes. Bringing people to account for their actions will not be easy, but at the moment, the international community is often in the position of doing nothing because none of the potential options are seen as militarily viable or politically palatable. Rethinking the use of surveillance drones in such situations would provide a viable option to the international community in such situations, in between doing nothing but condemning from afar and committing to full-scale military intervention. Simply knowing that one's actions *might* be observed and recorded by eyes in the sky could potentially curb and restrain perpetrators of human rights atrocities. That potential chance is more than enough to justify trying this low-cost, non-invasive option on behalf of the international community.

Acknowledgements

This article is based on the ideas set out by B.J. Strawser and D. Whetham, 'Eyes Over Syria: Using Drones to Monitor Atrocities', *RUSI Analysis*, 27 August 2013.

Disclosure statement

No potential conflict of interest was reported by the author.

Notes

1. David Whetham, 'Drones: the Moral Ups and Downs', *Journal of the Royal United Services Institute* (June 2013).
2. For example, B. Medea, *Drone Warfare: Killing By Remote Control* (London: Verso Books, 2013); B.J. Strawser, *Killing By Remote Control: The Ethics of an Unmanned Military* (Oxford: Oxford University Press, 2013).
3. Neil MacLucas, 'U.N. Says Syria Deaths Near 200,000', *Wall Street Journal*, 22 August 2014. http://online.wsj.com/articles/u-n-says-syria-deaths-near-200-000-1408697916

LEGAL AND ETHICAL IMPLICATIONS OF DRONE WARFARE

4. United Nations High Commission for Refugees, *Syria Regional Refugee Response*, November 16, 2014. http://data.unhcr.org/syrianrefugees/regional.php

5. J. Karlsrud and F. Rosén, 'In the Eye of the Beholder? The UN and the Use of Drones to Protect Civilians', *Stability: International Journal of Security & Development* 2, no. 2 (2013): 27, 1–10. DOI: http://dx.doi.org/10.5334/sta.bo

6. Human Rights Watch, 2011–14, *Human Rights in Syria*. https://www.hrw.org/middle-eastn-africa/syria

7. Ibid.

8. David Williams and Tania Steere, 'Lined Up and Executed, Their Severed Heads Put on Display as a Warning to Others: Horrific New Photographs of ISIS Atrocities', *Mail Online*, 8 August 2014. http://www.dailymail.co.uk/news/article-2719991/Horrific-new-photographs-ISIS-atrocities-prompted-Obama-act.html#ixzz3JFub32sd

9. Paolo Tripodi, 'Understanding Atrocities: What Commanders Can Do to Prevent Them', in *Ethics, Law and Military Operations*, ed. David Whetham (Basingstoke: Palgrave, 2010), 175.

10. Per-Olof H. Wikström, Andromachi Tseloni, and Dimitris Karlis, 'Do People Comply With the Law Because They Fear Getting Caught?', *European Journal of Criminology* 8 (September 2011): 401–20.

11. B.A. Olken, 'Monitoring Corruption: Evidence from a Field Experiment in Indonesia', *Journal of Political Economy* 115 (2007): 200–49.

12. One can see this intention 'to put an end to impunity for the perpetrators of these crimes and thus to contribute to the prevention of such crimes' declared in the preamble to the Rome Statute of the ICC. See http://www.icc-cpi.int/iccdocs/PIDS/publications/RomeStatutEng.pdf

13. For example, see Matt Steinglass, 'Lubanga Sentence Sets Legal Deterrent', *The Financial Times*, 10 July 2012. http://www.ft.com/cms/s/0/5c3ec040-cab1-11e1-89be-00144feabdc0.html#axzz3JGu3IuZ5. Reputational issues mean that actors who wish to govern post conflict may be induced to moderate their behaviour through a fear of indictment. See BA Simmons and AM Danner, 'Credible Commitments and the International Criminal Court', *International Organization* 64 (2010): 2.

14. Human Rights Watch, *Sudan: Satellite Images Confirm Villages Destroyed*, 18 June 2013. http://www.hrw.org/news/2013/06/18/sudan-satellite-images-confirm-villages-destroyed

15. BBC News, 'Marine Guilty of Afghanistan Murder', 8 November 2013. http://www.bbc.co.uk/news/uk-24870699

16. The role of misplaced peer-to-peer loyalty in such situations is explored in Stephen Coleman, *Military Ethics: An Introduction with Case Studies* (Oxford: Oxford University Press, 2012), Chapter 3.

17. Cris Burgess, *Risk-Taking Behaviour* (unpublished 2002).

18. Ministry of Defence, *International Defence Engagement Strategy*, 2013. https://www.gov.uk/government/publications/international-defence-engagement-strategy

19. Paul Robinson, Nigel de Lee, and Don Carrick, eds., *Ethics Education in the Military* (Aldershot: Ashgate, 2008).

20. See David Whetham, 'Expeditionary Military Ethics', in *Handbook of Military Ethics*, ed. George R. Lucas (Abingdon: Routledge, forthcoming 2015).

21. H.G. Grasmick, and D.E. Green, 'Legal Punishment, Social Disapproval and Internalization as Inhibitors of Illegal Behavior', *Journal of Criminal Law and Criminology* 71 (1980): 4.

22. M. Verkuyten, *Why Do People Follow (Formal) Rules?* (Rotterdam: Erasmus University, 1992).

23. Burgess, *Risk-Taking Behaviour*.

24. Verkuyten, *Why Do People Follow (Formal) Rules?*, 3.

25. D. Whetham, interviews with Organisation, Mentoring and Liaison Team members from Afghanistan (2010).

26. The link between knowledge of being observed and behaviour modification is not straightforward. In terms of CCTV and recorded changes in criminal behaviour, see Coretta Phillips, 'A Review of CCTV Evaluations', *Crime Prevention Studies*, Vol.10, ed. Kate Painter and Nick Tilley (Monsey, NY: Criminal Justice Press, 1999), 123–55.

27. Diana E. Schaffner, 'The Legality of Using Drones to Unilaterally Monitor Atrocity Crimes', *Fordham International Law Journal*, 35, No. 4 (2012): 1125.

28. See *Jus Post Bellum* in Whetham, *Ethics, Law and Military Operations*, 83.

29. Allen Buchanan and Robert O. Keohane, 'Toward a Drone Accountability Regime', *Ethics and International Affairs* (forthcoming, Spring 2015).

30. D. Whetham, 'Drones and Targeted Killing: Angels or Assassins?', in *Killing by Remote Control: The Ethics of an Unmanned Military*, ed. B.J. Strawser (Oxford: Oxford University Press, 2013), 135.
31. Jonathan E. Davis, 'From Ideology to Pragmatism: China's Position on Humanitarian Intervention in the Post-Cold War Era', *Vanderbilt Journal of Transnational Law*, 44, no. 2 (2011): 232.
32. David Whetham, 'Drones: the Moral Ups and Downs', *Journal of the Royal United Services Institute* (June 2013): 28.
33. This is a point acknowledged in United Nations Office for the Coordination of Humanitarian Affairs, *Unmanned Aerial Vehicles in Humanitarian Response* (OCHA Policy and Studies Series, June 2014), 11.
34. Human Rights Watch, *The Right Whose Time Has Come (Again)*, 2014. http://www.hrw.org/world-report/2014/essays/privacy-in-age-of-surveillance
35. Hyung-Jin Kim, 'Suspected North Korean Drones Reflect New Threat', *Huffington Post*, 4 April 2014. http://www.huffingtonpost.com/2014/04/04/north-korean-drones_n_5090150.html
36. C. Lynch, 'U.N. Wants to Use Drones for Peacekeeping Missions', 2013. http://www.washingtonpost.com/world/national-security/un-seeks-drones-for-peacekeeping-missions/2013/01/08/39575660-599e-11e2-88d0-c4cf65c3ad15_story.html
37. This may be part of the political calculation in the publicity surrounding the deployment of observation drones to the Ukraine by the Organisation for Security and Cooperation in Europe. See Jason Hovet and Jan Lopatka, 'OSCE Says Will Use Drones for Ceasefire Monitoring in Ukraine', *Reuters*, 10 September 2014. http://www.reuters.com/article/2014/09/10/us-ukraine-crisis-osce-idUSKBN0H50Q920140910
38. 'Exelis Demonstrates Detection Capabilities of New LWIR HIS Airborne Sensor', *Unmanned Systems Technology*, 14 May 2014. http://www.unmannedsystemstechnology.com/2014/05/exelis-demonstrates-detection-capabilities-of-new-lwir-hsi-airborne-sensor/
39. E. Isango, 'Drone Crash in Congo Kills 1, Injures 2', *Washington Post*, 3 October 2006. http://www.washingtonpost.com/wp-dyn/content/article/2006/10/03/AR2006100300778.html

Virtuous drones?

Caroline Kennedy and James I. Rogers

School of Politics, Philosophy and International Studies, University of Hull, UK

The use of drones in recent conflicts by Western states has proved controversial. Obama's 'kill list' and the use of remote 'execution' have inspired passionate debates about the ethics and use of these systems. Proponents of their use highlight their alleged 'precision' and make the point that such weapons may prevent the necessity for 'boots on the ground'; at least in certain contexts. In this article we wish to build on the idea of drones as both useful but also perhaps as 'virtuous'. We do not make this case for the universal deployment of drones but rather for the specific case of United Nations peacekeeping missions.

The use of drones is, as commonly recognised, increasing. The capacity of such technology to be ever more precise in targeting the enemy is often lauded, as in Kenneth Anderson's claim that 'drones are a major step forward towards much more discriminating use of violence in war and self-defence – a step forward in humanitarian technology'.[1] An additional and related argument, widely used by the Obama administration, is that drones provide a massive step up in intelligence capability, perhaps negating the use of human intelligence gathered at some risk in hostile environments with complex and persistent tribal rivalries. (This has been an argument for the widespread use of drones in Yemen since March 2012 for example, but also for intelligence gathering on Iran's nuclear progress.) Added to this is the pragmatic issue of cost. A Predator might cost around $4.5 million while a fighter jet around $150 million. Drones seem to provide value for money. However as P.W. Singer quite rightly emphasises, 'the introduction of unmanned systems to the battlefield doesn't change simply how we fight, but for the first time changes who fights at the most fundamental level. *It transforms the very agent of war, rather than just its capabilities*' [emphasis added].[2] This matters in the current context because the 'ethical character of war' has depended upon the sense that it is human beings that fight. This is important for a number of reasons. Those who sacrifice or are sacrificed in the service of the state bring a range of emotions to the activity of war and conflict. There are profound reasons as to why law, ethics and moral debate characterise soldiering and the taking of enemy lives. Indeed one could argue that since 1945, attempts at regulating the business of war, the primacy placed on war avoidance and an emphasis on universal human rights have all entered popular and scholarly narratives. The debate in the United Kingdom (UK) for example over the genesis of the Iraq War in 2003 demonstrates that popular feeling requires explanation not only for the deployment of men and machines into conflict but justification for the conduct of those conflicts. Consider the debate (for example) over the extent to which militaries should be allowed to prioritise the defence of their own soldiers against damage to a civilian population (a debate which was central to discussion over the actions of the Israeli defence forces against Hezbollah in 2006, but which was also central to NATO (North Atlantic Treaty Organisations) strategy in the war over Kosovo in 1999 and British actions in Afghanistan). Whatever position one takes on this it is clear that the relevant criterion is thinking about the importance of one set of human beings in conflict against another set. The very crass (and one is afraid to say, all too predictable) use of the terms 'bug splat' or 'whack-a-mole' to denote the killing of a 'terrorist' by drone strike obviously dehumanises those killed, and is clearly meant to achieve the idea that the enemy needs and deserves eradication without trial or observance of the rule of law. A disquieting assumption indeed.

It will be said, of course, that the benefits of drone technology are such as to render such philosophical or public objections null and void. Drones in so many ways can reduce the risks of conflict for liberal states which, after more than a decade of the 9/11 wars and the generally recognised failure of Counterinsurgency (COIN), understandably would rather use drones than boots on the ground.[3] Indeed, the argument that drone use saves a need to risk soldiers, or indeed civilians, in messy COIN activities seems compelling. So there are a series of serious justifications (as well as politically useful ones) for the increasing use of drones in contemporary zones of conflict and contention. After all, if the practise of lethal force for what we presumably think of as justified and legitimate goals is ongoing, we surely want our practice to be as effective and efficient as we can make it – and drones it would appear, help to do that. However (although related to notions of improving effectiveness and the ability to mitigate the loss of life through drone use) our argument here is set in a rather different context.

Specifically we look at United Nations (UN) missions in zones of conflict. While we are not naïve enough to believe that UN missions are always value neutral, a point we go on to discuss, we do argue that they may provide a different case for consideration in the debate on drones. Peacekeepers are after all not just drawn from liberal states, do not 'slaughter' or target civilians but have as their mission the sanctity of civilians however often that objective may prove to be illusory.[4] So, the argument here is that drones may even in complex and contested arenas be seen as 'virtuous'. Our use of 'virtue' is not entirely playful but reflects the idea that drones may be put to 'morally excellent' purposes in the service of the UN for the purpose of peacekeeping.

Peacekeeping

In 2009 it was declared that UN peacekeeping was 'at a crossroads' in regard to the 'future form of its missions'.[5] From policy development and capability development, to global field support and planning, critical shortages were identified as being 'manifest across many missions'.[6] These shortages continue. In the Department of Peacekeeping Operations (DPKO) and Department of Field Support (DFS)'s progress report (2011), it was stated that although some improvements had been made, there are a number of 'ongoing challenges associated with the growth in complexity and scale of United Nations peacekeeping and the continued impact of external resource and political developments'.[7] In short UN peacekeeping is overstretched. As a consequence, underperformance in 'providing security and protection in response to conflict' is an all too common occurrence.[8] The lack of vital resources, such as military helicopters, is one such example.

In regions where poor transport infrastructure and difficult terrains are a perennial challenge, these vehicles are a vital resource for the 'fulfilment of the civilian protection mandate'.[9] Without helicopters, UN personnel have little support on the ground and effectively no intelligence from the air. Deficiencies such as this contribute to failures in UN mandate fulfilment. This was evident in 2012 when a detachment of peacekeepers as part of the UN Stabilisation Mission in the DR Congo (MONUSCO) was expected to halt an army of M23 rebels – who had rapidly grown 'much stronger in size and capability' – from taking the city of Goma.[10] In this case, the peacekeepers made a 'value judgement' and chose not to engage precisely because of the shortages in equipment and personnel.[11] Such inaction led to the peacekeepers being labelled as 'les touristes' by the local population.[12] In response, the French Foreign Minister Laurent Fabius stated that it was 'absurd'[13] that the UN force did not have the necessary means, such as helicopter assistance, to defend Goma – a city of over one million people – from the rebels who committed 'human rights violations'.[14] This argument is surely compelling if the expectation is, unlike in Srebrenica, that peacekeepers should protect the population.

It is probable that if helicopters had been readily available (along with a robust political will), the rapid deployment of reinforcements could have taken place, and air support (in its various forms) would have been at hand to combat some of the human rights abuse. This view was reinforced in the 2010 'Report of the Secretary-General', which stated that:

> two of our missions, the United Nations Mission in the Central African Republic and Chad, and the African Union-United Nations Hybrid Operation in Darfur (UNAMID), are completing their deployments under difficult circumstances. Together with the United Nations Organization Mission in the Democratic Republic of the Congo (MONUC) [renamed MONUSCO] and the United Nations Mission in the Sudan (UNMIS), they also continue to lack key capabilities, in particular aviation assets, to enable full implementation of their mandates. Such shortages are especially critical since their mandates require peacekeepers to act rapidly and in a robust fashion across vast areas to implement critical tasks such as the protection of civilians.[15]

However, despite the report, critical shortages in equipment remain in many peacekeeping missions. Shortages increase the challenges and decrease the effectiveness of the DPKO as it attempts to fulfil proscribed mandates and protect civilians. One suggestion to combat these deficiencies is the introduction of unmanned drones. This is a relatively cheap option accounting for up to 50% of the cost of helicopter systems (even more so when the cost of training personnel to man these aircraft is taken into account).[16] As the Under-Secretary-General for Peacekeeping Operations Hervé Ladsous stated, the 'use of such drones during the recent crisis ... would have enhanced the capability ... to protect civilians by preventing violence and displacements'.[17] This in itself seems compelling. Yet there are concerns about the use of drones and the relationship to civilian populations. (The prevailing public perception of drones as a 'scourge targeting innocent civilians' remains prevalent.[18]) These concerns are addressed by the article in its final section. However, before we move into the labyrinth of drone related concerns, let us highlight the challenges to UN effectiveness which may, we suggest, be mitigated through a use of drones. Let us start with the fact that peacekeepers die in the service of the UN. This may seem unremarkable in itself but the recent trends should give us pause for thought.

Fatalities

UN peacekeeping is a dangerous business and has become increasingly so. Since its conception in 1948, peacekeeping missions have resulted in the death of 3250 peacekeepers.[19]

As can be seen in Figure 1, these fatalities range from malicious acts which account for 826, or 25%, of all fatalities, accidents which are responsible for 1229, or 38%, and illnesses which make up 1002, or 31%, of fatalities. The final 6% is accounted for under the category of 'other'. Such figures are interesting, especially when the illness and malicious acts categories are broken down into the trends which have characterised the proceeding seven decades.

In regard to illness, as Figure 2a and Figure 2b indicate, it is only over the last two decades that this category has become a prominent driver of peacekeeping fatalities. Specifically, in Figure 2a it is clear that during the first five decades of UN peacekeeping missions, between 1948 and 1988, illness was responsible for 139 out of 1002, or 18%, of all UN peacekeeping fatalities. This figure is relatively small when compared to the data highlighted in Figure 2b, where it can be seen that between 1989 and 2014 illness was responsible for 863 out of 2456, or 35%, of fatalities. Such an increase has been largely ascribed to inadequate training, but also to the fact that peacekeepers are increasingly deployed to regions of 'high-risk' endemic illnesses.

Specifically, malaria is a 'killer'. As volume two of the UN Infantry Battalion Manual (2012) warns, 'one of the most threatening insects encountered by peacekeepers is the mosquito which carries malaria'.[20]

As Figure 3 outlines, the deployment of UN peacekeepers within UNAMID, MONUSCO, the United Nations Mission in Liberia (UNMIL) and the United Nations Operation in Côte d'Ivoire (UNOCI), has resulted in a rise in the amount of peacekeepers that die of illness. Whilst deployed as part of UNMIL 80% of UN peacekeeper fatalities were due to illness, with 69% in UNAMID, 50% in UNOCI and 67% whilst on deployment as part of the MONUSCO mission. Of course, the fact that these nations are all classified as endemically malarial is no coincidence.[21] In theory, it should be relatively simple to safeguard peacekeepers against this threat. Although there is no vaccine, peacekeepers should take 'anti-malarial tablets' called malaria prophylaxis, they should wear 'clothing over legs and arms and liberally use insect repellent', avoid 'setting up camp locations near insect/arthropod breeding areas' and properly 'use mosquito bed nets when sleeping'.[22] In reality, lapses in standardised training across all UN contributing nations inhibits the level of peacekeeper compliance to these simple measures.

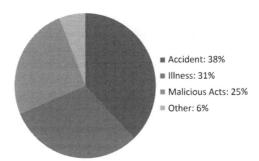

Figure 1. Percentage of UN peacekeeping fatalities 1948–2014. http://www.un.org/en/peacekeeping/fatalities/documents/stats_4a.pdf
Source: Self-generated graph. Data retrieved from Department of Peacekeeping Operations, *Fatalities by Mission, Year and Incident Type*, 2014.

LEGAL AND ETHICAL IMPLICATIONS OF DRONE WARFARE

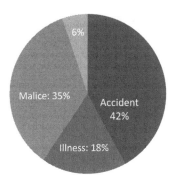

Figure 2a. Percentage of UN peacekeeping fatalities 1948–1988. http://www.un.org/en/peacekeeping/fatalities/documents/stats_4a.pdf
Source: Self-generated graph. Data retrieved from Department of Peacekeeping Operations, *Fatalities by Mission, Year and Incident Type*, 2014.

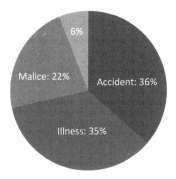

Figure 2b. Percentage of UN peacekeeping fatalities 1989–2014 http://www.un.org/en/peacekeeping/fatalities/documents/stats_4a.pdf
Source: Self-generated graph. Data retrieved from Department of Peacekeeping Operations, *Fatalities by Mission, Year and Incident Type*, 2014.

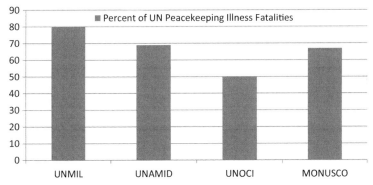

Figure 3. Percentage of UN peacekeeping fatalities caused through illness within UNMIL, UNAMID, UNOCI and MONUSO in 2014. http://www.un.org/en/peacekeeping/fatalities/documents/stats_4a.pdf
Source: Self-generated graph. Data retrieved from Department of Peacekeeping Operations, *Fatalities by Mission, Year and Incident Type*, 2014.

As Dorn's 2008 research into UN peacekeeper fatalities highlighted, the 'overall fatality rate for [peacekeepers from the] developing world [is] 77 per cent higher than for the developed world, mostly on account of illness. With almost 90% of the troops in the field drawn from the developing world, the UN may be wise to directly address the issue of illness.'[23] Such figures indicate inadequate levels of peacekeeper training. This leads to 'a general lack of awareness'[24] of the disease amongst peacekeepers, resulting in thousands falling victim.[25] (Facts which highlight the increasing ineffectiveness and resultant vulnerability of peacekeepers in these high-risk regions.) So one 'virtue' of drones would be to reduce the number of ground-based monitoring, observing, reporting and peace enforcement personnel needed in high-risk regions. Drone deployment would reduce threats to life and arguably improve the effectiveness of the mission. Yet this is not the only case for the deployment of drones. It is the case that UN peacekeepers are consistently the target of 'malice' or malicious acts.

Malicious acts

Within the 2009 'Implementation of the Recommendations of the Special Committee on Peacekeeping Operations' report, it was stated that:

> [S]afety and security of personnel in the field is an ever present and growing concern. Challenging security environments in places like Afghanistan and Darfur hamper the ability of the United Nations to deliver on its mandates. Globally, the nature of the security threats has changed and attacks on the United Nations have increased. International organized crime and local banditry, including kidnappings of national and international staff, are also part of this new threat picture. Recent attacks in Kabul and Darfur are examples, among many, of how United Nations personnel in the field have increasingly become the direct target of lethal attacks.[26]

The consistent risk of 'malice' is obvious when the data on UN peacekeeping fatalities is studied.

As Figure 2a and Figure 4a highlight, over the first five decades of UN peacekeeping the average number of UN peacekeepers killed as a result of malice was higher than that of the following two decades, averaging 35%. However, as Figure 4a shows, between 1948 and

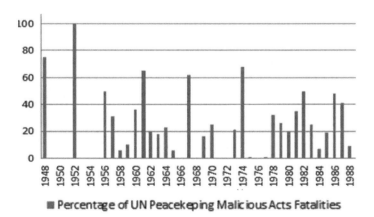

Figure 4a. Percentage of UN peacekeeping malicious acts fatalities between 1948 and 1988. http://www.un.org/en/peacekeeping/fatalities/documents/stats_4a.pdf
Source: Self-generated graph. Data retrieved from Department of Peacekeeping Operations, *Fatalities by Mission, Year and Incident Type*, 2014.

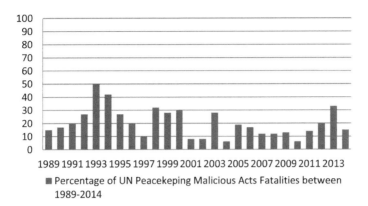

Figure 4b. Percentage of UN peacekeping malicious acts fatalities between 1989 and 2014 http://www.un.org/en/peacekeeping/fatalities/documents/stats_4a.pdf
Source: Self-generated graph. Data retrieved from Department of Peacekeeping Operations, *Fatalities by Mission, Year and Incident Type*, 2014.

1988 there were no clear trends formed in regard to the average amount of malicious acts fatalities. Instead, erratic peaks and troughs were evident throughout this period. This is in contrast to the period between 1989 and 2014, as displayed in Figure 4b. Here a clear and consistent trend, with comparatively few peak and troughs, can be distinguished. Specifically, this period levels out at a consistent 22% of peacekeepers killed as a result of malice over this period. We believe that this sustained level of 'malice' from 1989 onwards can help us put into context the nature of the current threat from malicious acts. This information may help us understand the threats and perhaps lead to a clearer understanding of risks on the ground.[27]

According to SIPRI, after 1989 fewer armed conflicts took place, with state war in steady decline.[28] Those wars that did take place were civil wars fought within weak or failing states. These conflicts were bloody and simmering and in some ways far more challenging for external actors. According to some scholars these conflicts had novel and bloody characteristics. So-called 'new wars', as Mary Kaldor labelled them, displayed a disturbing mix of endemic violence fuelled by powerful forces of globalisation.[29] The wars of the 1990s were often inconclusive, were quite often based around identity and were characterised by raids and massacres rather than set-piece confrontations. Any understanding of war as a continuation of politics by other means was arguably irrelevant in the midst of internalised and chaotic confrontations. Although increasingly scholars recognised the local and regional economic and political logic of such conflicts.

Civilian casualties have always formed part of war but by the end of the twentieth century, civilians as opposed to regular troops were, according to many scholars, bearing the brunt of conflict.[30] Although the actual statistics have been disputed and the overall thesis of 'civilian as casualty' has been challenged by scholars such as Edward Newman,[31] the range of innovative instruments of war against 'innocents' appeared novel. Hostage taking began to be commonplace as groups such as the children of Beslan were seized and murdered, or foreign nationals held to make a political point. (The holding and murder of foreign nationals and Christians in Algeria in January 2013 by militant Islamists and the execution of foreign journalists in Iraq during the summer of 2014 is part of a trend from the 1990s.) Much has been made in the American press of the use of surveillance drones when a child was kidnapped in 2013 in Alabama.[32]

The drones were used to apparently gather data both on the child and the kidnapper before a raid was undertaken to free the child. Given the preference exhibited by some gangs to take and hold foreign hostages, such a capability may prove to be useful.

Mercenaries, arms dealers, criminal gangs and 'radicalised' individuals all made their way into the landscape of these 'new' conflicts. Arguably these groups had little respect for the UN, its peacekeepers and their role. In West Africa for example, child soldiers would be fuelled with concoctions of cocaine, gunpowder and alcohol by commanders and sent to perform specific tasks, such as providing 'bait' for attacks. In 2012, 'Militias loyal to the former Ivory Coast president Laurent Gbagbo' carried out an attack in which they used 'small boys units', otherwise known as child soldiers, to scout and take part in an ambush on a unit of UN peacekeepers which resulted in seven of the soldiers being killed.[33] Drones may reduce these dynamics by providing surveillance evidence and therefore criminal attribution, thus making these acts more costly for the perpetrator and indeed may act as a deterrent.

The example above is not the only case of child soldiers and peacekeepers clashing during conflict. Since 2010, when the UN established its MONUSCO mission, it has faced the ever-present problem of fighting child soldiers who are part of the M23 rebel group. As MONUSCO's Chief of Child Protection Dee Brillenburg Wurth has stated, there are 'a couple of hundred children among the M23 ranks' and these children have been given 'very, very sophisticated training [and] very serious training' for conflict situations.[34] As a result, this has led to a number of situations where peacekeepers have faced children in the line of fire. The UN has held roundtable discussions and training workshops on how to deal with situations where peacekeepers are at risk and 'confronted with child soldiers during their field deployments'.[35]

As Michael Ignatieff has pointed out, 'what is a warrior's honor to a destitute orphan with a Kalashnikov or to some ethnic irregular who survives by pillage and predation? As states disintegrate, so do armies and chains of command, and with them, the indigenous warrior codes that sometime keep war this side of bestiality'.[36] Disparate and diverse bands of fighters, some with little political or ideological direction, others motivated by radical ideologies, inhabited the battlefield, seemingly with little respect for international organisations.[37]

Again, as Ignatieff has pointed out, human rights or norms had little or no purchase in 'this world of war'.[38] Respect for organisations such as the Red Cross or indeed the UN seemed absent. Arguably the nadir was reached when in 1995 the Bosnian Serbs took hostage French, Canadian and Dutch peacekeepers guarding the enclaves of Srebrenica and Zepa.[39] The subsequent execution of some 8000 Bosnian Muslim men demonstrated the lack of authority exhibited by the UN but also no respect for the mission. As MacKinley puts it; 'at the operational level, the soldiers on the ground found themselves in an environment which continued to grow increasingly complicated. Previously, the peacekeepers' operational space had been an empty desert between two inert armies, now it was crowded with independent actors, most of whom had an equally important role in the success of the peace process'.[40] Intervention in the bloody conflicts of the 1990s became more intense, with over 100,000 international troops involved by 1995.[41]

In the 1990s, operations shifted from what we might term *traditional* peacekeeping missions with the support of the major players on the ground for a UN deployment, to more contested roles such as 'peace enforcement' activities or a wider peacekeeping context. As Christopher Bellamy argued, it was possible to identify at least two other categories of operation outside traditional peacekeeping. The first was the deployment of peacekeepers in failed states where institutions had collapsed and the UN functioned as the 'only law in a lawless land'.[42] Here the mission was complicated precisely because the absence of a strong central authority meant that only the UN could be relied upon for the passage and delivery of aid, as in Somalia or Bosnia-Herzegovina. Also, because of the growing number of deployments across a range of complex theatres of deployment, governments and military forces were and are called upon to take greater risks in operations. So Belgian peacekeepers when deployed by the UN in Rwanda in 1994 were withdrawn after ten soldiers were killed and genocide engulfed the nation. The peacekeeping mandate at that point was not to engage in *fighting* an enemy. International opinion critical of such hesitancy to actually halt genocide contributed, along with the case of Srebrenica in 1995, to the creation of a rather more muscular mood for military action amongst the international community.

So traditional peacekeeping (that is the deployment of peacekeepers with the consent of the parties to a ceasefire) evolved into a broader definition that embraced the idea of peace operations in the *absence* of a ceasefire and the *absence* of consent of all the groups involved. If we take the example of intervention in Sierra Leone, during which the UK's forces were engaged in military action against the Revolutionary United Front (RUF), what the peacekeepers actually accomplished was a strengthening of the army in order to suppress the violent challenges to the authority of government. Hence external forces actually took sides in the conflict. So, as David Keen and others have stated, peace building by *consent* usually means the *consent* of key elites and often rests on various degrees of violent coercion against other groups. In short, peacekeepers now take sides.[43]

As Keen has pointed out, this has a series of consequences creating situations which are unlikely to be very 'pure' or very 'nice'. In fact the taking of sides is likely to institutionalise corruption.[44] If it did not institutionalise corruption in some form, those who had previously been violent would be unlikely to accept a diminution in their position.[45] In this sense, the deployment of peacekeepers distorts both the existing 'market' of violence and the behaviour of competing interests within the area and region. The various 'bargains' between the government and local warlords, factions and gangs will be affected by their reaction to the power and patronage of the UN. Violence or the promise to withhold violence by these groups may be the only instrument for exacting concessions. In this sense, war provides opportunities for some groups to maximise their influence and keep the resources from outside flowing in by claiming cooperation with Western institutions. Nowhere is this more obvious than in the War on Terror, when those who claim to oppose Islamic extremism and radicalisation benefit from Western friendship and patronage. Equally, those identified as the friends of extremism can expect to be sacrificed for the pursuit of global stability.

This market of violence operates in an ambiguous parallel to the UN agenda for political transformation. Cooper et al. have identified a key weakness in aid programmes operated by Western states or institutions. The Liberal Peace model was the dominant paradigm articulated by UN agencies and the powerful international financial organisations and states underwriting the peace agenda.[46] Neoliberal policies of open markets, privatisation, fiscal restraint and good governance policies relied and still rely upon instruments of state coercion and capacity building for any degree of success. Cooper et al. argue that the global economic crisis has discredited precisely such models of liberalism as espoused by the US and its European allies.[47]

So Cooper et al. identified a key weakness in Western programmes, a fragility replicated in aid programmes. Following on from the so-called War on Terror, aid towards some 27 developing countries affected by violence has increased over the past decade. In 2007–2008 aid reached $36 billion for that year.[48] While Iraq and Afghanistan accounted for some 38% of that total, Afghanistan alone received more aid than the combined total dispersed to the DR Congo, Liberia and Sudan combined.[49] One effect of aid was arguably that the ever growing gap between the elites and those excluded from the benefits created fault lines. While it is not the point of this article to examine the issue of aid as a cause of conflict, what we are interested in is the growing resistance to Western-style intervention and the imposition of governance structures across a number of conflict zones as well as attacks on UN staff and peacekeeping personnel.[50] As Michael Pugh, an astute commentator on such matters, has argued, it is almost inevitable that 'the asymmetries of power between peace missions and locals provoke tension. The arrivistes have the wealth, the vehicles, computers and access to the outside world'.[51] These sentiments could be applied to any numbers of conflict zones and bring with them resistance from those marginalised by aid and intervention processes.

In these very challenging and complex environments the immunity of aid workers and peacekeepers decreases. As the new wars literature indicates, there has been a disconcerting targeting of non-governmental organisations (NGOs) and affiliated workers by militant groups. In certain cases, the motivation appears to be material greed (as noted above) or opposition to what international NGOs represent or are perceived to represent: attacked because of their association with Western governments, institutions and militaries. When studied from this perspective, and backed by the data in Figure 4b, it is clear that the 'erosion of respect' experienced by peacekeepers in recent years is not a new phenomenon. Instead, since the end of the Cold War the landscape of conflicts, for all of those involved in conflict, including peacekeeping, has changed.

So from the study of UN fatalities data, although the reasons for death may vary, the fact that peacekeepers die in the service of the UN is a consistent and in some cases increasing trend. In regard to illness – due to the fact that peacekeepers are human – they will always be vulnerable to disease. Yet the risks are amplified when manifest lapses in training exist and they are deployed to high-risk regions. As for acts of malice, well it is safe to say (with their white vehicles and blue helmets) whilst deployed on the ground peacekeepers are an easily identifiable target. When this is mixed with the perceptions of the peacekeeper as a legitimate target and the fact there are critical shortages in vital equipment, it is clear to see why they are susceptible to malicious acts. However, such issues do not only impact upon the lives of peacekeepers. Endemic illness leads to a decrease in the effectiveness of peacekeepers operating in high-risk regions. Also, being the consistent target of malice, mixed with chronic equipment shortfalls, leads to civilian protection mandates being unfulfilled (as seen in Goma). Thus, these trends do not only affect peacekeeping in regard to fatalities, but also in regard to its overall effectiveness. As the 'New Horizon' report concludes; 'taken together, the challenges described above have stretched UN peacekeeping to its limits'.[52] Therefore, we suggest that one way to reduce peacekeeping fatalities and improve the effectiveness of UN peacekeeping missions, is through technological advancements such as drones. Specifically, we outline the virtue that could come from the introduction of armed drones as opposed to the unarmed variety.

Virtuous drones?

From controversial beginnings, the argument for the use of unarmed drones has moved forward to the point where they are currently being deployed within select UN peacekeeping missions on an experimental basis. As Ladsous states, these drones will be used as a 'tool for situational awareness' and will seek to increase the effectiveness of the UN missions by making them 'more proactive'.[53] This relatively quick progression from debate to deployment was catalysed by the controversies that surrounded the UN peacekeeping shortfalls against M23 rebels at the city of Goma. (It is no coincidence that the first deployment of these unarmed drones was to Goma on humanitarian grounds.) As Ladsous argued, unarmed drones are the 'tool of choice'[54] when it comes to mapping 'the movements of armed militias ... to protect civilians'.[55] As he concluded, 'we need to get a better picture of what is happening'.[56] However, there are a number of limiting factors to consider with the deployment of unarmed drones as opposed to armed drones.

There can be little doubt that through unarmed drone use a greater understanding of the landscape, movement and intentions of malicious actors can be constructed. Such intelligence is indeed useful and a 'better picture' would be distinguished. Human rights abuses could be observed, genocidal acts would be logged and if aggressors are identified approaching civilian settlements warnings could be transmitted. It is also the case that evidence of criminal activity (such as the trafficking of people, or the aforementioned use of child soldiers) could be obtained and used as means to increase the likelihood of prosecution at a later date. However, it is with Ladsous's argument that such technology can make peacekeeping more 'proactive' that this article draws its greatest concern. From the functionality outlined above, is the use of unarmed drones truly making peacekeeping as proactive as it could be? It would appear that such unarmed drones would only be able to ensure the UN is a reactive monitor of abuses with little increase in its ability to actively prevent them. In essence, a better picture may be available but unarmed drones do little to proactively address the manifest shortfalls and risks which we have outlined. They do even less to reduce the need for peacekeepers on the ground in high-risk regions and, if deployed as a sole entity (despite their ability to transcend the intertwined issues of terrain and speed of deployment) they are unable to directly intervene to protect vulnerable populations from genocide or human rights abuses.[57]

This is where the introduction of armed drones appears to come to the fore. To put what an armed drone may accomplish in perspective, let us take a look at the characteristics of leading high-altitude, long-endurance armed drones. Such drones, like most of the current generation of drone technology, can send out 'near-real-time high resolution imagery of large geographical areas all day and night in all types of weather' and 'direct weapons to attack both stationary and moving targets'.[58] In other words, the armed drone can transmit high-quality live images of regions under threat to intelligence analysts whilst it continues to fly day and night. Upon targeting being approved, the armed drone is then in an opportune position to intervene when and where approved. Thus the advantages of deploying armed drones in a peacekeeping context appear clear. Not only would the DPKO be able to monitor situations with greater intelligence, but it would be able to act (within the limits of a UN mandate) in real time to unfolding security issues. Yet, although the advantages of the drones deployment in a peacekeeping context may seem clear, we are not ignorant of the negative connotations which surround the deployment of armed drones. For many populations which have had to live under their deployment, the reality has left much to be desired.

As the Nobel Peace Prize winning Archbishop Emeritus of Cape Town Desmond Tutu stated in an open letter to the editor of the *New York Times*; 'I used to say of apartheid that it dehumanized its perpetrators as much as, if not more than, its victims. Your [America's] response as a society to Osama bin Laden and his followers threatens to undermine your moral standards and your humanity.'[59] Furthermore, in reaction to the proposed plans to 'only kill' non-Americans with drone strikes, Tutu adds '[d]o the United States and its people really want to tell those of us who live in the rest of the world that our lives are not of the same value as yours? That President Obama can sign off on a decision to kill us with less worry about judicial scrutiny than if the target is an American?'[60] As such, from his letter entitled 'Drones, Kill Lists and Machiavelli', Tutu is not only voicing his objection to the American deployment of armed drones for the offensive strategy of targeted killing, but also to the ease at which the life of a person in a 'foreign land' can be distinguished as potentially lesser and thus easier to kill. As he declares, 'I am deeply, deeply disturbed.'[61]

It is such perceptions of the American deployment of drones which has led to the aforementioned notion that drones are a 'scourge targeting innocent civilians'.[62] The often-cited figure that '474 to 881 civilians' have been killed through these drone strikes since September 2012 lends support to this notion.[63] Furthermore, such an offensive deployment of drones has led a number of like-minded reports to suggest that these American strikes cause 'harm to civilians and local communities, and may fuel anger toward the US in the aggregate'.[64] From these perceptions of American drone use for the purpose of targeted killing, it is clear to see the reasons why a negative public perception of drones may exist. However, it is the view of this article that just because the manner in which the US has deployed drones through targeted killing has led to a negative perception of the weaponry, this does not mean that if used in a less offensive and more regulated and restricted manner, the public perception of armed drones cannot change. The perception of a drone is surely a social construct? The way in which they are perceived depends upon how they are deployed, by whom and for what reason.

Drones, even armed drones, can be used in a virtuous manner to protect civilians in line with a UN mandate, just as much as they can be used in a manner which is perceived as immoral or unethical. Let us learn lessons from the public perception of drones in regions of Afghanistan, compared to the border regions of Pakistan, where 'signature strikes' epitomised a move toward a much more offensive and indiscriminate targeting strategy. Here armed drones were deployed against those whose behaviour was linked to 'militant activity' (aka a pre-defined 'terrorist signature').[65] This ambiguous notion led to an increase in collateral damage. As one probing *The Atlantic* report stated, '[t]he problem with signature strikes is that they open the door to a *much higher incidence of civilian casualties* [emphasis added]'.[66] Therefore, perhaps unsurprisingly, when drones are deployed in this manner they cause anti-drone and anti-American sentiment within the society upon which they are deployed. In contrast, in parts of Afghanistan the view of armed drones is distinctly more positive due to restrictions put on their use.[67]

In certain regions, drones were often used discriminately and proportionately to target specific people or groups who had been identified through a mix of human and drone intelligence. As the *New York Times* states, '[in Afghanistan] the coalition has drastically reduced the number of civilian casualties stemming from airstrikes, after adopting more rigid rules for such attacks'.[68] Although mistakes still occurred, the method of deployment led to a rather different societal perception of armed drones. As the Deputy District Governor for Nad 'Ali District, Helmand Province, declared, 'drones are very efficient'.[69] When asked what the Afghan civilians' perceptions of drones are, he stated, 'there are things the Taliban do that local people don't like. So, as far as the civilians are not harmed, I think the perception on drones will stay positive to a significant degree.'[70] Thus, armed drones are not innately evil or immoral weapons and if used in a manner which deters and prevents acts of genocide and human rights violations then they would likely be welcomed by a public under siege and in need of protection. In theory, this assertion can be applied to armed drone use more generally as long as they are used in this measured and restrained manner. Yet, when applied to the unique context of UN peacekeeping (and the justifications and consensus behind the use of force) such an argument has particular resonance and justification. Let us investigate this notion further by highlighting the virtue of armed drones in peacekeeping situations.

The UN stated in the 2010 Global Field Support Strategy: '[t]oday, the typical field environment is remote, austere and, increasingly, dangerous, sometimes openly hostile to a United Nations presence'.[71] With an armed drone the issue of increasing danger and the resultant ineffectiveness of the peacekeeper – from issues such as illness and hostility – is mitigated. As Schaffer has argued, 'remote piloting is particularly advantageous because UAV pilots cannot be injured or captured by enemy forces in the course of their duties'.[72] As such, if monitoring or peace-enforcement peacekeeping numbers were to be reduced in high-risk regions, in favour of armed drones, there would be fewer peacekeepers at risk in the field whilst the roles would continue to be effectively fulfilled. Furthermore, the issue of remoteness is 'solved' with the deployment of armed drones.

Unlike in current circumstances where once detected by an unarmed drone it may take hours or even days for ground-based peacekeepers to reach a specified location, with an armed drone means would be on hand to respond in a manner fitting to the specific UN mandate for the mission. When put into the context of a situation like that of the incident in Goma, it is obvious what the virtue of the armed drone may have been. Specifically within the MONUSCO mission, the DPKO is authorised under a UN Security Council approved mandate (Resolution 1925) to 'use all necessary means [to] ensure the effective protection of civilians, including humanitarian personnel and human rights defenders, under imminent threat of physical violence, in particular violence emanating from any of the parties engaged in the conflict'.[73] However, despite the fact the mission had almost 20,000 troops deployed, the sheer size of the country, mixed with the shortfalls in equipment and the dispersed nature of the operation, meant that when a situation occurred peacekeepers were powerless. Although not as extreme as the atrocities witness by powerless peacekeeping in the 1990s, in this instance children as young as five were killed and maimed[74] as a small force of 1500 peacekeepers decided to 'hold fire' against a large M23 force and 'observe what [was] happening', as they entered the city and, 'as anticipated', committed human rights violations.[75] Yet, this is not the only case of such shortfalls. One notorious example is that of the Central African Republic (CAR).

As the 2014 Amnesty International report on 'Ethnic Cleansing and Sectarian Killings in the Central African Republic' highlights:

> Concern over the increasingly sectarian nature of the violence in the Central African Republic led the UN Security Council in December 2013 to authorize the deployment of peacekeeping forces in the country ... Yet they have been slow to fill the power vacuum created in mid-January when interim President Michel Djotodia resigned and the Seleka began withdrawing from these areas. International forces failed to swiftly deploy to these areas to protect civilians, allowing anti-balaka militias to assert themselves. In town after town, as soon as the Seleka left, the anti-balaka moved in and launched violent attacks on the Muslim minority. These developments were entirely predictable, given the deep-seated anger of both the anti-balaka and of large sectors of the Christian community, who largely held the Muslim minority responsible for Seleka abuses. Already, in December 2013, Amnesty International had warned of this danger.[76]

In this instance, or in future situations, if armed drones are deployed, not only might they act as a potential deterrent against such attacks, but in some case the drone could be used to halt the rebel and militia advances in line with a specific UN mandate to protect civilians and peacekeepers.

As Schaffner argues, the deployment of drones may 'constitute a legitimate intermediary humanitarian interference mechanism given their ability to provide useful atrocity response services'.[77] Thus although armed drones are not a panacea to all UN peacekeeping problems, their introduction could reduce the need for large numbers of peacekeepers on the ground in regions at high-risk from illness and malicious acts. Arguably drones could improve the performance of the UN DPKO in its protection of civilians. In itself this could be a virtuous outcome. As Jean-Marie Guehenno, a former Under-Secretary-General for Peacekeeping Operations, argued, 'we are the firemen of the world, but we have to build a fire truck when there is a fire'.[78] Although armed drones may not be the whole fire truck, they are an effective hose with which to douse the flames whilst reducing the cost to peacekeeping lives and increasing the effectiveness of civilian protection.

Conclusion

This article began by highlighting some of the most pressing areas of concern facing UN peacekeeping. The self-confessed 'critical shortages' in equipment, outlined by the UN in its 2009 New Horizon report, were addressed. The case of human rights violations occurring in the city of Goma, whilst peacekeepers stood to one side unable and ill-equipped to react, was an example of such deficiencies. The issues of peacekeeping fatalities and the vulnerability to illness and malice in the field were outlined. Here, the case was made that due to the changing nature of warfare since the end of the Cold War and the changes in regions of deployment to high-risk malarial nations, UN peacekeepers had an increased risk of death in the field. In an attempt to address these issues, it was suggested that the armed drones should be deployed to replace the number of peacekeepers in monitoring and peace-enforcement roles in regions of high-risk. Specifically, it was concluded that with the ability to monitor vast swathes of land, even whole countries, drones are the weapons of choice to improve the effectiveness of UN peacekeeping missions by replacing the vulnerable and often ill-equipped and under-trained peacekeeper. Overall, from a lack of vital equipment, such as helicopters and the consistent risk of malice faced by peacekeepers, this article has clearly identified some of the pressing issues facing UN peacekeeping. In reaction to this, we suggest that drones, in particular armed drones, could be deployed as a means to improve the effectiveness of peacekeeping, reduce the cost to peacekeeping lives and improve mission effectiveness.

Disclosure statement

No potential conflict of interest was reported by the author.

Notes

1. K. Anderson, 'Written Testimony Submitted to Subcommittee on National Security and Foreign Affairs: Rise of the Drones: Unmanned Systems and the Future of War', 23 March 2010. http://digitalcommons.wcl.american.edu/cgi/viewcontent.cgi?article=1002&context=pub_disc_cong
2. P.W. Singer, *Wired For War* (London: Penguin Group, 2010), 194.
3. See for example the outrage expressed by Frank Ledwidge in *Losing Small Wars British Military Failure in Iraq and Afghanistan*, over the absence of training and kit. F. Ledwidge, *Losing Small Wars British Military Failure in Iraq and Afghanistan* (New Haven, CT: Yale University Press, 2011).
4. By illusory we mean that in current conflicts it is quite often difficult to understand who or what may be the innocent parties. In areas of conflict, for example, the presence of children or, more specifically, child soldiers can complicate intervention while it is not unknown for peacekeepers to find themselves caught in complex emergencies in which 'truth', 'justice' and notions of 'rights' are highly contestable. See D. Keen, *Useful Enemies* (New Haven, CT: Yale University Press, 2012).
5. DPKO and DFS, *A New Partnership Agenda: Charting a New Horizon for UN Peacekeeping* (New York: DPKO & DFS, 2009), Foreword.
6. Ibid., v.
7. DPKO and DFS, *The New Horizon Initiative: Progress Report No. 2* (New York: DPKO & DFS, 2011), 26.
8. DPKO and DFS. *A New Partnership Agenda*, 5.
9. UN News Centre, 'Senior UN Officials Highlight Diversity and Challenges of Peacekeeping', 21 February 2012. http://www.un.org/apps/news/story.asp?NewsID=41321#.VBsRefmwIn5
10. A. Boutellis, 'Will MONUSCO Fall With Goma?', 3 December 2012. theglobalobservatory.org/analysis/394-will-monusco-fall-with-goma.html
11. Ibid.
12. J. Verini, 'Should the United Nations Wage War to Keep Peace?', 27 March 2014. http://news.nationalgeographic.com/news/2014/03/140327-congo-genocide-united-nations-peacekeepers-m23-kobler-intervention-brigade/
13. J. Irish, V. Buffery, and L. Ireland, 'France Urges Review of U.N. Mandate in Congo', 20 November 2012. http://www.reuters.com/article/2012/11/20/us-congo-democratic-fabius-idUSBRE8AJ13520121120
14. Boutellis, 'Will MONUSCO Fall With Goma?'
15. United Nations General Assembly, 'A/64/573: Implementation of the Recommendations of the Special Committee on Peacekeeping Operations', 2009. http://www.un.org/en/ga/search/view_doc.asp?symbol=A/64/573, 2.
16. This is for the system alone, without the extra cost of training personnel to operate the craft. See, Center on International Cooperation and United States Global Peace Operations Initiative, 'Assessment of Helicopter Force Generation Challenges for United Nations Peacekeeping Operations', December 2011. usun.state.gov/documents/organization/179150.pdf, 4–6.
17. UN News Centre, 'Senior UN Officials Highlight Diversity and Challenges of Peacekeeping', 21 February 2012. http://www.un.org/apps/news/story.asp?NewsID=41321#.VBsRefmwIn5
18. J. Masters, 'Targeted Killings', 23 May 2013. http://www.cfr.org/counterterrorism/targeted-killings/p9627
19. Figures correct of 6 August 2014. See, Department of Peacekeeping Operations, 'Fatalities by Mission, Year and Incident Type', August 2014. http://www.un.org/en/peacekeeping/fatalities/documents/stats_4a.pdf
20. United Nations Department of Peacekeeping Operations, *United Nations Infantry Battalion Manual: Volume 2* (New York: United Nations Department of Peacekeeping Operations, 2012), 292.
21. See, *The Guardian*, 'World Malaria Day: Which Countries Are the Hardest Hit?', 25 April 2011. http://www.guardian.co.uk/global-development/datablog/2011/apr/25/world-malaria-day-data#data. Also see, World Health Organisation, *World Malaria Report 2012* (Geneva: WHO Press, 2012).
22. United Nations Department of Peacekeeping Operations, *United Nations Infantry Battalion Manual: Volume 2*, 290–3.
23. Walter Dorn, 'Dying for Peace', in Center on International Cooperation, *Annual Review of Global Peace Operations 2008* (London: Lynne Rienner, 2008), 70.

24. UNGA, 'Manual on Policies and Procedures Concerning the Reimbursement and Control of Contingent-Owned Equipment of Troop/Police Contributors Participating in Peacekeeping Missions (COE Manual)', 27 October 2011. http://www.un.org/en/peacekeeping/sites/coe/referencedocuments/COE_manual_2011.pdf, 100.
25. United Nations Department of Peacekeeping Operations, *United Nations Infantry Battalion Manual: Volume 2*, 290–3.
26. United Nations General Assembly, 'A/64/573: Implementation of the Recommendations of the Special Committee on Peacekeeping Operations', 2.
27. To provide clarity it must be stated that the graphs in Figures 4aand 4b are constructed of percentages of fatalities, not the total number of fatalities. As such, the increased number of peacekeepers deployed over this period has no impact on the findings as the percentage allows us to construct an unbiased average over the time period.
28. Stockholm International Peace Research Institute, *Global Patterns of Major Armed Conflict 1989–95: SIPRI Yearbook 1996* (London: Oxford University Press, 1996), 15.
29. M. Kaldor, *New Wars Organized Violence in a Global Era*, 2nd ed. (London: Polity Press, 2012).
30. J. Black, *War and the new Disorder in the 21st Century* (London: Continuum, 2004).
31. E. Newman, 'The "New Wars" Debate: Historical Perspective is Needed', *Security Dialogue* 35, no. 2 (2004), 173–89.
32. BBC, 'FBI Uses Drones for Surveillance Over US Soil', 19 June 2013. http://www.bbc.co.uk/news/world-us-canada-22976598
33. M. Mark, 'Ivory Coast Mercenaries Train Child Soldiers for Attacks across Liberia Border', 10 June 2012. http://www.guardian.co.uk/world/2012/jun/10/ivory-coast-child-soldiers
34. N. Michelle, 'Children Lured from Rwanda to Fight with Congo Rebels – U.N.', 5 October 2013. uk.reuters.com/article/2013/10/05/uk-congo-democratic-rwanda-children-idUKBRE9940CD20131005
35. UNITAR, 'Round Table Discussion on African Peacekeepers and Child Soldiers', October 2012. http://www.unitar.org/round-table-discussion-african-peacekeepers-and-child-soldiers
36. M. Ignatieff, *The Warrior's Honor: Ethnic War and the Modern Conscience* (New York: Henry Holt and Company, 1997), 6.
37. W. Reno, *Warfare in Independent Africa* (Cambridge: Cambridge University Press, 2011). See also J. Gettleman, 'Africa's Dirty Wars', *The New York Review of Books*, 8 March 2012. Caroline Kennedy and Thomas Waldman, 'Wars of War in the 21st Century' in *21 Century World Politics*, ed. Mark Beeson and Nick Bisley (Palgrave Macmillan, 2013), 92–105.
38. Ignatieff, *The Warrior's Honor*, 6. See also Christopher Kinsek and Malcolm Hugh Paterson, eds, *Contractors & War* (Stanford, CA: Stanford University Press, 2002).
39. T. Onea, 'Putting the "Classical" in Neoclassical Realism: Neoclassical Realist Theories and US Expansion in the Post-Cold War', *International Relations* 26, no. 2 (2012): 152.
40. J. Mackinlay, 'Defeating Complex Insurgency. The Conwallis Group X: Analysis for New and Emerging Societal Conflicts', 2005. thecornwallisgroup.org/pdf/cx_2005_03-MackinlayJ.pdf
41. On the challenges posed to UN missions in the 1990s, see Christopher Bellamy, *Knights in White Armour: The New Art of War and Peace* (London: Hutchinson, 1996).
42. Ibid., 88.
43. D. Keen, *Conflict and Collusion in Sierra Leone* (New York: Palgrave, 2005).
44. Ibid., 240.
45. Ibid.
46. N. Cooper, M. Turner, and R. Paris, 'The End of History and the Last Liberal Peacebuilder: A Reply to Roland Paris', *The Review of International Studies* 37 (2011): 1995–2007.
47. Ibid.
48. Y. Matsumoto, 'Young Afghans in "Transition": Towards Afghanistan, Exit or Violence?', *Conflict, Security & Development* 11, no. 5 (2011): 555–78.
49. Ibid.
50. Please note that much of the middle section of this article was inspired by the debate in *The Review of International Studies* in 2011 between Roland Paris and Neil Cooper, Mandy Turner and Michael Pugh. Please see Neil Cooper, Mandy Turner and Roland Paris, 'The End of History and the Last Liberal Peacebuilder: A Reply to Roland Paris', *The Review of International Studies* 37 (2011): 1995–2007. Of considerable background interest was David Chandler, *Empire in Denial: The Politics of State Building* (London: Pluto, 2006).

51. M. Pugh, 'Accountability and Credibility', 2010. kms2.isn.ethz.ch/serviceengine/Files/ EINIRAS/123563/ ... /5.pdf
52. DPKO and DFS. *A New Partnership Agenda*, 6.
53. H. Ladsous, 'Transcript: Department of Peacekeeping Operations Press Conference', 6 February 2013. http://www.un.org/en/peacekeeping/articles/USG%20Ladsous.PC.transcript.060213. final.rtf.pdf
54. BBC, 'UN Starts Drone Surveillance in DR Congo', 3 December 2013. http://www.bbc.co.uk/ news/world-africa-25197754
55. M. Ladsous, 'Remarks of Mr. Hervé Ladsous Under-Secretary-General for Peacekeeping Operations to the Special Committee on Peacekeeping Operations', 2012. http://www.un.org/en/ peacekeeping/articles/HL_Speech_C34_Delivered_21022012.pdf
56. BBC, 'UN Starts Drone Surveillance in DR Congo'.
57. Of course, the use of unarmed drones to gather intelligence before a peacekeeping intervention brigade is deployed could be argued to be a proactive role for this technology. Yet, although this would highlight a limited increase in making peacekeeping 'more proactive', such assistance does not reduce the need for peacekeepers on the ground in high- risk regions and does not address the issue of manifest shortfalls in the training, equipment and number of these peacekeepers. More can be done to proactively mitigate the cost to civilians and peacekeepers with armed drones.
58. Northrop Grumman, 'RQ-4 Block 40 Global Hawk', 2012. http://www.northropgrumman.com/ Capabilities/GlobalHawk/Documents/Datasheet_GH_Block_40.pdf
59. D. Tutu, 'Drones, Kill Lists and Machiavelli', 13 February 2013. http://www.nytimes.com/ 2013/02/13/opinion/drones-kill-lists-and-machiavelli.html?_r=0
60. Ibid.
61. Ibid.
62. Masters, 'Targeted Killings'.
63. Ibid.
64. Columbia Law School and the Center for Civilians in Conflict, 'The Civilian Impact of Drones: Unexamined Costs, Unanswered Questions', 2012. civiliansinconflict.org/uploads/files/publications/The_Civilian_Impact_of_Drones_w_cover.pdf
65. D. Greenfield, 'The Case Against Drone Strikes on People Who Only "Act" Like Terrorists', 19 August 2013. http://www.theatlantic.com/international/archive/2013/08/the-case-against-drone-strikes-on-people-who-only-act-like-terrorists/278744/
66. Ibid
67. A. Ahmed, 'Drones and Taliban Attacks Hit Civilians, Afghans Say', 8 September 2013. http:// www.nytimes.com/2013/09/09/world/asia/two-deadly-attacks-in-afghanistan.html
68. Ibid.
69. Deputy District Governor for Nad 'Ali District, Helmand Province, personal interview, University of Hull, March 2014.
70. Ibid.
71. UNGA, 'Global Field Support Strategy: A/64/633', 2010. http://www.un.org/en/ga/search/ view_doc.asp?symbol=A/64/633
72. D. Schaffner, 'Legality of Using Drones to Unilaterally Monitor Atrocity Crimes', *Fordham International Law Journal* 35, no. 4 (2012): 1121–64.
73. United Nations Security Council, 'Resolution 1925 (2010)', 28 May 2010. http://www.un.org/ en/ga/search/view_doc.asp?symbol=S/RES/1925(2010)
74. H. O'Malley, 'Children Maimed during M23 Attack on Goma', 2012. http://www.telegraph.co. uk/news/picturegalleries/worldnews/9700172/Children-maimed-during-M23-attack-on-Goma. html?frame=2408501
75. Boutellis, 'Will MONUSCO Fall With Goma?'
76. Amnesty International, *Ethnic Cleansing and Sectarian Killings in the Central African Republic* (London: Amnesty International Publications, 2014), 6.
77. Schaffner, 'Legality of Using Drones to Unilaterally Monitor Atrocity Crimes'.
78. J.M. Guehenno, 'NPR Radio Interview Transcript', 21 September 2010. http://www.npr.org/ templates/story/story.php?storyId=130021491

Index

Page numbers in italics refer to figures.

accountability: applicable law 48–9; compliance with principles of 51–2; international law 63; methods of warfare 40; military chain of command 2; Obama administration's drone policy 13–5
Afghanistan: aid programmes 115–6; civilian casualties 40–3; 'kill lists' 55–6; potential violations of international law 50–3; public perception of drone use in 118–9; signature strikes 57; surveillance 11; targeted killing research 31; transparency and accountability 48; UN report on civilian casualties 30; *see also* Uruzgan province
aid programmes 115–6
Air Force: Afghanistan, operation in 51; civilian casualties 62; Joint and Coalition Operational Analysis reports 42–3; signature strikes 57
al-Nusra front 4
al-Qaeda: Authorization to Use Military Force 4–5, 7; combatant status 9; identifying targets 80; target identification 10
al-Shabaab 10
Al-Skeini and Others v. The United Kingdom 47
Alston, Philip 7, 48, 84
Amanulluh, Zabet 56
American citizens, strikes against 5
Amin, Muhammad 56
Amnesty International 77–8, 85, 119
Anderson, Kenneth 107
anticipatory self-defence 6, 7–8, 18, 79–80
arbitrary killing prohibition 47–8
Afghan military 98
Armed Activities on the Territory of the Congo (International Court of Justice) 47
artillery guns 25, 30–1
assassinations 4, 7, 15–7, 31, 100
associated forces 4, 5, 10, 14
assumptions and the means-method paradox 58, 60, 61, 62, 63
The Atlantic 118
attribution theory 58

Authorization to Use Military Force 4–8, 10, 78
al-Awlaki, Anwar 5

Bacardi, Arturo Jimenez 12
Ban Ki-moon 95
behaviour modification 97–8
Belgium 103
Bellamy, Christopher 114
beneficial uses of drones 98–104, 118–20
Bergen, Peter 32
Best, Geoffrey 25–6
biological agents, detection of 102–3
blast areas 54
Bousquet, Antoine 30
Braun, Megan 17, 83, 86–7
Brennan, John 1, 5, 81–2
British military 97
Brodie, Bernard 25
Brodie, Fawn 25
Brunstetter, Daniel 12, 17, 83, 86–7
Buchanan, Allen 100
Bureau of Investigative Journalism 28, 42
Burgess, Cris 97
Bush, George W.: al-Harethi targeted killing 77–8; Authorization to Use Military Force 4; ethics of war 76; strategic-legal justification for drone use 79–80; target identification 10; unlawful combatant status 9
Bush Doctrine 79–80

Carney, Jay 14
Caroline case 8, 79
Carvin, Stephanie 2
Central African Republic 119
Central Intelligence Agency, US: civilian engagement in lethal operations 52–3; legal-normative justification for drone use 83; signature strikes 57; strategic-legal justification for drone use 78; transparency and accountability 14–5, 40, 51–2
Chad 95–6
chemical agents, detection of 102–3

INDEX

child soldiers 114
China 17, 101
Civil War, US 24–5
civilian casualties: Afghanistan 40–3; drones *vs.*
manned aircraft 62; human rights protections
84–7; legal-normative justification for drone
use 83; means *vs.* method of warfare 28–33;
personality strikes 56; proportionality 12,
86–7; public perception of drone use 118–9;
signature strikes 10–1; target identification 9;
United States human rights claims 73; *see
also* collateral damage
civilians: engagement in lethal operations 52–3;
international humanitarian law 44–5;
precautions 46; psychological effects of
drones 11–3, 87; risk transfer 80–1, 108
classified information 48
co-belligerents 10
cognitive closure 58–9, 60
cognitive consistency 58–60, 61, 62–3
collateral damage: Air Force rules 50;
international humanitarian law 80, 82;
means-method paradox 63; proportionality
44, 45–6; public discussion 95; *see also*
civilian casualties
combatant status 8–9, 44–5, 80–1, 108
commercial satellite images 96–7
compliance with international law 50–7
Congo 103, 116, 117; *see also* United Nations
Organization Stabilization Mission
(Democratic Republic of the Congo)
Congress, US 14
consent and peacekeeping missions 115
continuing threat 86
Cooper, Neil 115
costs of drones 107
Counterinsurgency (COIN) 108
counterterrorism: Authorization to Use Military
Force 4–8; and the human rights community
84–7, 88–90; intelligence gathering 31–2;
legal-normative justification for drone use
81–4; strategic-legal justification for drone
use 77–81
courts, American 14
Crawford, Neta 79
Creveld, Martin van 24, 30
crimes against humanity 98–104
Cronin, Audrey Kurth 31
customary international law 8, 15–6, 43, 47, 49,
75

data: civilian casualties 42–3; 'data crush' 54,
59; misinterpretation of 41; research issues
32–3
decision-making: intelligence gathering 54;
means-method paradox 58–60; signature
strikes 56
dehumanising effects of drones 2

democratic reforms 90
Department of Justice White Paper (US) 7–8,
85–6
detachment *see* distance and detachment
deterrence 98–104, 119
discrimination, principle of 17, 45, 98
disease-related peacekeeping mission fatalities
110, 116
distance and detachment: drone operators 2–3;
historical precedence for drones 25–8;
means-method paradox 58, 59; negative
features of drones 54–5
distinction: compliance with 50–1; human rights
community 86; international humanitarian
law 44; principle of 27; signature strikes 11;
target identification 9; targeted killings 85
Djotodia, Michel 119
domestic law 48
'double-hatting' 52
Drone Accountability Regime 100
'dynamic targeting' 56

East Africa 31
economics 83, 89–90
effectiveness studies 32
egocentrism and decision-making 59
Emmerson, Ben 29–30, 49, 87
endurance capacity of drones 11, 40, 53, 61, 63,
117
equipment shortages 108–9
European Convention on Human Rights 47
European Court of Human Rights 47
European Parliament 48
excessiveness 45–6, 50
Executive Branch transparency and
accountability 15
extra-judicial executions 85
extraterritorial operations 28, 47–8, 100
Exum, Andrew M. 31

Fabius, Laurent 109
fact-finding inquiries 49
failed states and peacekeeping missions 114–5
fatalities, peacekeeper *110,* 110–2, *111, 113,* 116
Flynn, Matthew 79
frames of legitimacy 74–7

Gaddafi, Muammar 4
Gatling, Richard Jordan 25
Geneva Conventions: indiscriminate attack 29;
international humanitarian law 44–5;
transparency and accountability 48–9
geographic limits, lack of: Authorization to Use
Military Force 4, 5–6; human rights
protections 84–5, 88
Germany 30–1
Global Field Support Strategy, UN 119
Goldsmith, Jack 7

INDEX

'Gorgon Stare' 53
GPS-guided bombs 54
Graham, Robert 78
gray area between war and peace 16, 17
Greenwood, Christopher 27
Gross, Michael L. 31
Guantanamo Bay military tribunals 9
Guehenno, Jean-Marie 120

Hamdi v. Rumsfeld 4
Haqqani network 10
al-Harethi, Abu Ali 77, 78
al-Harithi, Ali Qaed Senyan 40
harm and proportionality 87
Hayden, Michael 8
Heller, Kevin 56
Hellfire missiles 54
Heyns, Christof 85
Hezbollah 108
historical precedence for drones 24–8
Hitler, Adolf 31
Holder, Eric 4, 81
hostage taking 113–4
'How to End the Forever War?' (Koh) 89–90
human rights: drone use to protect 95–6,
    98–104; duty to intervene 6; international
    human rights law 84–7; legal-normative
    justification for drone use 81–4; mass
    atrocities and perceptions of impunity 96–8;
    means *vs.* method of warfare 28–33; norms
    regarding drone use 88–90; strategic-legal
    justification for drone use 77–81; United
    States, claims of the 73
human rights community: human rights
    approaches 73; international human rights
    law 84–7; on the killing of al-Harethi 77;
    norms regarding drone use 88–90; reports
    28–9; satellite images of mass human rights
    abuses 96–7
Human Rights Watch 28, 29
humanitarian intervention 6, 118–20
humanitarian organisations 26, 27–8; *see also*
    human rights community
humanity and guided weapons law 26–7
hypotheses and the means-method paradox
    58–60, 62, 63

identifying targets *see* targeting errors; targets
Ignatieff, Michael 114
illegal weapons, detection of 102–3
illness and peacekeeping missions 110, 116
imminent threat 7–8, 79–80, 85
indiscriminate attack 29
insurgents: economics 90; inadequate signature
    criteria 57; legal status 41–2, 45; observation
    of 60; target status 4, 8–9
intelligence: accuracy of and personality strikes
    55; beneficial drone use 99–101; features of

drones 53–4; humans *vs.* drones 107; means-
    method paradox 61; targeted killings *vs.* 31–2
International Committee of the Red Cross 26, 45
International Court of Justice 7, 46–7
International Covenant of Civil and Political
    Rights 47
International Criminal Court 96, 99, 103
International Criminal Tribunal Yugoslavia 29
international human rights law: applicable law
    46–8; conflicting human rights narratives
    73–4; drone strikes in Afghanistan 41; human
    rights community 84–7, 88–90; legalistic
    justification for drone use 75–6; strategic-
    legal justification for drone use 77–81;
    transparency and accountability 63
international humanitarian law: applicable law
    43–6; conflicting human rights narratives
    73–4; drone strikes in Afghanistan 41; human
    rights community 84–7, 88–9; legalistic
    justification for drone use 75–6; legal-
    normative justification for drone use 81–4;
    proportionality 29; signature strikes 56;
    strategic-legal justification for drone use
    77–81; transparency and accountability 63
international law: compliance with 50–7;
    legalistic grounds for drone use 75–6; means
    vs. methods of warfare 38–40; target
    legitimacy principles 26–7
international organisations and transparency 49
International Security Assistance Force 41
International Stabilization Afghanistan Forces 30
intervention, duty of 6
Iraq: aid programmes 115; associated forces and
    co-belligerents 10; surveillance 11
irregular fighters, status of 8–9
ISIS 96
Islamic Movement of Uzbekistan 10
Israel 17, 108

Jackson, Patrick 74
Johnson, Jeh 5, 81
Joint and Coalition Operational Analysis 42–3
Joint Special Operations Command (JSOC):
    strategic-legal justification for drone use 78;
    transparency and accountability 14–5, 40,
    51–2
jus ad bellum: normative justification for drone
    use 76; principle of 27; targeted killings 85
jus ad vim 17
jus in bello: human rights community 87;
    normative justification for drone use 76;
    principle of 27; proportionality and
    discrimination 17; targeted killings 85
just war: gray area between war and peace 17;
    human rights community 88–9; legal-
    normative justification for drone use 81–3,
    81–4; normative justification for drone use
    76–7; Obama, Barack 1–2

127

INDEX

Kaag, John 12, 17
Kaldor, Mary 113
Kaplan, Edward H. 32
Keen, David 115
Kegley, Charles W., Jr. 79
Keohane, Robert O. 100
kill lists *see* targeted killings
'kill lists' 55–6
Koh, Harold 5, 9, 81, 89–90
Kosovo 108
Krebs, Ronald R. 74
Kreps, Sarah 12, 17
Kunar province 41

Ladsous, Hervé 109, 116
law of armed conflict 3, 8–11; *see also* rules of
    engagement
Lawrence, T.J. 23
legal authority 4–8
*Legal Consequences of the Construction of a
    Wall in the Occupied Palestinian Territory*
    (International Court of Justice) 46–7
legalistic grounds for drone use 75–6
Legality of Nuclear Weapons (International
    Court of Justice) 46
legally inadequate signature criteria 56, 57, 60
legal-normative justification for drone use 87,
    88, 89, 90
legitimacy, frames of 74–7
lethal force and international human rights law
    86
lex specialis 46, 48
Liberal Peace model 115
Liberia 116
Libya 4
limited events *vs.* regular events 11–2, 13
lingering ability of drones *see* endurance
    capacity of drones
linkage to recognised combatant groups *see*
    associated forces
long-range artillery 25, 30–1
Luban, David 81

malicious acts and peacekeeping missions *112,
    112–6, 113*
manned aircraft and civilian casualties 62
mass atrocities 95–104, 119–20
means and methods of warfare: drone debate
    28–33, 38–40; international humanitarian law
    44; means-method paradox 57–63;
    personality strikes 55–6; positive and
    negative features of drones 53–5
militants, legal status of 45
military advantage 45–6
military and the beneficial uses of drones 101–3
military human rights abuses 97
military tribunals 9
mind-sets 60

misperception and the means-method paradox
    58–63
MONUSCO *see* United Nations Organization
    Stabilization Mission (Congo)
moral distance *see* distance and detachment

narratives, human rights 73–4
National Security Strategy (US) 79, 81
necessity: guided weapons law 26; human rights
    community 86; international humanitarian
    law 44; target identification 9; targeted
    killings 85
negative features of drones 54–5
neoliberal policies 115
New America Foundation 79, 83
'new' conflicts 114
'New Horizon' report 116
'New Silk Road' 83, 84, 89–90
New York Times 17, 118
Newman, Edward 113
non-combatants 80–1, 108
non-governmental organizations 116; *see also*
    human rights community
non-interference rights 6
normative justification for drone use 76–7

Obama, Barack: human rights community's
    letter to 85–6; just war 1–2, 76–7; legal
    authority 4–8; legal-normative justification
    for drone use 81–4; rules of armed conflict 3;
    signature strikes 11; strategic-legal
    justification for drone use 78, 80; target
    identification 9–10; transparency and
    accountability 13–4, 48
observation *see* surveillance
overconfidence and the means-method paradox
    58, 61

Pakistan: Amnesty International report 85; CIA
    programmes 51; drone strike studies 42;
    legal-normative justification for drone use 83;
    linked groups 10; proportionality 86–7;
    public perception of drone use in 118–9;
    signature strikes 57; strategic-legal
    justification for drone use 79, 80; surveillance
    11; target identification 32; targeted killing 31
Panetta, Leon 5
Pashtun population 31
pattern-of-life observation 63
peacekeeping missions: beneficial uses of
    drones 102, 104, 118–20; critical shortages
    108–9; drone use to aid 96; fatalities *110,
    110–2, 111*; malicious acts *112, 112–6, 113*;
    surveillance by unarmed drones 100–1
perceptual sets 60
personality strikes 55–6
personnel shortages, peacekeeping 108–9
'Playstation mentality' 2, 55, 59

INDEX

political issues 99–101
positive features of drones 53–4
precautions: compliance with 50–1; international humanitarian law 46; personality strikes 56; targeting errors 53
precision 54, 107, 108
Predator drones: civilian casualties 41; cost 107; endurance 53; precision 54; surveillance 11
premature cognitive closure 58–9, 60
Preston, Stephen 81
prevention *vs.* preemption 79; *see also* anticipatory self-defence
prisoner of war status 8–9
proportionality: human rights community 86–7; international humanitarian law 45–6; means *vs.* method of warfare 29–30; personality strikes 56; principle of 27; psychological effects of drones 12–3; self-defence and standards of 7; target identification 9; targeted killings 85; targeting errors 53
psychological issues: human rights 87; means-method paradox 58–63; surveillance 11–3
public relations 14
Pugh, Michael 116

Raymond, Gregory A. 79
real-time observation 56, 60, 61, 63
Reaper drones 11, 53, 54, 103
reconnaissance drones 98–104
regular events *vs.* limited events 11–2, 13
research issues 32–3
responsibility and remote killing 26
Responsibility to Protect doctrine 6
Revolutionary United Front 115
'rhetorical coercion' model 74
Rice, Condoleezza 78
right to life: human rights community 87, 89; international human rights law 47–8; transparency and accountability 49
risk transfer 80–1, 108
Royal Marines 97
RQ-1A Predator drone 11
rule-breaking 97–8
rules of engagement 50–1, 52, 55, 61, 83; *see also* law of armed conflict
Rwanda 115

St Petersburg Declaration 26
Schaffner, D. 119, 120
Schmitt, Michael N. 27
security transition 89–90
Segal, Howard 25
self-defence 7–8, 79–80, 81
Senate Intelligence Committee 78
Sheehan, Michael 5
siege mentality 31
Sierra Leone 115

signature strikes: improper targeting criteria 40; methods of warfare 56–7; precautions principle 50; target identification 10–1
Singer, P.W. 107
SIPRI 113
'soda-straw effect' 54, 59
soldiers and risk transfer 80, 108
Somalia 10, 101
sovereignty violation 100–1
Special Committee on Peacekeeping Operations 112
spying 15
Sri Lanka 48, 49
Stockholm International Peace Research Institute *see* SIPRI
strategic defeat of al-Qaeda 5
strategic grounds for drone use 74–5
strategic-legal justification for drone use 77–81, 88, 89, 90
Stufflebeem, John D. 41
success, definition of 32
successor groups *see* associated forces
Sudan 116
surveillance 11–3; beneficial use of 97–104; hostage taking situations 113–4; means/method paradox 40; peacekeeping missions 117; positive features of drones 53–4; real-time observation 56, 60, 61, 63
Syria: associated forces and co-belligerents 10; Authorization to Use Military Force 4; beneficial drone use 99; mass atrocities 95, 96

Taliban: Authorization to Use Military Force 4; combatant status 9; target identification 10
target legitimacy and international law 26–7
targeted killings: and assassinations 15–7; human rights community's response to 85; just war principles 76–7; kill lists 80; 'kill lists' 55–6; legalistic justification 75–6; Obama administration policies 18; research on 31; strategic-legal justification 77–81; transparency and accountability 48, 49; Tutu, Desmond, letter of 117–8
targeting errors: examples 41–3; means-method paradox 57–63; personality strikes 55–6; potential violations of international law 53; signature strikes 10–1, 40; types of 56; as war crime 29
targets: difficulty in identifying 32; international humanitarian law 44–5, 44–6; law of armed conflict 8–11; nature of 8–11; non-combatants 80; transparency and accountability 51–2
Taylor, Letta 29
temporal scope of the Authorization to Use Military Force 5, 88
Tenet, George 78
terrorists, legal status of 45

INDEX

Tesón, Fernando 85
Third Geneva Convention 8–9
Tiedemann, Katherine 32
training camps 10–1
transnational enemies 4
transparency: applicable law 48–9; compliance with principles of 51–2; human rights community's call for 85; international law 63; methods of warfare 40; Obama administration's drones policy 13–5
Tutu, Desmond 117–8

Ukraine 104
UN Department of Peacekeeping Operations (DPKO) 102, 117, 119, 120
UN General Assembly 48
UN Human Rights Committee 47
UN Human Rights Council 48
unarmed drones, beneficial uses of 99–104
unintended effects 103
United Nations: beneficial use of drones for peacekeeping missions 118–20; Global Field Support Strategy, UN 119; malicious acts and peacekeeping missions *112,* 112–6, *113*; peacekeeping mission fatalities *110,* 110–2, *111*; peacekeeping mission shortages 108–9; reports 28, 29–30
United Nations Assistance Mission in Afghanistan 42, 51
United Nations Organization Stabilization Mission (Democratic Republic of the Congo) 102, 109, 110, 114, 119
United Nations Security Council 100–1, 104

United Nations Security Council Resolution 99, 101
United States: government drone strike reports 42–3; human rights claims 73; legal-normative justification for drone use 81–4; public perception of drone use 117–9; strategic-legal justification for drone use 77–81; *see also* Obama, Barack
unlawful combatant status 9
unnecessary suffering, principle of 27
Uruzgan province 41, 57, 59–60, 61, 62
US Central Command 42
US Special Operations Command 52
usage of drones 11–3
U.S.S. Cole bombing 77
utility-maximisation 74–5

Walzer, Michael 17
war crimes, targeting errors as 29
Watapur district strike 41, 50
weapons: historical precedence for drones 24–8; means *vs.* method of warfare 29–30; regulation of 28
weapons treaties 26
Wolfowitz, Paul 77, 80
World War I 25
World War II 31
Wurth, Dee Brillenburg 114

Yemen: CIA programmes 51; drone strike studies 42; signature strikes 57; surveillance 11; targeted killing research 31

Zhawar Kili strike 57